X

May you always
" STAND APART ! "

all the best,

Kim LaBuche

STAND APART

THE
WORLD'S LEADING EXPERTS REVEAL THEIR SECRETS TO HELP YOUR BUSINESS STAND OUT FROM THE CROWD TO ACHIEVE ULTIMATE SUCCESS

Published by CelebrityPress®, Orlando, FL

CelebrityPress® is a registered trademark.

Printed in the United States of America.

ISBN: 978-0-9895187-5-8
LCCN: 2013950067

Most CelebrityPress® titles are available at special quantity discounts for bulk purchases for sales promotions, premiums, fundraising, and educational use. Special versions or book excerpts can also be created to fit specific needs.

For more information, please write:
CelebrityPress®
520 N. Orlando Ave, #2
Winter Park, FL 32789
or call 1.877.261.4930

Visit us online at: www.CelebrityPressPublishing.com

STAND APART

THE

WORLD'S LEADING EXPERTS REVEAL THEIR SECRETS TO HELP YOUR BUSINESS

STAND OUT FROM THE CROWD TO ACHIEVE ULTIMATE SUCCESS

CONTENTS

CHAPTER 1

I GIVE YOU THE KEYS, TO STAND APART LIVING

BY DAN S. KENNEDY

There are six key strategies I find virtually all exceptionally successful individuals use to Stand Apart. Different contributors to this book exemplify different keys, but every one of these fascinating people you're meeting here own and use at least one of the keys. Most rely on several. Before handing over the keys as I know them, I would like to briefly define what "exceptionally successful" means, and tell you just a little bit about my own Stand Apart life.

Decades of my business life have been all about association with and intimately working with hundreds and hundreds of from-scratch millionaire and multi-millionaire entrepreneurs as well as 7-figure income business owners, professional practice owners, sales professionals, authors, speakers and celebrities. They have raised themselves up by, in part, following my business models and methods, and with my consulting, coaching and other assistance. I have *not* been observing these people from afar, like many authors who write about them. In fact, one of the ways that I personally Stand Apart from most "experts" on the subject of successful achievement who write and lecture and opine as information gatherers and reporters is that I am not only an authentic made-from-scratch multi-millionaire myself but that I work with hands dirty, right alongside hundreds of these people and have ample opportunity to see what they're made of and how they really function, behind closed doors, in good times and in difficult times. In

15

short, the keys I'm giving you here are *not* made of ideas and theory or motivational and metaphysical mumbo-jumbo and psycho-babble that lifts you up in a seminar room but lets you down, often hard, outside, in the real world. This isn't cotton candy. It's steak.

I have been a Stand Apart guy pretty much my whole life. In multiple businesses or careers, I have defied the rules and norms and expectations of others to rise. This is not an autobiography, so I'll make brief mentions of my own experience as we look at the keys. I'll just say that in several different environments, I've made myself one of the highest paid individuals, against high odds. And, while income and wealth aren't everything, they are a legitimate scorecard measurement of how the marketplace views you and assesses you. Having money and the ability to create it at will also makes everything else easier and more exciting. The price of freedom, of security, even of the best health care is written on the tags in dollars and cents.

One of the ways that "exceptionally successful" and Stand Apart fit is in the conduct of business and of life as you decide, rather than as others dictate. For example, at this time, I am a very highly paid consultant, business coach and copywriter, I deal with very successful clients – but I do not own a cell-phone, I rarely take an unscheduled incoming call, my assistant organizes most of my phone conversations as pre-set appointments on just one day a month which people may wait weeks to be booked on; I am not personally connected to the internet and have no interest in being connected, and do not accept or send e-mail, nor "play fetch" and go examine things online. (I do make a lot of money for myself and clients having the Internet used as a marketing media, but I also do that with mail and even with the Yellow Pages, and I don't hang out down at the post office or in the forest and at the sawmill or read the Yellow Pages an hour a day either.) I militantly safeguard my time, which I've written about in detail in one of my NO B.S. series books, *No B.S. Time Management for Entrepreneurs, 2nd Edition*. So, you *can't* call me or e-mail me or text me at random, on whim, or at all. There are very limited means of access that I impose on the world.

If this sounds high-handed, strange or impossible to you, then bluntly, you don't know or work with many exceptionally successful people. You may know pretenders, you may know high income but zero net worth types, but you would not be surprised by this at all if you knew a lot of highly exceptional people. Not necessarily with the same specific details, but in principle and practice, they Stand Apart by decision and determination from the unfettered and random access by all that the overwhelming majority of people embrace. 7-figure income and truly rich entrepreneurs and professionals are the least surprised by my 'rules of engagement', and are rarely offended by them, for they have their own. It is all the "little people" – like speaker and literary agents with little power of their own – who are most upset.

This is just one way of many in which those who Stand Apart, as 1%'ers, or 5%'ers, surprise, annoy and offend the 99%, the 95%. The masses envy, resent and fear those with the rare courage to live a Stand Apart Life on their own terms. Seeing someone do this makes those who aren't earning top incomes and aren't satisfied with their lives confront evidence that they could be, and that is not welcome confrontation. Which brings us to the first of the six keys:

THE EXCEPTIONALLY SUCCESSFUL STANDARD APART BY EMOTIONAL DETACHMENT FROM WHAT OTHERS THINK ABOUT THEM

Stand Apart Living is *not* for everybody. You don't have to actually be arrogant or obnoxious or unreasonable, but you do have to be okay with being thought of as those things and more and worse. Everybody who watches someone like Larry Ellison, sitting on the deck of his epic-sized yacht as it makes its way through a harbor does not admire him, and think, "There goes a guy who has made himself fabulously successful, worked hard and smart, created tens of thousands of jobs and provided thousands more with opportunity as investors along the way." Most of them are thinking very different, darker thoughts. Some hate him on sight without even knowing who he is. A few wish him dead. A father points him out to his young son, and says: "See him? He's a crook. Behind every fortune there's crime!" Almost without exception, the more you Stand Apart, the more you will be thought badly of by many. If you are visible enough and successful enough at Standing Apart, you will even be subject to *mass* criticism.

Dr. Maxwell Maltz, with whom I co-authored the book *The New Psycho-Cybernetics* taught, beginning back in 1960, **the criticality of immunity to criticism,** whether directly made or as gossip behind your back. He found that unsuccessful, unhappy people with fragile egos and weak self-images were constantly worrying about, guessing, checking on, and hyper-sensitive to others' skepticism, disapproval, dislike, envy and jealousy, and criticism. This sabotages successful achievement in the making, and it ruins it for many who do rise above others in their family, people they grew up with, neighbors and, most of all, professional or industry peers. It even puts people in real jeopardy.

Not long ago, a high-paid, promising, starting quarterback on an NFL team, maybe one of the most coveted jobs in all of sports, actually asked his coach to be benched and then left his team in mid-season *because he couldn't stand being booed by the fans*. The tipping point was when he had fumbled the ball away as he was driven to the ground and was lying on the field with an injury (from which he would quickly recover) and he heard thousands booing him as he lay there and was then supported by men on both sides and helped off the field.

I still have a news clipping about an actor many considered promising who committed suicide and, in his suicide note, referred to a particularly savage negative review of his first night's performance in a Broadway play.

Exceptionally successful people in every field are booed, one way or the other. Few react as visibly and dramatically as the quarterback who quit or the actor who put a gun in his mouth and pulled the trigger. Most people surrender quietly and un-dramatically, so that the world around them takes no notice. They meekly submit to mediocrity and timidity and a life lived obsequiously, and over time, regretfully, even bitterly. They kill themselves very slowly with the poisons of procrastination, self-doubt, disappointment and frustration, instead of a gun and a fast bullet. They learn to stand in place, in the group, in servile conformance. Those who Stand Apart, strive, succeed, do so by building emotional distance between their self-appraisal and others' opinions.

THE EXCEPTIONALLY SUCCESSFUL STAND APART BY LEAP-FROGGING AND UTTER DISREGARD FOR THE ESTABLISHED RULES OF ORDER

Whether you like seeing the ads or not, the freedom for lawyers to advertise exists because one guy took on the entire legal profession's establishment, challenged its rules, and changed everything. You have choices of phone service providers because one guy challenged AT&T and long established FCC policies and changed everything. These are two of many, many individuals who listened carefully as the Establishment explained its Rules of Order, then spit in the Establishment's eye.

Leap-frogging is a particularly interesting, and very often, very offensive to others, practice used by those who Stand Apart. I borrow the term from my friend, Robert Ringer, who originally made himself a New York Times bestselling author by running full-page newspaper ads for his first book, *Winning Through Intimidation*, and forcing demand into bookstores before he had a real publisher – at the time a most radical approach. In most fields of achievement, there is an Establishment, a Bureaucracy, people with badges or hats or titles or apparent authority, who tell new people they must be patient, must grovel, must crawl before they walk, must climb one rung at a time. I have heard this every place I've ever gone to achieve anything and ignored it, often to the dismay and disapproval of both the Establishment and all those they'd convinced to grovel.

You know Sly Stallone. You may not know how he leap-frogged. He wanted to be a leading man actor and made the rounds and was roundly rejected, as too Italian, too dumb looking, with too "thick" a speaking style, and no discernible acting ability, but maybe most of all, no long time put in, in acting school, endless auditions, begging lowest level agents and casting directors, taking miniscule parts (although he did famously appear in a soft porn video). Stallone wrote the script for the movie 'Rocky', and a number of producers instantly recognized it as a potential blockbuster, and offered to buy it – at a time when Stallone was dead broke, with a pregnant wife, a baby on the way. He had people offering him good-sized sums for the script, but they wanted nothing to do with him as an actor. He refused to sell the script unless he could play Rocky himself. After countless rejections, some producer finally gave in. Leap-frogging is often done by forcing someone to let you do one thing because they want you to do something else. It's a high pressure game of who blinks. It's a form of extortion. It is a way of getting things done.

You know Rush Limbaugh. I am a fan, you may hold an opposing opinion, and that doesn't matter. His success is undeniable. His is a Stand Apart Life in every imaginable respect. Back when his syndicated radio program was young and unproven as a vehicle for brand advertisers, he could have plodded along, groveling in front of Madison Avenue ad agencies' masters for ad dollar crumbs, being patient and persistent, waiting for respect. Instead, he picked a then little-known, regional-only drink brand, Snapple®, and without signing them as an advertiser; *without even telling them or obtaining permission*, he began doing commercials for Snapple® on his show, telling listeners to go to their grocery stores and get it, and if their stores weren't stocking it, to demand it. When Snapple® sales soared, Limbaugh had leap-frogged to the top of the ad media food chain, and quickly became rich. **Most people spend entirely too much time waiting for respect and asking for permission.**

Another leap-frogging play, somewhat similar, is as a kind of Svengali or consigliore. I leapt to speaking on the #1 public seminar tour in America, as the only constant along with Zig Ziglar in 27 to 29 cities a year for 9 years, with audiences from 10,000 to 35,000, sharing the platform with four former U.S. Presidents and a who's who of celebrities by being a consultant to the tour's owner and dealing with the question of what might be done to somehow squeeze more revenue out of each day. One of those answers: add a bonus speaker who sells resources at day's end, after the official end time of the event. It can be somebody of no fame, but who can sell. Next question: who might I suggest? Answer: me. Far more experienced and more widely known and better credentialed speakers were standing in line, all begging, cajoling, delivering demo tapes, fighting for auditions, trying to get on that tour. I stood apart and leapt on.

I sold one of my companies by acting as a consultant and advising a client about his objective of broadening from a niche expert, author and publisher to reaching a much larger and broader audience. His means of achieving that goal – instantly: buy my company. I could have, instead, gone through the normal processes and channels for readying a company for sale, paying brokers and lawyers, taking months or years, and suffering numerous failed negotiations before getting the job done. Instead, I by-passed all that and just did a deal.

The biggest Svengali Leap Frog ever belongs to Dick Cheney. Dick Cheney was the man in charge of finding and selecting the person to be George W. Bush's Vice-President. When that process ran its course, the last, best candidate standing to be recommended to the future President by Dick Cheney was Dick Cheney. Imagine that. It has never happened before in presidential politics. The head of the V.P. selection committee has never become the V.P., and I'd guess, no such selection advisor has ever even included himself as a possible candidate. It takes what I respectfully call: brass balls.

Recently, I stood – smirking and shaking my head – at the back of the room at a mystery writers' convention and listened as a panel of well-known wise elders, much published writers and officious agents sternly lectured the room full of hopeful authors about ever so patiently paying their dues and suffering rejection and groveling and never daring to so much as call an agent, and only e-mailing as instructed and submitting query letters prepared just-so. They spoke to this room of people as if royals to peasants. The entire audience should have stood as one and walked out. Instead, they meekly scribbled notes.

In 2013, I leap-frogged to my first published mystery novel, as a co-author with a much celebrated and published detective series author. I employed no agent, I circulated no query, no proposal. I did not know him before directly approaching him with both a story idea and a proposition. You can get the book, *Win, Place Or Die* by Les Roberts with Dan S. Kennedy at all booksellers, including Amazon. If the agent-ocracy knew what I did, they might all get torches and pitchforks and hunt me like the townspeople pursuing the werewolf. Had I strode to the front of that room and revealed my leap-frogging, I'd have had my microphone turned off and been hustled out the back, never to be seen again.

I had an eerily similar experience many years ago, in speaking, after making $100,000.00 my first year figuring an unorthodox plan out on my own, I eagerly traveled to the trade association's convention to learn from the famous name pros how to do it right. There, I heard the same warnings about expecting to starve for years, about begging agents and bureaus to get one to grudgingly and skeptically add you to their list, about groveling at the feet of the elders and masters. I also discovered that hardly anybody dispensing this advice was making $100,000 a year. Some were stunned by my revealing that I was, my very first year. Some, after quizzing me for details, quickly criticized what I was doing as 'unprofessional.' They actually tried persuading me to give up my plan that was working in favor of theirs that wasn't!

Every place is loaded with people eager to tell you what you can't do *because they can't do it.* Most literary agents are, by the way, frustrated, unpublished or unsuccessful writers. Most speakers bureau operators can't function as speakers. Most professors giving grades can't do anything *but* teach – this is especially true of business professors. The can't-do-ers tend to create and support complex bureaucracies designed to prevent anybody circumventing their authority. It's important to recognize that they have an agenda.

The legendary CEO, Jack Welch said, "It's best to HATE bureaucracy." Every industry, every field of endeavor, every association has one. Stallone could have surrendered to the film industry bureaucracy, Limbaugh to the ad media industry bureaucracy, I to several different bureaucracies. Instead, I hate them and I have disdain for them and I derive joy from leap-frogging over them.

Willie Nelson tells this story: "There was a guy named Ben Dorsey who used to work for Johnny Cash, and he had a bunch of fancy suits that Johnny had given him. He was walking down the street in Nashville in front of the Grand Ole Opry, and this guy came up with a guitar in his hand and thought Ben was one of the stars because he had on Cash's suit. He said, "How do you get started in this business?" And Ben said, "Ain't but one way, hoss. You start at the bottom, you go right on to the top. Don't mess with that in-between shit."

THE EXCEPTIONALLY SUCCESSFUL STAND APART BY REJECTING INDUSTRY NORMS

If you are unsure of how to proceed with a career or business, the first thing I suggest is making as complete a list of the industry norms as possible – then trying to figure out a contrarian strategy that defies every one of them. *Majority equals mediocrity.* That's a simple, mathematical fact. If your ambition is average, then you can copy what the majority of others in your field of endeavor are doing. If your ambition is to excel or dominate or enjoy extraordinary income, wealth, prominence and power, then you *must* reject the norms.

When Ray Kroc chose to franchise the McDonald brothers' hamburger stand rapidly, selling territorial rights and pushing franchisees to open multiple locations, he defied the industry norms of slowly and methodically opening company-owned restaurants, using profits from one to build the next. Recently, I helped a conversion franchisor in the chiropractic field zoom from 4 to over 360 operating clinics in under 40 months, defying all known speed limits, by rejecting franchise industry norms and rules about the routine process for selling franchises. Also, in chiropractic, years back, I was a leader in teaching and promoting patient pre-pays, then a radical and controversial strategy – which often transformed struggling, cash-poor $5,000.00 a month practices into powerful $50,000.00 a month practices almost overnight.

That big Apple store you see thriving exists because Jobs threw out his industry's whole rulebook about product distribution.

Place Strategy is a way of challenging industry norms. My client, Guthy-Renker, has made billions of dollars by re-locating acne treatment products from the drugstore shelf to TV infomercials and in-mall vending machines, and by re-locating skin care and cosmetic products from the department store beauty counter to infomercials and home shopping channels. Bezos has wreaked havoc with bookstores by first moving books to an online store with unlimited space, selection and inventory, then to the Kindle. **Price Strategy*** is another disruptive and powerful force. In the information marketing industry, I led the continuity and forced continuity revolution, which in many cases has ten-timesed the price of a newsletter or other subscription, eliminated the cost of soliciting subscription renewals, and extended the longevity of subscribers. There are still Establishment companies' owners and executives who refuse to even acknowledge the superiority of this model. **Process Strategy** is another means of defying norms. Clients of mine who are single industry marketing innovators and coaches like Craig Proctor in real estate, Ben Glass in law, Bill Gough in insurance, Iron Tribe Fitness in gyms, and many others literally lead insurrections and revolutions in their respective industries, replacing, for example, sales prospecting with my *Magnetic Marketing System*® to attract prospects; replacing one to one with one to many selling; replacing selling of services with my Trust-Based Marketing*, etc. Technology has become a most disruptive force, for good and bad. I'm a founder and shareholder in a software company, Infusionsoft, which has dared to defy

---

*I have whole books about these critical subjects. *No B.S. Price Strategy*, co-authored with Jason Marrs, *The Man Who Competes With Free. No B.S. Guide to Trust-Based Marketing*, co-authored with Matt Zagula.

all norms for product and sales process in the CRM software space, with magnificent success.

Most people either harness and leverage a disruptive force or forces or are victimized and harmed by such forces. Much of that depends on their basic attitude about industry norms. If you view norms as law to be feared or as best practices to be honored, you will likely never go beyond the median point in your field, if you rise that far. If you view norms as the consensus opinions of mediocre achievers and unimaginative followers enshrined thanks to the meekness of the majority, you will react to them creatively. If you understand that norms are limited, limiting beliefs and practices reinforced by bureaucracy, you will never be intimidated by them. It's *not* about the norms. It's about your way of thinking about them.

One of my great heroes, Walt Disney, violated so many norms and violated so many rules, it's impossible to catalog them all. When a technology didn't exist to do what he wanted to do, that no one else was doing, he invented it. When every amusement park in the world had open access, multiple entrances and exits and per-ride pricing, he first built his with only one entry and exit point, then quickly converted to per day pricing – against every expert opinion. When cartoons were "shorts", to fill time before a movie started, he produced feature length animated films, then films mixing live actors and animated cartoons. On and on and on and on.

Most people entering a place, a group, an industry or profession, a field, get there, look around, asking "How are things done around here?" - *so that they can conform*. The ambitious think about doing things incrementally better. Hardly anybody arrives and asks the same question for the express purpose of finding ways to violate every norm, dis-prove every tradition, break every rule and outrage every authority. Only true Stand Apart-ers do that.

THE EXCEPTIONALLY SUCCESSFUL STAND APART BY OWNING AN ULTRA HIGH VALUE SKILL

If you don't recognize the name Buddy Rich, you might go Google or Wikipedia him, to better appreciate this story from the actor Al Pacino: "I went to see Frank Sinatra in a concert. His opening act was Buddy Rich. So Buddy Rich came out, and I wondered about him because he was in his sixties and all he was doing was playing the drums. I know he's a good

24

drummer. But I'm thinking, I'm going to sit here and listen to him drum for a while and twiddle my thumbs until Frank Sinatra comes out. But once he started and then kept going and going and going, he transcended what I thought he was gonna do tenfold. It became this *experience*. When Sinatra came out, he said, very simply: 'You see this guy drumming? You know, sometimes it's a good idea to stay at *a* thing.'"

The legendary martial artist Bruce Lee said that he had no fear of the man who practiced 10,000 kicks 10 times or of the man who practiced 1,000 kicks 100 times, but he feared the man who practiced *one* kick 100,000 times.

Most people never rise to the level of mastery of any one thing. But, on the earned income side of the wealth equation, and often, to some extent also on the equity side, it is the person who masters a single, highly valuable skill who earns the most for his time and has the most power to live on his terms. I bill my time at $2,000.00 an hour, but often earn more per hour than that with project fee pricing in place of hourly billing, and with leverage of various kinds, including royalties on clients' gross revenues tied to my advice and my copywriting. But at $2,000.00 an hour, I'm billing at a significantly higher rate than the lawyers at the biggest firms in the city, the accountants at the top C.P.A. firms, even the celebrity doctors at the big name hospital. And when professionals in those fields, with degrees and certifications and alphabet soup after their names learn of my fees, many are shocked, many are dis-believing, some are angry. They do not understand the power of being positioned as THE master in a category of one, versus one of many in a crowded category. Still, they all earn far more than the fast food counter clerk or the barber or the jack-of-all-trades lawyers, accountants and doctors, because they have at least made a point of developing higher value skills.

Warren Buffet mastered the analysis and selection of industries and companies to invest in. Trump mastered what he calls "the art of the deal". The comedian Bob Newhart mastered dead-pan, hang-dog humor. If you are too young to know Newhart, try finding the 2013 episode of 'The Big Bang Theory' in which he guest stars and steals the show. You can watch a master at work. Elmore Leonard mastered a very particular style of mystery-writing, spare of detail, driven by dialogue. One of his terse pieces of writing advice: leave out the parts readers skip. These people all rose to pinnacles of peer respect – even if grudging, of power in their fields, of fame with and affection from their publics, and of wealth on the strength of mastery of a high value skill.

This is *the* path open to anybody and everybody – regardless of childhood, upbringing, background, formal education, financial situation, physical disadvantage. The public library is free. With as little as an hour a day of intense study, you can become a world class expert in just about any marketable skill in two to four years. With self-managed intense practice, you can become adept at it in about the same amount of time. I taught myself direct-response copywriting, and began earning a 6-figure income from it while learning, now a 7-figure income. I taught myself professional speaking and platform selling, began clumsily and ineptly, but got good in 2 years, and never earned less than a 6-figure income doing it. I went from ignorant and inept to knowledgeable and competent, then on to mastery in exactly the same way open to anybody: I hunted, found, gathered and studied information; I found and observed and analyzed the most successful people in these fields; I drilled and practiced, drilled and practiced; and I went to work.

There is NO real excuse for remaining ignorant and incompetent and devoid of a high value skill in America. None. Not poverty, not absent parents, not bad neighborhoods. Og Mandino went to the library first as a drunk and street bum, using it as a dry and warm place to kill time. He discovered things there and discovered himself there. He became one of the great personal development authors of his time, and lived a life as a celebrated and respected thought leader, with prosperity, a home in a beautiful place of his choosing. The minimum wage worker who claims to be "stuck" in a dead-end job that fails to pay a "living wage" and rails against this injustice drives near a library while commuting to and from his lousy job – but on his breaks, he will not be caught reading a how-to-succeed book or studying a higher value skill.

Mastery can make you "*the* go-to guy or gal", at which point, you can name your price, set your terms, and the marketplace will acquiesce.

In my own life, I have mastered and become known for two specific, high value skills. One is selling as a speaker from the stage. No less than Zig Ziglar said I was the best platform salesperson he'd ever seen. For more than a dozen years I earned over

$1-million a year with this skill, with my speaking only a part-time endeavor, feeding a more complex business. Many exceptionally lucrative speaking opportunities came to me without my having to chase or create them, because I was known for this skill. The other is writing direct-response advertising copy that sells. I have been and am the highest paid freelance copywriter anybody knows of, routinely commanding upwards from $100,000.00 per project, plus royalties. This skill allows me a 3-minute commute, working at home or wherever I please, on my schedule, with every client coming to me so I avoid travel. There are other things I'm good at, and still others I'm competent at, but these are the two that have enabled me to Stand Apart from all others and be compensated accordingly.

I should point out that having mastery of a high value skill alone can prove of little economic value. The next item on my list is nearly always required to capitalize on it. But without it, even mastering the next item can prove disappointingly unproductive.

THE EXCEPTIONALLY SUCCESSFUL STAND APART BY MASTERY OF <u>PERSONAL</u> MARKETING AND SELLING

The higher up the income and autonomy pyramids you go, the more you are paid for *who* you are and who you are perceived to be, rather than for *what* you do. Manufacturing a highly valuable, highly marketing "Who" for yourself, i.e., a persona, a story, positioning, etc., and then selling *it* is the Stand Apart way.

This is a reality that many people suffer by denying. The author who believes he has written the best book, the inventor who believes he has the superior product, the business owner who think his company delivers superior service, the professional who believes he has the best credentials are all bitterly disappointed when their work fails to equate, automatically, to recognition and reward. An owner of a bankrupt restaurant told me that they served the best and most authentic Italian food in the entire city, and I agreed. Yet he was bankrupt. How could this be? Everyone who Stands Apart knows the answer.

There is not a single Hollywood insider including the highest paid actors and actresses who will claim that *the best* actors are the most sought after or highest paid. That's just not the way it works. It is the actors of greatest interest to the public, who can be counted on to draw audiences and produce top box office revenues who have the most power. Mostly, they must also have highly developed acting chops. But if they aren't good at or willing to sell themselves to the public, skill or even talent alone won't carry them far. This is even truer in most other professions and businesses.

When asked to name the best singers, both Sinatra and Dean Martin named people other than themselves – far less famous, far less prosperous. I recently saw an interview with the country-western superstar Toby Keith, who is also one of the richest stars, when he was asked the same question. He also named a less famous, working-for-a-living person the public is pretty much unaware of. I can definitely name better speakers than I am who've barely made a living and have created no wealth at all. I can't name a living direct-response copywriter better than I am, but I'll wager there are some out there. Success solely on the intrinsic or core merits of a person's talent or skill, a product's originality or superiority, or a company's excellence at what it does are rare.

Of course, there are notable exceptions, where the individual is virtually unknown, and a product or company is very successfully promoted, marketed and sold on its own. The Harry Potter fortune was made via brilliant marketing, but with J. K. Rowling in the background. But the Chicken Soup for the Soul brand, now iconic, was built from a much-rejected idea and one book grudgingly put out by a tiny publisher because its co-creators, my friend Mark Victor Hansen and Jack Canfield, personally and relentlessly sold themselves to the media.

A lot of traction comes when someone learns to distinguish their deliverables exchanged for money from what they are actually selling. People who can't understand that tend to stay at very low incomes, and are very vulnerable to commoditization. You need to know what business you are really in. Although there have been and are many deliverables for which I receive money, I've long been in 'The Dan Kennedy Business.' Trump still gets much of his money from points in real estate deals and in properties his company develops, and a lot of money from licensing his name and brand outside of real estate – there is Trump apparel, Trump mattresses, etc., and deals with Macy's and others – but he is in The Donald Trump Business. He gets up every morning publicizing, promoting, marketing and selling himself, as do I. And as do many, in many fields. Not what we do. Who we are.

For many people, this is a very *uncomfortable* thing. It once was for me, and it has never become natural. Automatic now, but still not natural. If you try to Stand Apart without being very effective and assertive if not aggressive at personal marketing, you'll likely just find yourself standing apart, alone and ignored. Napoleon Hill is famous and loved for his book titled *Think And Grow Rich*. People *like* the idea of thinking a certain way and getting rich. His failed and obscure book was titled *Sell Your Way Through Life*. People do not like that fact. If you do not train yourself to embrace and love and respect selling, I frankly think you are doomed, and nothing else will matter much.

For many people, this is a *philosophically difficult* thing. They believe in false entitlement. They believe their higher education and credentials or their pure souls and generous hearts or their expertise and providing of true-blue service or the superiority of their products or some other merit *should entitle them to* top success – without the grimy, hands-dirty work of selling themselves. They see others of less merit succeeding wildly while they are, they feel, ignored by the marketplace, and they describe it as injustice, as a world gone mad; they blame the marketplace. In this, they jail themselves in the prison for Those Of Great Merit Who Refuse To Know How Success Really Works. It's a very, very crowded prison.

Because I am a high school graduate with no credentials for any of the things I do, I have occasionally had someone openly express disbelief, outrage and resentment about my activities or commanded compensation. I've *often* had that expressed behind my back, too. This is akin to countless practicing psychologists' bitter disapproval of Dr. Phil, countless speakers' jealousy toward Tony Robbins. All across the country, there are chefs graduated from the finest culinary schools sitting on their couches watching some celebrity chef on a reality show or on The Food Network and, in unison, telling their spouses what a total moron and douche-bag the star is. *I get it.* Of course it annoys me that somebody like the star of Duck Dynasty sells 300,000 copies of his book the first week while I, the serious author of useful books, must struggle so mightily to sell far fewer copies. But I remind myself, if superior credentials or content or other such merit alone governed compensation, school teachers might be rich and the Kardashians might be poor. And if grandma had wheels she'd be a race car. And if turnips were watches, every man would wear a Rolex.

*You **can** disapprove of the way the marketplace chooses its victors and awards its spoils if you must, but you will not persuade it to change nor will you be rewarded for your disapproval. You might as well disapprove of the way the weather operates and distributes clear skies and sunny days, vicious tornados and hurricanes, calm waters and tsunamis.*

Or you can get in sync with the reasons why money moves from person to person and place to place, described in my book *No B.S. Wealth Attraction in the New Economy.*

A player can vehemently disapprove of the way professional football is played and refereed, and he will rust on the bench or find himself traded to the worst team in the league. Or he can get in *the* game.

A lot of my work is with information marketers; self-appointed experts, self-published authors, independent publishers, consultants, coaches, who, following my business models and advice, routinely rise to 7-figure incomes and wealth, and celebrity and authority in their fields. I say that **I am responsible for fathering the largest legion of *utterly unqualified* multi-millionaires on earth**. One of the things they must all learn is to Stand Apart from the crowd in their space, by personal marketing and selling. But they are far from unique.

If you examine people who live Stand Apart Lives, live much as they please, and achieve extraordinary things, you will usually find that they are master salesmen and promoters of themselves. In my newest book, *No B.S. Brand-Building by Direct-Response* (2014), I have a chapter titled *The Mouse And The Bunny*, describing the many commonalities of Walt Disney and Hugh Hefner. Both built entire worlds of their choosing. With 20//20 hindsight, I realize a point I failed[**] to directly and clearly make in that chapter is the extent to which both men were master salesmen and promoters of themselves, as well as master salesmen and promoters of ideas.

Warren Buffet, a master promoter of himself, perceived and celebrated as "the world's greatest investor", although the facts do not support that title. There are more successful investors and investment managers concealed in oblivion. Yes, Buffet has a highly developed skill as an

---

[**] (There is always the book you intended to write, the book you wrote, and the book you wish you'd written. Being okay with that is essential. It's part of being comfortable in your own skin, discussed here, later.)

investor. But he is also half P.T. Barnum. Steve Jobs was a master promoter of himself, so that the public automatically accepted anything *he* held up as breakthrough and beneficial innovation they had to possess, to the extent of sleeping outside on the ground all night to be ahead of others in getting it – and were perfectly willing to forgive each new product's flaws, and defend Apple to the death. Jobs' replacement at Apple, Tim Cook, has not been given the same "all hail The Wizard" reception. If he thinks 'product' can give him that, he is sadly mistaken, and totally misunderstands the magic of the late Steve Jobs.

THE EXCEPTIONALLY SUCCESSFUL STAND APART BY RESOLUTE DETERMINATION AND RESILIENCE

When I was doing a lot of speaking, up to 70 engagements or so a year, for several years I was on a number of programs with Christopher Reeve. He was paralyzed from the neck down as a result of spinal cord injury from a riding accident, an irony of sorts as he was best known as the actor who had then played Superman in the movies. What he had to go through just to be gotten out of bed in the morning would destroy most people. Just the fact that he traveled – or more accurately – was transported to a site, and wheeled on stage, and aided by a breathing device, was able to deliver an uplifting speech was a super-human miracle. He definitely Stood Apart from just about everybody in the resilience and resolute determination departments.

I frankly doubt I'd be half as heroic. But, compared to most, I am a very determined and resolute and self-disciplined and resilient cuss. The Napoleon Hill Foundation even awarded me its Persistence Award in 2012. I pride myself on going back into 'places' I'm thrown out of – and buying them. Anyway, instead of being persistent, most people are paralyzed by their problems or by roadblocks put in their way by others.

Reeve said: "Some people are walking around with full use of their bodies and they're more paralyzed than I am." People are stalled, stopped and paralyzed by all sorts of comparatively small things. Getting rid of *that* behavior is critical for exceptional success. No one who lets himself be stopped by disadvantageous circumstances ever gets very far. I teach two axioms. One, that people good at making excuses are never good at making money. (If you have such a person around you, fire them – today, distance yourself from them, avoid them, for they are contagious and toxic.) Two, that there is always *something* you can do, right now, to move forward. Although I've had a serious back injury from a racing accident, I've never had anything anywhere close to Reeve's, and hope and pray I never do, but I have been flat broke, bankrupt and financially embarrassed. I started from zero, with only one stick – but then you can go in search of the second stick you need to rub two together, and if you have one, you have a head start. There is always *something* you can do, now.

Another Reeve quote: "We all have many more abilities and *internal* resources than we know. My advice is that you don't need to break your neck to find out about them." Even if you are starting or starting over from worse than zero, or everything has been lost, you still have you. You always have your internal resources. It is better to have external ones too, but you are never without your internal resources – and it's good to condition those and keep them strong all the time.

I am very troubled and disappointed by the ever-growing weakness and wimpiness I see in the majority of people. If there's no app for it, they lack the initiative to do it, let alone persistence. And they better really, really, really love their little magic phones, because that's about all they'll ever have. I have yet to find the exception, when exceptional success could be had without overcoming some serious obstacles and resistance, getting knocked down and having to get yourself back up, usually more than once, and having to break through closed and locked doors. That does not contradict leap-frogging, by the way. It is part of the process.

Joan Rivers, who I've worked with and written for, and respect as much or more than any other person I've ever met, saw her fame evaporate and career crash, after the loss of her late-night show on Fox and her husband's suicide. She also, then, discovered she was virtually broke. Joan says: "Walk through *any* door." She started over, working for scale, in a square on The New Hollywood Squares. But she also leap-frogged, by becoming very entrepreneurial, and getting a jewelry business begun on a card table going on QVC, the home shopping channel. Huge income followed fast. Although some in her peer community looked down their noses, then, at home shopping TV, walking through that door not only solved her financial difficulties, but reinvigorated public interest in her. More recently, her taking the gig on Trump's *Celebrity Apprentice* skyrocketed her fame. She is now quite rich, very popular, on her own

TV shows and a guest on many, packing theaters as a comic. I know her to be intense, resolute and resilient. You do not want to be standing around in the doorway she's decided to go through. I urge going online and finding and renting and watching the recent documentary about her, with unprecedented access, titled 'A Piece Of Work.'

I've had Ivanka Trump, George Ross – The Donald's right-hand man of decades, and Donald Trump himself on event programs I've organized, and where I've also been a featured speaker. Everything I've learned about Trump from the backstage conversations and observations, I like. One of my favorite Trump stories is from his worst financial time. He tells it:

"I was walking down Fifth Avenue with Marla Maples in 1991. This was at the peak of the bad real estate market. Equity had disappeared leaving just debt. Across the street I saw a man in front of Tiffany with a tin cup, selling pencils. I looked at Marla and said, 'You know, right now, that man is worth $900-million more than I am.'" He adds, *"When I told Marla this, she didn't run away. Of course, I would have saved a little money if she had."*

THE EXCEPTIONALLY SUCCESSFUL STAND APART BY BEING COMFORTABLE IN THEIR OWN SKIN

One of the best top-level executives of our time has been Jack Welch. Under his leadership, from 1981 to 2001, GE's profits increased by 600% - a stunning number when you note I said profits, *not* grosses, and that GE is no wiz-bang high-tech company selling magic wands, but an old-line industrial-based, manufacturing-based company. Fortune Magazine named Jack 'Manager Of The Century' in 1999. Like most leaders, he has long had raving fans and vocal, even vicious critics. He has had a public scandal, late in his career, involving an extra-marital affair apparently begun impulsively with a female journalist interviewing him; she is now his wife. Overall, his track record in business and, ultimately, at creating a life entirely to his liking, is solid. Jack says**:**

"When you're comfortable in your own skin, you can do anything. You're not worried about what somebody else has or what you don't have, or what somebody else thinks. You just like you. Not in a braggadocio way. You just like you."

I've worked at this, at being comfortable with me. It's very stressful trying to be somebody you are not. That was a lot heavier work, back when I tried that. That doesn't preclude deliberate self-improvement – in fact, it requires it, but it liberates you from putting on false airs, from incessantly worrying about and responding to other peoples' expectations. A lot of people perceived by many as successful are actually sweating bullets all the time, struggling to own the home, drive the cars, wear the clothes, do the things, live, as they think others think they should. They are literally working for others' expectations.

I have many rich clients who come to consulting days at one of my homes, and it is a modest and decidedly unimpressive home with my office in its basement, and there is clutter because it is a workplace, and I have no staff present to bring us ice water in a crystal pitcher on a silver tray. I never give a thought about anybody being put off by this. I have, on occasion, been told of gossip about it. I don't care. For the record, I prefer putting my money into money, and my racehorses and a few classic cars, not my mansion. Others in my position, doing my work, with my clients would feel compelled to have a fancy mansion with a grand circular drive with a fountain in its center. Feeling compelled to do anything because of what others may think is a bad place to be, a bad way to live.

I know people who race around cleaning up their house – before the maid service people get there! Now *that's* being controlled by worry over what others may think of you!

I work with 20 entrepreneurs involved in information marketing businesses, each with businesses from several million to $30-million a year, in a mastermind group setting, for 2 or 3 days at a time. They can tell you, I do not edit myself at all in this setting. In my one to one work with clients, I am the same. One client, now with a company doing over a billion dollars a year, who has been with me for more than 20 years, brought a group of his "young guns" in for a meeting with me, and halfway through the day I, joking, said something about him that I might better not have said with this group. A few minutes later, I tried mopping up a little, reminding the group that the CEO and I went back a long ways and that left room for the liberty to, frankly, be a bit of an asshole once in a while. He piped up and said that I'd been an asshole from the very beginning. This is the way I want to work, and the kind of people I want to work with, so I do.

My friend Mike Vance, who worked closely with Walt Disney for many years, said that the thing he admired most about Walt was his **"authenticity"**, and Mike believes most people are themselves very, very inauthentic, and are subconsciously if not consciously searching for someone with the confidence to be authentic. My own experience in creating and sustaining successful relationships with both a limited clientele and a large audience of followers and fans verifies his thesis.

Ultimately, having a Stand Apart Life with all its benefits (and its price tags) is a matter of *decision*.

It's not a destination you journey to.

It's definitely not something you patiently pursue permission from others for.

It's something you *do*.

About Dan

DAN S. KENNEDY is a multi-millionaire serial entrepreneur, sought after and trusted marketing and business advisor, author of over 20 published books (www.NoBSBooks.com) and is integrally involved with GKIC, the leading international membership organization of marketing-oriented entrepreneurs, business owners, professional practice owners and sales professionals as well as authors, speakers and thought leaders. (Information at www.DanKennedy.com). As a speaker, he has regularly appeared with Zig Ziglar, Brian Tracy, Jim Rohn and Tom Hopkins, celebrity entrepreneurs like Gene Simmons (KISS), Kathy Ireland, George Foreman and 'Body By Jake' Jake Steinfeld, as well as former U.S. Presidents and world leaders and Hollywood and sports celebrities. He is a celebrated direct-response copywriter working in all media, from direct-mail to TV infomercials to online video and webcasts. Ads of his making have appeared in over 250 different magazines ranging from Forbes to Mother Earth News, his clients mail millions of sales letters he's written every year, and online media utilizing his scripts is also viewed by hundreds of thousands and annually generates over a billion dollars. His work has been favorably recognized by Entrepreneur, Inc. and Success Magazines, he has received the Copywriter of the Year Award from American Writers & Artists, the Persistence Award from the Napoleon Hill Foundation, and is on the Advisory Board of the School of Communications at High Point University. 2013 was his 40th Anniversary in the field of information-marketing, in which he is a recognized leader. (Information about the Information Marketing Association at www.info-marketing.org.)

Personally, he lives a definitively Stand Apart Life. He owns racehorses competing in 3 states and drives professionally in over 200 harness races a year, lives in Ohio and Virginia but has his assistant's office in Arizona, owns and drives 4 classic cars including Dean Martin's Rolls-Royce, is married to his 2nd and 3rd wife, and they jointly parent The Million Dollar Dog. There are also two grown children and six grand-children.

Dan is available for a very limited number of interesting speaking engagements, customized seminar engagements, or guest appearances at coaching/mastermind groups; consulting engagements; and copywriting assignments, and may be contacted directly (only) via fax: 602-269-3113.

CHAPTER 2

THE SECRET TO CREATING A BUSINESS MODEL THAT STANDS APART IN ANY COUNTRY AND IN ANY MARKET – NO MATTER WHAT!

BY ANTHONY FORD

Every kid has an imaginary friend, right? Well, at least that's what I thought growing up as a kid. My imaginary friend's name was Mr. Blue. Mr. Blue was a tall, handsome muscle-bound strong yet gentle man that only appeared to me when no one else was around. Although he didn't say much of anything, he always assured me of the fact that he was there to comfort me and to protect me. Mr. Blue stood about 6'4" and weighed in at a solid 275 lbs., he had a looped earring in one of his ears and all he did most of the time was stand in front of the door to my room folding his arms while he'd watch me play with my toys – smiling at me! Every now and again he'd play with me or help me clean my room, but more times than often he just guarded my door. As I think about it, he resembled "Mr. Clean" from the Pine Sol commercial! It really disappointed me that no one else could see Mr. Blue except me. I tried to get him to reveal himself to others but for some reason he would not!

It wasn't till later on in life, some 20 years later that a good friend of mine, who is a Psychologist, revealed to me that when a child develops an imaginary friend, he/she is looking for validation in areas of lack. She went on to explain to me how our minds are very powerful tools and that one of the main attributes of the brain is that it will go into "protective" mode when it sees fit to do so. Our subconscious minds create imaginary figures to cope with unbearable truths within our realistic minds. In other words, because Mr. Blue was a comforter- protector – those were the areas of my childhood life that I so desperately needed an intervention to take place in.

You see, I'm the eldest of my parents' five children, so being lonely and not having enough people to play with was never an issue. For I was dealing with more severe issues than that; issues that consisted of feeling alone and having no voice, unsupported, thoughts of being shot and killed while playing basketball at the neighborhood park...all of the things that kids shouldn't have to worry about at age 9. Hence the psychological makeup of "Mr. Blue", who I later discovered was created to be my bodyguard!

YOUR PERSONAL PAIN BIRTHS – YOUR PERSONAL AMBITION

If you're admiring a person's ambition, just know that you are also admiring their pain. ~ Anthony Ford

At the age of sixteen I started managing and running my dad's lawn care company while he took two part-time jobs to increase the family's revenue. I loved mowing lawns, but boy was it hard work! I didn't like the job because of the labor; for what teenager you know would like manual labor? I loved the job because it was the only place that I could escape the mundane routine; the responsibility of changing my little siblings diapers or having to boil and mix baby formula while my friends lived a carefree life, it was the one place that I could escape to! Aside from that, I wasn't too thrilled about my job; I'd rather work at McDonalds with my friends than to be working in Texas' 100-degree heat. My company benefits were elaborate; it provided severe heat exhaustion, time away from my friends and a permanent suntan! However, just like the subconscious mind will create coping mechanisms as needed, in order to remain faithful to my dad's business, my subconscious mind did just that! I'd be so hot while mowing the grass that I'd trick myself into thinking that if I finished mowing the lawn in record time that I'd be rewarded by having the rest of the day off and be able to lounge around in a pool for six hours –and that actually worked; it kept me focused on what was to come rather than what the current situation was. Because I was able to psyche myself out as I did, I began to grow my dad's business just as well as he did when he was in his prime. When I took over the business my junior year in high school, my dad was at 82 accts/lawn contracts; by the time I graduated high school, we were at 134 accts. If you didn't know any better, you'd think that I was obsessed with working. That wasn't the case however, but rather I was eager to leave my poverty-stricken neighborhood to go and work in the suburban areas of my town where love and wealth seemed to so graciously abound.

I remember on one Sunday afternoon when I was loading up some construction debris for one of my dad's customers (a very wealthy banker), when he said, "Son, why do you choose to come out and work on a Sunday, you could've waited 'til Monday to do this job. Your dad told me that Sundays are your favorite day of the week because you get to be off from work and play basketball in the neighborhood instead." I began to explain to him that when I'm at work, I get to see a different atmosphere – one that many of my peers didn't think existed. I went on to tell him that I love working because it's about the only place where I could actually hear the sounds of nature rather than the sounds of firearms, abusive language and police sirens. He began to get choked up as he nodded his head in agreement. As a result of that conversation, he found work for me to do each and every weekend – without him really realizing that he was feeding the ambition inside of me!

YOUR CURRENT SITUATION DOES NOT DICTATE YOUR FINAL DESTINATION

Although I lived in a tough, rugged inner city neighborhood where your first life lessons were to learn how to fight, shoot a gun and how to outsmart the cops; I knew that this was not my destiny! Because I had been on the "other side" (the neighborhoods where I mowed lawns), I was certain that life was going to soon be mine. I remember observing the lifestyles of the affluent families that I worked for; they looked so happy, they ate dinner together, they went on family vacations together; their kids smothered them with hugs and kisses as they returned home from work. I remember saying to myself, "I want that lifestyle!" It was several years before I had the chance to experience that lifestyle, but my current situation became a little more bearable being that my hope and aspirations were fixed on that particular destination.

You may ask yourself what does this have to do with business. Well, believe it or not, the best businesses are created from the owners' personal struggles! There are three points to take from what we've discussed so far:

Lack - Lack creates the desire to have whatever it is that you're lacking. If lack is perceived in the right manner it could serve as a tremendous driving force that will catapult you to new heights!

Ambition - Lack paired with ambition is a force to be reckoned with! Lack fuels ambition and ambition keeps the drive just as a battery cranks the automobile, though the alternator is what keeps the engine and the entire car from dying.

Vision - It's one thing to lack something and another to have ambition, but how do you know how long to keep the ambition? Vision makes you aware of how long the ambition has to stay around so that the said goal could be achieved.

MR. BLUE REINCARNATED

The idea that Mr. Blue was created and formed based out of my needs is the same concept that one must apply when deciding on what product and/or services that their business will provide! That's if your business is going to STAND OUT in any country and will stand the test of time! Every business that I've ever started derived from a problem, and for which my company provided a solution.

The secret to ensuring that your business will be successful, unique and will stand apart in any country, market, city or state, is to ask yourself the following questions:

• *What is it that I enjoy doing?*

• *What special gifts do I posses?*

• *What do I have to offer someone?*

• *What would I attempt to do if I knew that I could not fail?*

• *What type of contribution can I make to people lives?*

Use the answer to these questions to develop your business plan!

MY COMPANY – THE REAL ESTATE CONCIERGE

The Real Estate Concierge – We are an investment firm that acts as a personal concierge service for regular people who'd like to invest in real estate, but lack the time, the resources, the knowledge and the experience to do so themselves. I started investing in real estate when I was 23 years old; the first flip that I participated in gave me a net profit of $45,000. When my peers and colleagues heard that I knew how to "flip" properties they began to marvel at me as if I were some type of superhuman! That couldn't have been further from the truth than the east is from the west; I was just an ambitious young man that had experienced his fair share of lack – which I was sick and tired of – and therefore my ambition drove me to just jump out there and do it! I didn't know what I was doing entirely. I just knew where I wanted to be financially and that was enough motivation for me!

So, as I began to tell people about the property that I had just flipped, people began to make comments about how they could never do anything like that and how they've always wanted to invest, but were afraid of all that could go wrong within a project. Some people would tell me how they loved to watch HGTV and how they subscribed to various magazine publications that centered around home improvement, etc. But all of these people had one thing in common: they had the desire, but for some reason or another they lacked the resources to make such a desire come to fruition. This problem sparked a very big interest within me. I just had to provide a solution to this problem!

To this day, my company has invested in close to 900 rental properties and have flipped over 700 properties and has helped thousands of investors develop their real estate portfolio and go on to be very wealthy in doing so. All of these people had one thing in common: *their desire was to invest in real estate but they lacked the resources and proper knowledge to be able to do so.* The company that I created has helped these individuals to do something extraordinary; something that they wouldn't have otherwise had the privilege of doing if it weren't for my company. These individuals have two options:

Option#1: We could hold their hand through the investment process by mentoring them every step of the way.

Or

Option#2: We could act as their personal concierge and do all of the work for them while they sit back and enjoy the profits. They get to choose which option they'd like to explore. The thing that has made my business so successful is the fact that I simply provided a solution to a problem that every "investor hopeful" faces!

CLIFF PAUL VS. CHRIS PAUL

Have you seen the State Farm Insurance commercial featuring Chris Paul and his twin brother Cliff Paul? One twin assists 7-foot giants in the NBA and the other twin assists regular homeowners with their insurance needs. "They both were born to assist!" Well I'm the real estate Chris & Cliff Paul wrapped up in one! I found myself not only leading people through the investment process, but I also began to lead them through life. Because many of my clients consider me to be a real estate guru, they automatically consider me a guru in life itself. You'd be surprised as to the number of clients that have come to me with their relationship problems, financial woes and family issues – wanting me to "flip" their issues/problems around just as I flip properties for them. At first I thought that this was an odd gesture, but when I began to look at myself through their eyes, I began to see why they thought of me as they encountered life's hurdles. For through showing them how to invest in real estate, I was also the one that has helped them to gain financial freedom, the one who helped them open up their first business, to take their families to exotic destinations, etc. No wonder they were both comfortable and confident in having me to solve their personal issues and, just like anything else, Mr. Ford was up for the challenge!

ALLOW OTHER PEOPLE'S PROBLEMS TO STRETCH YOUR VISION AND DICTATE OTHER POSSIBLE BUSINESS OPPORTUNITIES

Because I have helped several families not only attain wealth but also attain healthy solid relationships with their spouses, kids, colleagues and parents, I've started a counseling practice. Within my practice I counsel those dealing with anger management problems, those that are having dating and career issues, and those who suffer from what I call the "failure to launch syndrome."

As you can see there are no limitations to what you could do in the business world...So remember these three points as this chapter comes to a close.

#1: Seek out people's problems and create a business that offers the solutions to those problems.

#2: Never allow yourself to think that it's too late to start a new business/concept. My counseling practice was officially birthed less than 16months ago.

#3: Take some time to get away and analyze life. Let life speak to you in terms of what your purpose on this earth is, and be sure to own up to it, for prosperity and financial freedom will soon follow.

About Anthony

ANTHONY FORD is widely referred to as "Mr FordHustle" because of his keen work ethic and the fact that he has owned several businesses in and around the Houston Texas Metropolitan Area. Anthony is a life coach to several corporate figures and has bought and sold several hundreds of real estate properties over the past decade.

Anthony began his journey from a very humble beginning. He grew up in a rough, urban inner city neighborhood in Houston, TX – where poverty, prostitution and drugs were a common scene. Yet Anthony's parents still found a way to instill in him strict morals that taught him how to survive on the rough streets of his community, while never being detached from his strong moral background.

Well it wasn't too long after Anthony began to receive such teachings from his parents that he started to take an active approach of his own to ensure that the next generation of "Fords" would have these same sentiments. He named this approach the #fordhustle movement. This movement consists of two components: The first component was Mr. Ford teaching and mentoring his two kids and younger siblings on how to become entrepreneurs by taking what the streets have taught them; in terms of being tough, trustworthy and the ability to think two steps ahead of their opponents; while comprising it with what they've learned scholastically and becoming valiant business owners. The second component consists of Mr. Ford teaching his family to pay it forward by giving back to the community that "made" them who they are today - successful business owners and pillars in the community.

Currently Anthony has a Non-Profit Organization that mentors inner city youths, owns a Real Estate Investment Concierge Firm, A Real Estate Brokerage, runs an Anger Management Resolution Operation and is a Life Coach.

For more information on Anthony Ford, visit him on the web at the websites listed below.
www.AnthonyFord.net
www.recHouston.com
www.ivyleagueproperties.com

To connect with Anthony Ford via social media, follow him on Instagram and Twitter @fordhustle.

CHAPTER 3

5 SECRETS TO MARKETING YOUR BUSINESS ONLINE

BY JENN FOSTER

MY BACKGROUND

I grew up in an entrepreneurial family. My grandfather started one of the largest gas station chains in the western United States. His nephew also created a very large gas station chain that eclipsed the size of his business. If you've traveled very far inside the United States you probably purchased gasoline from one of his stations. Needless to say, my background growing up was very business-oriented. I then married an entrepreneurial-minded person and we built a business owning numerous retail stores. It seems that I have always been surrounded by entrepreneurial people and I was destined to follow that path.

Almost a decade ago, I wrote my first book about how to create your own home-based business and make money online by drop shipping products. In the book I used the real-life examples of individuals that established a legitimate business through online sales. Interestingly, up to that point, I had never done what I wrote about. Instead, I wrote about the successes of others. Based on the advice I offered in the book, I found a product, built my own website, and began selling drop-shipped merchandise which became a successful business for me. This was a way for me to be a stay-at-home mom, home school my three children, and still contribute to the family budget.

Through this process I discovered how much I enjoyed building websites and I was very good at it. When the word spread about my website-building expertise, I began building sites for friends and local businesses. As others learned of my talent, requests began continuously streaming into my developing business. I quickly realized that web sites can be made to look awesome, but if no one can find them, then they are just taking up virtual real estate and not serving any real purpose. That realization led me into becoming a Search Engine Optimization (SEO) expert and to the discovery of video marketing and its importance in SEO.

After learning video marketing, I began to help my web site clients develop an SEO strategy that would get them on the first page of a Google search for video and local marketing. This portion of my business grew exponentially as I employed various networking strategies. Nine years later, I have a highly successful business of helping others achieve marketing success in their business.

A WORD TO WOMEN ENTREPRENEURS

As I have networked with others in my trade, I have noticed there are a lot more men than women. So, I am functioning in a very male-dominated industry. Over the years I have talked with many women who lack confidence in their ability to build a business of their own. I want to let women know they **CAN** be successful entrepreneurs. They can be empowered to make their own way. I want to encourage women entrepreneurs who may doubt their abilities and their dreams. Anyone can make their own mark on this world if they really want to: women, men, young, old, married or single. It's just a matter of putting your mind to something and doing it.

Being limited financially can be very debilitating in many ways. Sometimes people stress over their lack of money, but don't want to take the initiative to do anything about it. Now, creating your own business can give you the ability to have more control over your time and your finances. If you find something you like to do and can make money at it, you have the best of both worlds.

I've always liked computers. When I was young my family purchased an Amiga computer. It was one of the first computers with a mouse. There were two games and a coloring book feature that I always used. I loved to be on the computer. That was the beginning of my "connection" with the computer. When I started creating websites for family, my friends, and myself, I found my passion. Find something that you like and build a business out of it. One of my favorite quotes is from Henry Ford, "If you think you can do a thing or think you can't do a thing, you're right." A lot of times women think they can't, but if they have enough determination, they really can.

MY TOP 5 SECRETS FOR MARKETING YOUR BUSINESS ONLINE

Today I help businesses expose their industry presence to their local community and beyond depending on their desired geographical reach. What I have learned through formal education, personal research and years of experience can be highly beneficial to your online business marketing strategy. I want to share with you my top five secrets for marketing your business online. If used properly, these points will help you achieve online star power:

Top Secret #1 - Local Marketing

The most important step you can take in local marketing is to make sure your Business Google Map is claimed or verified. If you are on your phone and search for a particular business, the Google Map is what will come up first. If you're not on the top 5 listings of that map, then you're not doing yourself any favors. Having a verified Google Map is essential to people finding you. You should make sure all your business information is filled out and accurate – such as your picture, logo, business descriptions, phone number and web site address.

You can also encourage your clients to write a positive review for you. You may want to give them an incentive such as, "If you leave a review about us, we'll give you 10% off your next purchase." By asking your best customers you will very likely have multiple positive reviews. You should also have someone consistently managing your reviews. If you happen to get a bad review, don't ignore it. Make sure you comment on it and take care of the problem with your dissatisfied customer. If you do get a bad review, go out and get several more good reviews. You want to make sure you have many more positive reviews than negative reviews.

Top Secret #2 – Mobile Marketing

Make sure your website is mobile friendly. This is imperative because almost everyone has a tablet or a phone today. Many websites today are "responsive." That is, your website will fit the size of screen on which it's being viewed (i.e. desktop, tablet, mobile device, etc.). Having a responsive or mobile friendly website is key in the present market. If you don't currently have a website that can be viewed by all devices, you can easily obtain a mobile version of your website inexpensively and without having to change your current website.

You also want to make sure your mobile site has "click to call." That is, all your customer has to do is click the phone number on their mobile screen and it will automatically place the call. If you have a physical store location, you must also have a "click for directions" option so people can easily find out how to get to your location. These are features your customer expects to see.

Top Secret #3 – Social Media Marketing

The majority of business owners think social media is so amazing that they get myopically focused on venues such as Facebook and Twitter, only to find their efforts are not resulting in much profit. They end up spending hours upon hours on social media without adequate return on investment. Make sure you don't concentrate all your online marketing efforts on social media.

Google wants to show the most **current, consistent** and **relevant** content. When a potential customer uses a search engine to find something in your industry and you have the correct key words posted on your social media platforms consistently, you will be on the first page of the Google search results. That's the reward for being **current, consistent** and **relevant**.

The biggest secret to social media is to be consistent. Many businesses tell me, "Yes, we have a Facebook fan page. Someone created it for us a year ago, but I don't know what's on there." When you look at their page you find that no one has posted anything on there for about four months. That doesn't do that business any good at all.

I recommend that you concentrate on the top three to five social networks that make the most sense for your business. You don't need to be everywhere, but you need to be in the places you know where your clients are looking.

Social media can be very time consuming. Thankfully, there are many tools available to help you stay current with your social media posts. If you can't afford to hire someone to do your social media or have an employee do it, then you have to find some kind of a tool. Tools such as HootSuite enable you to manage all your social media in one place. You can set it up once a week and schedule all your posts for that week. Then you can have someone monitor your social media pages to respond to comments you may receive in response to your posts.

Instagram is another great resource, especially if you have a business with a specific tangible product such as art or fashion, because it's so easy to take a picture and in one click, Instagram will post it to Facebook, Twitter, Flickr, Foursquare and Tumblr.

As a business owner, you also need to be on LinkedIn. Not only can you create a profile of yourself linking you to your industry, but you can also have a business page. You can set up a page describing your business and identify the products or services you provide.

Top Secret #4 – Text and Email Campaigns
If you set up a text and email auto-responder campaign, you can generate a lot of business and a lot of leads. This will involve having a lead capture page or a website that has a video and a place to enter your potential customer's name and email address in order to receive a free offer you make available. Your offer might be to get an informational white paper you have written, to receive your monthly newsletter, or to get videos on a particular subject. This is a great way to expose others to your business by giving them something tangible. Let's face it; everyone likes the word "free."

Text campaigns work very well for restaurants. You may have seen a restaurant advertise "text this number to us and receive 10% off your next meal." You don't have to have a huge corporation to have a successful text campaign. By using an auto-responder you don't have to personally respond to all the texts or emails. An automatic response is sent to your new potential customer and you have just obtained a new lead. You can then follow up with that client in numerous ways.

Top Secret #5 – Video Marketing
I've saved the best for last. Video is everywhere. Google bought YouTube because it was the number two Search Engine and continues to be today. People often prefer to watch something instead of reading

it, and YouTube provides them with that option.

Video is important for many reasons, not just to have a presence on YouTube. Video on your website can be very beneficial to your business. When people see you or your employees on video, they identify you as being more reputable, they will trust you more and will have a greater likelihood of doing business with you. It gives them something tangible with which they can identify. It puts a face with a name, so to speak.

Video is also extremely important to your online marketing strategy because it ranks really well and helps boost your SEO if you have the proper titles, descriptions and key words. If you do it right, your video will rank very high on the search engines, especially in your local market. Remember, Google wants *current, relevant* and *consistent* material and video can be a tremendous resource to help you.

Many people get stalled right out of the gate when it comes to creating videos because they can't think of compelling content. Here is a simple way to create great content. Write down the 10 most frequently asked questions about your business, then answer those questions in ten 1-minute videos. Now you immediately have 10 videos to post. Post one video per week or two videos per month. Not only will this help your customer to better understand your business, it will also have a positive impact on your SEO.

Next, write down the 10 questions your customers "should" be asking about your business. Now you have 10 more videos to help your customers understand your products or services. You can see how very quickly you can create 20 videos that you can spread out over the next 5 months.

With video, you must capture your audience's attention in the first 10 to 30 seconds. If you don't capture their attention they are going to go somewhere else. You want your video to be between 1 and 3 minutes in length.

After you have provided the content of your video, make sure you conclude with a *call to action* (CTA). Tell them what to do next. It may be "visit our website" or "call us today" or "visit our store." Whatever you decide for your call to action, make sure it is very clear.

You will want to make sure on each video that there is a title and description. In your description you will also want to make sure you have a link to your website and your phone number. After someone watches your video they may want more information and this provides a very convenient way for them to obtain it. Make it easy for them to find you, or they will find your competitor.

After the video is created, then you will want to transcribe the video into text. Now you have information that you can use in social media posts, email messages, text messages, newsletters or blogs. So you take one piece of content (your video) and create more content (written). You can also do the opposite, that is, take any current written content you have available and use it to create great video content.

SEE YOU AT THE TOP

While the world of online marketing can become very complex and technical, you don't have to be overwhelmed or succumb to information overload. Take it a step at a time. Experiment with various aspects of online marketing to find out what will work best for you. If your budget will allow, seek out the advice of an online marketing expert. Sometimes it is more cost efficient to outsource this part of your business so you can focus on your core business.

Whatever form of online marketing you use, always remember to be current, consistent and relevant. I look forward to seeing your business on the top of Google!

About Jenn

Jenn Foster, one of today's national leading online and mobile marketing experts, is the founder and CEO of Biz Social Boom, a company dedicated to helping business owners of all sizes thrive in today's highly technical world of product and service promotion. From local brick and mortar stores to online entities to large international corporations, Jenn's years of experience and expertise has helped hundreds become front-page news on all the major search engines. She is dedicated to helping businesses use powerful new online and mobile marketing platforms to get visibility, traffic, leads, customers and raving fans.

A graduate of Utah State University, Jenn is an award-winning web designer, author and sought after speaker. She has been a featured speaker at such events as the Kim Flynn's Internet Marketing Boot Camp, Utah Crowd Funding Association, the Sandy Area Chamber of Commerce and the Saratoga Springs Chamber of Commerce among others. She was also an expert guest on The Teach Jim Show on Blog Talk Radio. Jenn has been named one of America's Premier Experts® and will soon be highlighted in a major national publication.

Coming from a family of successful entrepreneurs, Jenn grew up around thriving businesses and understands from the ground up what it takes to create, run and promote winning companies. Combining her education, knowledge and life-long experience, today Jenn teaches people and businesses globally how they can get found in today's virtual world, how they can engage prospects on their terms and how to continue to connect and follow up with prospects to convert them to customers. By utilizing her proven techniques, Jenn confidently guarantees her clients will be on the first page of Google Search in their local market.

When she is not helping her clients, Jenn enjoys spending time with her three children, sewing with her family 4-H club, experiencing the great outdoors and she loves Zumba. Additional information about Jenn and her business can be found at: www.BizSocialBoom.com or by calling her directly at: 801-901-3480.

CHAPTER 4

CONDOMINIUM ASSOCIATIONS AND HOMEOWNERS ASSOCIATIONS: HEAVEN SENT OR HELL-BOUND?

BY MOLLY PEACOCK

WHAT MAKES A COMMUNITY STAND APART, AND HOW CAN YOU HELP YOURS DO SO

This Chapter discusses how communities can stand apart in our locality, state, nation and world. First some background. A few decades ago, someone figured out that local communities should be in charge of maintaining their own common areas, roads, and amenities. This scheme seems obvious in the case of condominiums: the owners of the condominium units should share the cost of maintaining the roof, exercise room, insurance, legal needs, etc. At the request of municipalities, developers began creating what are known as community associations, which include homeowners associations, condominiums, and cooperatives. Homeowners in a community became responsible for maintaining common areas and governing themselves in a manner that supported property values.

So, are community associations good for society or are they a plague? That's an easy one! They are great. And they are reality. So if you are a disgruntled homeowner, let me be clear about my biased opinion: the key to success for any homeowner to prevail in an argument against the association is education. If you want to make a difference in your community, then follow three important steps: get involved, educate yourself, and stay ahead of problems. For Board members, managers and service providers reading this: Thank You for your service. This chapter is written for you. Figuring out how to make your community stand apart in excellence benefits you and your neighbors, and leaves a legacy of positive consequences that are far-reaching. Read on to continue your education, and be on your way to further improving your community.

REAL TALK

When I attended a seminar in early 2013 held by Community Associations Institute, the motivational, informative speaker, Adolph Brown, coined a term "Real Talk." He is right—the benefits of Real Talk include that it gets right to the truth/facts of a matter without unnecessary drama. This Chapter is intended to give you Real Talk.

Examples of what communities hear frequently from their members include: "Who is going to pay for this water damage to my condominium unit, certainly not me!" "All I want is a beautiful deck, which will add value to my home and enjoyment to my family's and my use of our house." "All I want is to feel secure that the construction next door is not going to damage my condominium unit." "All I want is more transparency, responsiveness and accountability around here!"

This feedback may feel grating at times to the leadership and/or management of a community association. However, it is worth listening to. These statements represent the sentiment, "This is my home, please do not unreasonably interfere with my use of it; furthermore I am paying the monthly dues so I would like to know that money is being used properly." From that vantage point, most concerns from homeowners can be addressed in a manner that results in a resolution of disputes without incurring unnecessary cost and without having to have a nervous breakdown over the argument.

IF YOU CAN'T BEAT THEM, JOIN THEM

If you are a disgruntled homeowner feeling angry with your association's Board of Directors, you may feel you want to sue them. Be Advised: If you sue them, you will be paying your lawyer and your opponent's lawyer with an uncertain outcome. As much as I love a good fight, litigation can become expensive, time consuming, and deleterious to property values. If you are contemplating incurring the cost and energy of a lawsuit, a potentially less nuclear option is to get yourself onto the Board of Directors and effect change from the inside out.

Now assume you are on the Board of Directors. You and your property management team, if you have one, may hear statements like those listed above; you might also hear complaints that are the result of a lack of understanding or knowledge. (I hope you also receive compliments? Don't answer that.) Please put yourself in the homeowners' shoes when you hear from them, i.e., "join them" in wanting to improve property values, making sure money is handled properly, and creating a well-run community.

Whether or not you take this advice, and regardless of the feedback you receive from the membership, it is also true that you:

- are in charge of properly overseeing the management of everyone's monthly dues

- have a legal responsibility to properly maintain the common areas and facilities

- must comply with the myriad laws that apply to community associations

- are supposed to know what the rules are and enforce them properly

- are expected to manage service providers in a manner that decreases your workload rather than increasing it!

Meanwhile you are not paid, have a day job, hobbies, a family, other interests, and maybe own other property. Finally, you have the highest level of responsibility there is: a fiduciary responsibility.

How on earth are you supposed to accomplish all this? Are you really expected to know exactly what that fiduciary obligation means, what that duty entails and what personal exposure you might have? Is this list for real? Shouldn't the laws change?

Answer: yes the list is for real, and yes the laws change often.

Fortunately, yes is also the answer to whether it is possible to live up to that list plus all the other requirements your community may have of you as a Board member. How? This chapter is written to help answer how.

GET EXCITED AND GET EDUCATED

It is helpful to not only understand, but also be enthusiastic about your role as a Board Member. The primary goals of a Board of Directors of a community association are twofold:

1. Enhance, maintain high property values;
2. Promote, preserve and protect a high quality of life for homeowners, unit owners and residents.

It is not easy to achieve those goals, and sometimes they seem to conflict! However, those goals are helpful to ask yourself when you are not sure what to do, AND if there are moments when life as a Board member gets you down. It can be a thankless job.* But you are at the ground level of protecting property values, enforcing rules fairly, seeking to streamline operations, thereby trying to effectuate a happy community—by both giving residents the freedom to not worry about unfair rules, or unfair enforcement, and by providing and maintaining amenities or parties that may be enjoyed at everyone's leisure. These tasks are the ingredients of not only a successful, Stand Apart community, but also I daresay, of a region, town, city, state, country, and world. Thus, your efforts as an educated steward of your community make you a quintessential public servant, and give you the ability to leave a significant, positive legacy. How?

STAY AHEAD OF THE PROBLEM

One of the things that makes a Board of Directors stand apart in excellence is the amount of space its team can create for it to stay ahead of problems. Lawyers like to say "pay me now or pay me (more) later."

---

* I have known Board members to go to lengths for the sake of their community; for example one Board member cancelled a vacation in order to address an urgent situation that could have had an intense impact on property values. Because of his sacrifice, a potentially expensive argument was resolved before escalating, and potential damage to the beauty of the building was avoided. No one (except me) knew or thanked him for giving up his beach trip, but his efforts paid off.

Identifying problems early can reduce their cost to the community. The more you know about your community's rules and laws, the better able you are to know a problem when you see one. The help of a quality team is essential: team members include property management, engineering, insurance, lawyer(s), accounting, landscaping (and more). The community's property management and lawyer exist to help educate Board members and the membership—so does an entity called Community Associations Institute ("CAI" for short), mentioned above. CAI is a valuable resource not only for Board members but also service providers and community members.

The good managers (and lawyers) figure out solutions to problems that are sometimes as creative as they are effective. The good lawyers (and managers) help the Board look around corners and establish systems so that when disaster strikes, the cost is lower than it otherwise would be.

FOR EXAMPLE

Situation: I am a Board member of a condominium and received a call at 2:30 a.m. from an angry unit owner who sees water dripping through her ceiling. Her unit appears damaged, and water might be flowing to other units and common elements. What do I do; who is responsible for the damage, and for fixing the water leak?

Answer: Anyone involved should take action to stop the flow of water; call a plumber; mitigate damage. Once danger to person or property is averted, determine, with an expert's help, what caused the water leak. Then identify who is responsible for what repairs based on the facts and the law (which includes the condominium's covenants). This identifying may be a collaborative effort among the property management, plumber, and legal counsel. If a claim is made to insurance, and a deductible is involved, it may be appropriate to pass the cost of the insurance deductible to a unit owner if the source of the leak is a unit component— if your rules permit you to do this.

Still awake? Water leaks happen often in condominiums. If your lawyer sets things up well, you might be able to apportion the costs of damage from water leaks directly to the responsible unit owner(s), including having the unit owner pay for any deductible associated with a claim the condominium makes on its master policy. (Unit Owners be advised, usually you can get insurance for this.) This magic trick could save (tens of) thousands of dollars yearly. To pull it off, educating the members on a regular basis is essential, as is a close study of the recorded covenants and bylaws, and creation of appropriate policy resolutions and systems.

Situation: Someone is asking for a deck that is not permitted by our rules. How am I supposed to promote high quality of life when letting this deck get installed would reduce property values probably?

Answer: Congratulations, it is good that you have advance notice of a desired deck. As experienced Board members will know, the first step in this case is to make sure you know exactly what your governing documents require, if anything, related to this request for a deck, including deadlines, and specifications. Each community is different. Your property manager and legal counsel will be able to answer questions you may have as to what is required and not allowed, and what the Board's deadline may be to respond to a request to install The Deck.

A universal truth which helps promote a constructive relationship (pardon the pun) with deck requests and--almost anything--is to set up a system where the requesting homeowner receives acknowledgment that the request was received, and an estimated time for when a substantive response will arrive. Your lawyer can help identify how to acknowledge receipt without giving permission to install the deck!

Once you have all relevant information, if The Deck is not permitted by the rules, respond to the requester with this information, denying permission, and giving the reasons why The Deck cannot be built because of XYZ rule(s).

The most important angle of this scenario is to make sure your community association grants and denies permission in a uniform manner pursuant to clear rules. Depending on the size of your community, you may need a system to be put into place to ensure this consistency. A tool some Boards find helpful is to call a town hall meeting on a regular basis to tell the community what the architectural rules are, and invite feedback. Sometimes the rules are twenty years old and need updating—so update them.

Situation: Someone already installed a deck. It is a monstrosity, the neighbors are complaining, it is non-compliant with our rules, the homeowner never requested permission, it is already installed, one of the neighbors is threatening to sue Board members because they wanted to install a deck that was half this big, and they were denied permission.

Answer: This situation is an excellent illustration of "Pay me now or pay me later." Here, the facts suggest that certain systems were absent which could have caught this now-large problem when it was a smaller problem. Those systems include:

- Taking active steps, such as yearly information meetings, open Board meetings, regular distribution of the rules, to try to make sure community members know they must ask permission before installing a deck.

- Conducting regular property inspections that could enable the Board to learn of the deck installation and take mitigating action before it is completed or begun.

- Having Policy Resolutions stating what must happen when a homeowner wants to improve his/her property, and what happens when rules are broken.

Yes Molly, thanks for the lecture about how to avoid this situation in the first place, but what do we do about the Taj Mahal deck that is now a liability? In typical lawyer fashion, I tell you the answer depends on the personality of the community. The universal truth is that some form of dispute resolution should be used, probably with the help of legal counsel. Dispute resolution can range in formality, and may occur inside or outside the courtroom. The whole situation can then be used as a wake-up call to this community: time to devote energies to building a proverbial fence in front of the railroad tracks rather than having ambulances waiting on the other side. Once you resolve the argument as best you can, proceed with vigor to install systems that can enable the Association to avoid expensive messes like this one.

Situation: There is significant construction about to begin next door to my condominium building. How will the Board make sure the condominium is protected against damage that might happen when a big crane is used, the ground is hammered, and construction dust is everywhere?

Answer: The condominium's engineer, insurance advisor and property manager can swoop in to take proactive steps to prevent and mitigate any trouble. These steps include: having a building/engineer inspect the condominium, take pictures, make a record of the state of the building prior to the next-door construction. Seek to establish a relationship with someone affiliated with the next-door construction, such as the head of the construction company, owner of the site. Have the property manager or Board member communicate regularly with a designated person to exchange updates. Invite residents to write down problems that arise and communicate those in a timely manner to the property manager. Know the municipality's noise rules, construction rules (for example, no jackhammering from 7:00 pm to 7:00 am and on weekends), publish these around the condominium, and inform the construction company of the expectation that these rules will be complied with.

CONCLUSION

There is enough sadness and badness in the world - both inside and outside of community associations to fill several volumes of books. The good news is you have an opportunity to change some of that within your community. As you can probably tell, my experience working with hundreds (thousands?) of Board members and managers indicates that advance planning and gratitude are essential ingredients to a successful community. Thank you, Board member, for being *stand apart* individuals, investing in your communities by continually educating yourself. Thank you, community managers and service providers who help the Board make its community thrive. Community associations were established to promote and foster harmonious living.

Getting involved + Educating Yourself + Staying Ahead of the Problems = Creation of a Stand Apart Community.

About Molly

Molly Peacock founded the Peacock Law Firm, a law firm that focuses its practice on condominiums, cooperatives and homeowners associations. She believes her clients are the fabric of this nation. Her clients are people with diverse daytime obligations who have a common goal: to make their community a great place to live. As Molly likes to repeat, the work that her clients accomplish also improves the property values within their communities. The ripple effect of this work is a better condominium, home, street, neighborhood, town, city, and world - yet her clients do all this on a volunteer basis. Money cannot buy the level of commitment required for certain institutions to work well. She feels honored to work with people who care for the physical, financial, and intangible assets of their community.

Molly graduated from The College of William and Mary with a BA in French and Government in 1999. She graduated with a JD from the University of Richmond in 2002, a semester early, and went on to work as a law clerk for the Honorable Judges of the Alexandria Circuit Court in Virginia, Judges Haddock, Kloch, and Swersky. Molly learned much about litigation, dispute resolution, and opinion-drafting during her two-year tenure as one of three Judges' Law Clerks. At the conclusion of the clerkship, Molly began her private practice at an insurance defense firm in Arlington, Virginia, continuing her thorough education in litigation, appellate work, and dispute resolution. From insurance defense, Molly moved into the realm of community association law, joining the law firm of Chadwick Washington in 2006.

Molly's father is a retired Brigadier General in the Army; her brother is currently a Major General, leading the 82nd Airborne Division in Ft. Bragg. Having been brought up in a military family, Molly has had the privilege of growing up with a special appreciation for duty, honor, country, and service. She herself was awarded an Army ROTC scholarship and was commissioned as a Second Lieutenant at her college graduation in 1999. Though a medical issue cut her military career short, Molly remains drawn to people who care enough for their communities to dedicate themselves to enabling due process, protecting freedom, and thinking creatively about the best prevention of, and solutions to, problems.

Problem solving and fun planning is an integral part of home life for Molly while not working. She and her handsome, funny, husband Glen are parents to three fast-growing sons. Her hobbies include going to plays with one or more of the boys, going to the park, visiting vineyards in Virginia and beyond, attending wine tastings on weekends (and weeknights), and determining which champagne is really her favorite.

CHAPTER 5

CREATING A BUSINESS — AND A LIFE YOU LOVE BY FINDING YOUR VOICE

BY PAM HENDRICKSON

The day we found out my mom was going to die, we were sitting in a crowded examining room in the doctor's office with the door open and a flood of doctors and nurses rushing by.

It was one of those rare moments in which my mom and I weren't talking to each other. What do you say when you're both waiting for the biggest moment of your lives together?

When the doctor finally did come by, he didn't even shut the door. He just stood in the doorway, looked at my mom and said, "It's not good. The tests came back and the fluid around your lungs is completely full of cancer."

My mom closed her eyes, opened them and said, "How long?"

"I'm going to refer you to the oncologist," he said, "but I'm hoping for 6-12 months."

Three days later, she was in a hospital bed just out of the ICU. The oncologist came in after having reviewed all her charts, took one look at her sleeping in the bed, and started shaking his head. He told my brother and me, "I want you to be prepared. She's not gonna make it through the night."

My brother left the room to go get something to eat, and there I was alone with my mom for what I thought might be our last moments together.

I recorded what happened next in my journal:

"Last night I went into the hospital and crawled into bed with her. And when I did that, she was half-conscious, but she stirred, and I said, 'Mom, is this okay?' And she said quietly, 'I love it.'

And then I whispered in her ear everything that's in my heart. I told her I know she's sad and scared, and I am too. But more than the pain, I am grateful. I would not change one day or do one thing different for the opportunity for her to be my mom. I reminded her that she and I had a special bond and a connection that goes well beyond the physical and into the spiritual. And I reminded her that the spiritual connection would never go away.

I told her I'm so grateful she's been here for me for every major life event you can imagine—growing up, concerts, plays, school graduation, the tough times, high school, college, my wedding, the birth of my boys. How lucky am I for that? I told her that I'll miss her so much, but I promise to keep the memories alive for me, for the boys, and for my family.

And I said, "Most of all, mom, I just want you to know that who I am comes from you. It's inseparable. It's how I'll live my life. It's the wisdom I'll use to raise my boys. It's how I'll know what to do when times get tough."

One of the last things she said to me was, "Life is fleeting and that's what makes it so precious." Then she recited her favorite quote from Dr. Wayne Dyer: "You come into this world with nothing. You leave this world with nothing. All you have is what you give while you're here."

Before my mom was diagnosed, I always thought that the whole secret to success and happiness was achieving. I believed that it was the answer not only to a successful life, but that it would make everyone around me happy.

To say I've changed my thinking would be an understatement.

It's not that achieving isn't important. It's incredibly important to have goals and accomplish things in life that make you a better person and help you contribute more to the people you care about.

What you achieve, however, has to connect with what makes you happy—and what you want your life to stand for. Otherwise, you'll get caught up in all the little things you didn't accomplish and you'll miss the big picture. You'll miss the joy in life.

This is especially important if you're an entrepreneur. Your journey won't be a straight line—and it will have its ups and downs. However, as long as you're making some kind of progress toward what you want— and what you're here to give—then you're in great shape. Fantastic shape, even.

The key is to get yourself to the point where you can embrace every part of the journey—the heartaches, the triumphs, the mistakes, the small miracles and the cliffhangers—and move forward with the lessons each has to teach you.

This will also help you spot opportunities that you encounter along the way. Unexpected opportunities are often the most powerful ones. If you're focused so tightly on achieving your goals to the exclusion of everything else, you might miss something important. Try to keep yourself fully present and open to the things that life lays out in front of you.

During this journey, your most powerful tool is clarity: specific, detailed, written, refined, compelling, passionate, personal clarity about what you really want from your life.

One of the gifts my parents gave me is their love for personal development. I was sure that I was the only kid who listened to Earl Nightingale on family road trips. Recently I had to clean out the house I grew up in, and in the basement I found three tall and wide shelves full of cassette tapes, videos and books by all the masters, including Dale Carnegie, Napoleon Hill, Norman Vincent Peale, Jim Rohn, Jack Canfield, Tony Robbins and many, many others. If you asked me what they all have in common, I'd tell you that they all believe strongly in the importance of defining what you want specifically and clearly and then associating to that vision vividly on a consistent, ideally daily, basis.

There's incredible power when you have a crystal-clear vision and everything in your life is working together toward the same goal.

It's very simple to get started:

1. **First, pick an area of your life or business and write down a goal that's important to you.** Make it specific and measurable.

2. **Then, rewrite that goal, but make it an even more clear, vivid and precise image.** The act of writing and rewriting will help clarify it in your mind.

3. **Now add as much detail as you can to your description of your goal.** For example, if it's a tangible item, write down the size, shape, color, height, length, texture or fabric, style, etc. The more comprehensive you can make it, the stronger your association and the more likely that this goal will motivate you to consistent action.

4. **Brainstorm 3-5 (or more) specific, small actions you can take to help move you toward this goal.** If you come up with a list of larger actions, try breaking them down into more manageable bites.

5. **Schedule a specific time each day where you will read, think about and associate vividly with your goal.** Ideally, you can find 2-3 times a day to do this. Imagine you've already achieved your goal and what your life will be like having achieved it. This will give you a strong connection to the emotions of success and help you make this goal a part of your reality that you'll fight for.

As you go through this process, make sure your business goals are set up to be an extension of what you want in your life. When your business contributes to your highest vision for yourself, you'll find passion, drive and satisfaction in your work. You'll also create an amazing life for yourself, one that you treasure and enjoy each day.

But here's the key: **you have to build a business whose primary products and services aren't *you*.** Otherwise, you'll end up trading your time for money. That's a challenging equation—and it almost always results in you working more to make more money. That, in my opinion, is missing the point.

There are countless product ideas you could pursue. One of my favorites—and one that I've focused on during the last 20+ years of my career—involves making an information product out of what you know. When I started in this field, these products often took the form of books and cassette tape sets. These days, the diversity is impressive. I've seen online training courses, software, apps and complete CD/DVD home study kits, to name a few, and the possibilities are truly endless.

Whatever form it takes, creating a product out of what you know will allow you to build a business that doesn't rely on your physical presence to operate.

This will give you the power to . . .

Leverage Your Time: If you find yourself showing people how to do the same things repeatedly, why not create a training product that teaches these lessons without you having to be there? Instead of sharing a lesson with a single person, you could create a video that can impact thousands—even millions—of people around the world. You film it once and it can be viewed over and over again while you record more advanced lessons, pursue other passions, spend more time with your family, etc.

Monetize Your Expertise: By developing products that can be applied without your presence, you will put yourself in the position to make money while you sleep—and exponentially grow your income. And once you have this single puzzle piece in place, your momentum will start to build. New opportunities will appear—such as licensing your content, product endorsements, media and speaking opportunities and much more—raising your visibility and your credibility to an even higher level.

Build Your Legacy: When you create products and services for your marketplace, they can be consumed by anyone in the world, anywhere and at any time. Instead of only being able to train one-to-one or at a 'live' event setting, you can put yourself in a position to have a positive impact on many more people's lives without the potential barriers of time or travel. Creating a product allows you to scale your impact and create a legacy beyond what you are able to physically do as an individual.

No matter who you are, where you live or what you do, if you're here reading this book right now, I know you have a message to share. This message can change other people's lives for the better and shape their trajectories toward a brighter future. Those people need to hear what you have to say—and it's your birthright to share this knowledge with us.

I've worked with thousands of clients in nearly every field imaginable: personal and professional development coaches, sales and marketing experts, university professors, venture capitalists, video producers, personal fitness trainers—the list goes on. Each one of them used the clarity of what they wanted in their lives to create a product for themselves, and a thriving business around that product.

It's not only possible, it's simpler than you think. It starts with what I call the "Six Magic Questions." These six questions will sharpen your vision for the product you'd like to make.

You may not know all the answers right this moment, and that's okay. Carve out some time each day over the next week to go through these six questions and start discovering the answers.

1. *Product:* What problem can you help people solve with your expertise, background or experience? What pain can you alleviate? Brainstorm some product ideas and then narrow it down to the one that's easiest to implement and that will add the most value.

2. *Market:* Who are you going to sell it to? What are some qualities of the people you can help most?

3. *Price:* How much will you charge for your product? If you're uncertain, take a look at your competitor's products, or ask yourself how much someone would pay a professional or consultant to cure the problem.

4. *Income:* What is your goal for how much money you want to make with this product or service in the first 12 months?

5. *Sales:* How many products do you need to sell to achieve this?

6. *Reasons:* Why is this important to you? What will you do—and who will you help—with this money?

On Day 7: Once you have answered the Six Magic Questions, make some final decisions. From those decisions, write down 2-3 interim goals you can act on quickly and commit to a date for completion.

Once you accomplish these goals, set another series of goals to guide you (and don't forget to date each one)!

As you do this, the most important question is the last one, as it associates you to your big "why"—your ultimate purpose for creating both a product and your own business. This "why" will inspire you to take daily action and follow through on your dreams and passions.

For me, my greatest inspiration was my mom. I would give up many things in my life for the gift of more time with her. And yet, because of her passing, I have many gifts that I'm able to share on a greater scale and I'm grateful to be able to help extend her legacy in this way.

By the way, my mom lived six weeks after the oncologist declared she wouldn't make it through the night—long enough to see her grandchildren, long enough to go home, and long enough to pass on her terms, not anyone else's.

We had 500 people in the sanctuary for her funeral. We had to live feed the video into a reception hall because we couldn't get everyone into the sanctuary itself.

Because the day was so emotional, it's hard to remember all the details of what happened, but I can tell you the one thing that stood out:

As I looked around into the people's eyes, I realized something very profound. Every single person in that audience, without exception, didn't just "know" my mom. They'd been deeply and profoundly touched by her in some way. She believed in them when no one else did. She helped them through a time when they didn't know where to turn. She celebrated their greatest victories and mourned their greatest losses.

You see, my mom was never afraid of dying. She was afraid of any of us not really living.

And so I lost my mom that day, but it's also the day I found my voice. It's the day I stepped into my own gifts. It's the day I declared that courage would win over fear, that somehow, someway, I'd figure out a way to give back and continue her message of all the good she has done.

And this is my wish for you—that as you go through the trials and tribulations of building your business, you never lose sight of what, or who, it's for. I've given you the tools to get started in this chapter—and I can't wait to see what you do with them.

About Pam

Pam Hendrickson has been producing, launching and marketing highly profitable products for many of the top names in the personal and professional development industry for over 20 years. In addition to consulting with entrepreneurs, celebrities and CEOs, Pam spent almost twenty years at Robbins Research International, Inc. where she worked directly with Anthony Robbins as the Executive Vice President of Content & Product Development.

Pam is the best-selling author (along with her colleague Mike Koenigs), of *Make, Market, Launch IT: The Ultimate Product Creation System for Turning Your Ideas into Income.* A magna cum laude graduate of Brown University, Pam has grown her consulting and product development businesses to seven figures in just under two years. In 2012, she received the Bronze Stevie Award for "Female Entrepreneur of the Year."

Pam lives in San Diego, CA with her husband and two sons.

For more information, visit: PamHendrickson.com

CHAPTER 6

WHY 3D MAIL GETS SUCH GREAT RESULTS IN ANY MARKETING CAMPAIGN, FOR ANY BUSINESS

BY TRAVIS LEE

When it comes to 3D Mail, 3D says it all. A regular envelope has length and width, but very little depth. 3D Mail has length, width and depth. It truly is three-dimensional. It can be an envelope with something in it that makes it three-dimensional. We call those items grabbers. We've mailed plastic toy scissors, compasses, boomerangs, silver platters, real and fake money and dozens of other items over the years.

3D Mail can also be a mini garbage can, or a real vinyl bank bag, a message in a bottle, a treasure chest, or a pill bottle. We call these items self-mailers because you don't need to put them in an envelope or a box. Imagine a real treasure chest or garbage can showing up in your mailbox, you just have to open it!

IF YOUR MAIL DOESN'T GET OPENED AND READ, IT CAN'T BE SUCCESSFUL

The biggest challenge we face in marketing and advertising is being seen, heard, or read, and direct mail is no different. In fact, if your mail isn't opened and read, you can't make a sale, it's that simple. I've yet to

71

see or hear of a business owner sending a mail piece, have nobody read it, and have it produce a positive return. It simply cannot happen. So when you use 3D Mail, you virtually guarantee that your mail will get opened and read, almost instantly.

3D MAIL CUTS THROUGH THE CLUTTER

Because people are overwhelmed with the amount of advertising and marketing they see today, it is absolutely imperative that you cut through the clutter and boredom and give your prospects or clients something interesting and out of the ordinary. People are so overwhelmed, that they often spend 3.5 seconds or less with information they've requested! If you can't keep your message in front of your prospect, you're done.

If you think that's bad, some studies show that business recipients throw out 48% of their unsolicited mail without opening it! Any message that isn't opened can never be acted upon. When an envelope shows up with a grabber inside, or a self-mailer arrives in the mailbox, your client or prospect MUST open it. They simply have to know what's inside.

IF A STACK DOESN'T STACK, IT CAN'T BE A STACK

Whether you're at home or at the office, we all get a stack of mail every day. One sure fire way to cut through the clutter is to make sure your mailing piece ends up on the top of the stack. If your mailing is in a regular envelope it can end up anywhere in the stack.

But what if your mailing piece is a bank bag? Or, what if your mail piece is in a mini-garbage can? Or what if you mail a plastic message in a bottle? Or what if your mailing is in an envelope with a bag of shredded money or a boomerang inside? If it gets put anywhere other than on the top of the stack, it will fall over. Neither the postal worker nor the receptionist or gatekeeper (whether at the home or office), can stack a stack that doesn't stack.

3D MAIL HAS STICKING POWER

Let's face it, most days nothing different happens. Nothing worth talking about happens either at work or at home. So a mailing that is different, innovative, and maybe a little humorous ends up being talked about. 3D Mail has sticking power. People show it to their spouse, neighbor, friend or coworker. It happens all the time. When two or more people see an offer, one may decide not to take advantage of it. But the other person sees the possibilities. So they start talking about all of the things they and you could do, and you make a SALE!

BUT DOESN'T 3D MAIL COST MORE?

Sure, 3D Mail will normally cost more than a mailing that is not 3D, but not all the time. All you should be interested in is the return on the investment of your campaign. In almost every instance, the results from 3D Mail are a better return on investment than the same mailing without the 3D item. In addition, we highly recommend that you send laser targeted mailings, multiple times, rather than sending out more pieces of untargeted, non-3D mail. In this case, less truly is more. If you're on a marketing budget (and what small business or entrepreneur isn't), we've never seen a case in which multiple 3D mailings to a smaller list hasn't outperformed one boring, same-as-everybody-else mailing to a large list.

HERE ARE JUST A FEW THINGS THAT 3D MAIL CAN DO FOR YOU

Generate Leads

We all know how hard it is to get new clients through a cold mailing. However, it's extremely important to stand out with your advertising and be sure your mail is opened and read. 3D Mail does that. It is not unusual for your prospects to be so amazed with your mailing that they actually call to find out where you got the idea! Talk about cutting through the clutter!

Reduce Returns

One problem any business runs into is return rates. This is also called buyers remorse. After the initial purchase you can send follow-up 3D mailings (often called a 'stick' campaign) to reinforce the purchase your client has just made. But why would you send 3D mail when you can send regular mail? For all the reasons we've already outlined. Remember, if a mailing doesn't get opened, it can't be read or acted upon. It is every bit as important for your follow up marketing to be opened, read and acted upon, as your initial mailing to get the order.

Reactivate Lost Clients

This is where 3D mail can really get fun, and profitable! Lost clients are those people who made a purchase from you at some point, but have not bought again over a defined period of time. This period of time varies by industry. If you're a car salesman, it may be 3-5 years. A real estate agent, it may be 5-10 years. If you own a restaurant, it may be 30-60 days. For a high-end jeweler it may be one year. In one business I work with (a B2B distribution business), we deem a client lost after six months of inactivity.

It is often reported that it is anywhere from 10 times to 100 times more costly to get a new client than it is to sell again to an existing client. A 'lost' client is the second easiest client to sell to (behind those clients who are continually buying from you).

A very successful 3D mail 3-step campaign used by our clients includes a Boomerang with a headline "We Want You Back." A compass with the headline "Are you Lost?" In the third step, a small plastic bug is inserted into the envelope with the headline, "This is the last time I'm going to bug you!"

Drive Traffic to a Location

3D mail can be very effective in getting your clients or prospects to come to your store, restaurant or other retail or office location. One of the best we've seen for driving traffic to a retail location is the treasure chest mailer.

Our client, Stuart Spencer in Laguna Woods, CA owns a hearing aid store. He wanted to run a client appreciation event over a weekend and wanted to invite all his past clients and unconverted leads. He decided to mail a real treasure chest (5" x 2.5" x 3" – about the size of a small jewelry box). He mailed the chest locked, with a small note attached to the top (the entire package was inside a box). The note said that there was a valuable prize inside, anything from a $25 gift certificate to be used at the store, up to a free cruise, and many others.

He instructed them to bring the box to his store over a specific weekend to be unlocked and to reveal the prize they had won. Not only did they have an amazing client appreciate event, he can directly attribute over $80,000.00 in sales from this one mailing!

Stimulate referrals

Using 3D Mail is also a great way to stimulate referrals from your existing clients. One that I really like is a small boomerang inside an envelope with the headline, "Most of Our Business Comes Back to Us From Great Customers Like You." You may want to consider offering a premium (free gift) for those clients who do refer new clients.

Get more business with current clients

There is one big problem all businesses face when trying to get more business from existing clients. Even though they know you and trust you, it's very hard to get their attention and get them to act, even though they've ordered from you in the past. You need to use 3D mail that demands attention. It must cut the clutter and get though to the client. A bank bag, message-in-a-bottle, or small item stuffed in an envelope (that all invoke curiosity), will get your client's attention. It gets them involved and interacting with the mailing. This gives you a much better opportunity to sell to them again.

Find qualified prospects at a trade show

Trade show attendees are often bombarded with pre and post show advertising. It comes from the show organizers themselves, your company, and your competitors. It can get downright overwhelming for prospects. This is a time when you have to be out-of-the-box, unique and willing to stand out from the crowd. A simple, standard size postcard won't cut it. Be daring and stand out.

For pre-show advertising, be creative. Use 3D mail to cut the clutter and give them a reason to stop by your booth. You can use a free gift or show specials to entice them to visit. If you're doing either, try to tie the promotion in with your 3D grabber or self-mailer. For instance, if you're doing a drawing for a free trip, try sending a small toy airplane with the headline, "We'll send you anywhere in North America just for stopping by and saying 'Hi'." The treasure chest mailer discussed above is another great way to drive traffic to your booth with pre-show advertising.

For post-show advertising, it's just as important to stand out. Again, you may want to tie in your promotion from the show. But most importantly, you want to remind them that they had stopped by your booth, and now it's time to get the sale.

Tips for Creating a Successful 3D Mail Program

1. Does 3D mail work for your business?

3Dmail has many uses in both consumer and B2B businesses. However you need to ask yourself if this is right for your business. If you are in B2B marketing with products/services that sell for a few hundred dollars or in an affluent type of consumer product/ service, then 3D mail is for you. If you have a product or service that sells for a lower dollar value, then the incremental cost of a 3D mail program may not be the right fit. However, if that product or service is consumable and being sold over and over again to the same client (in either B2B or consumer marketplace), then it is appropriate for you.

2. What are your goals for your 3D mail campaign?

What do you want to achieve with this 3D direct mail campaign? Is this a one-step sale or lead generation? Do you want to set up a phone call, a face-to-face meeting, a website visit or a direct sale? What are your monetary goals? What kind of sales and responses do you need to make the mailing successful?

3. It's about ROI, not cost, or even response rates!

It is very important to think of 3D mail sequences and campaigns in terms of ROI and not cost or even response rate. 3D mail can cost more than regular flat mail packages. But 3D Mail is not a regular package that gets regular results. Some will base their budgets on the cost to acquire a new customer. Do the math to see if you feel you can hit the optimal ROI for your business. Remember, you put money in the bank, not response rates.

One of my most successful mailers in terms of return on investment had what many would consider to be a horrible response rate. But I was selling $10,000 worth of computer hardware and software. I only needed one response to make the campaign extremely successful. We got more than one response, and it generated a 35 to 1 return! The slightly higher cost of 3D mail almost always warrants the use of it when measuring ROI.

4. Targeting and segmenting your list.

This is a key aspect of any marketing effort, especially 3D mail. Average copywriting sent to an extremely targeted list can get incredible results. Superior copywriting to an inferior list, with little or no targeting will get you inferior results. This is true whether you use 3D mail or regular mail.

5. Make sure the copy, the grabber and the package all tie together.

Integrating the entire package (copy, grabber, package, and target) seems simple enough but all too often the various elements are not connected. Make sure each element of the package from the copy and graphics to your target market and physical container are all communicating your message, especially the 3D item. Keep the recipient of your package in mind, what their needs are, your unique selling proposition and communicating it 3 dimensionally.

6. Test

As with any form of marketing, testing your 3D mail package is a very important step. Many entrepreneurs' and business owners get lazy with this, especially when things are going well. Even if you have a winning sales letter or campaign, always be sure to test something in at least some small way. Change the headline. Spruce up the offer. Try a new creative piece. In any case, don't rest on your laurels. What once worked won't work forever.

7. Multiple touches

To make a 3D mail campaign work, simply sending out the letter and the package sometimes isn't enough to ensure outstanding results. Whether you have a sales team making follow up calls, you're sending emails, or other forms of contact, don't forget to work those into your overall campaign. It's also a good idea to integrate e-mail and direct prospects to a website or a specific page on your website. This can maximize the impact of your package in both the 3D mail pieces and the follow up pieces you send. Contacting your prospects multiple times over multiple different media is essential for direct mail success.

In addition, there is a direct mail rule that says: *If you send the same offer with just different words a second and a third time, the response of #2 and #3 will match the results of the 1st mailing.* So, if your first mailing is a success, run your numbers to determine if you want to do a second and a third.

About Travis

Travis Lee is internationally known as the expert in getting direct mail delivered, opened and read. As co-founder and president of 3D Mail Results, he generates huge returns for thousands of businesses each year that use his innovative and effective marketing strategies. His unique, yet tested marketing methods have helped add millions of dollars in sales to a wide variety of businesses, from "kitchen-table-run" sole-proprietors, to National and Multi-National businesses mailing millions of pieces of mail a year. His techniques and strategies move seamlessly between the business-to-business and business-to-consumer worlds and consistently provide positive returns of 200% to over 3500% for his clients.

Travis is the "Go-To-Guy" for many of the top marketers in the country for 3D Mail ideas and implementation, including Dan Kennedy, Bill Glazer, Frank Kern and Alex Mandossian. He is also a sought-after speaker, speaking to thousands of business owners each year throughout the country.

He has spent the last 8+ years creating some of the most successful direct mail campaigns, specifically designed to give small businesses and entrepreneurs a leg-up against the competition. He is the creator of the *3D Mail Direct Marketing System,* through which his company provides specialized direct mail and ready-to-use sales letters to thousands of clients around the world. To learn more about this one-of-a-kind system, visit: www.3DMailSuccess.com.

When he isn't working, Travis loves spending time with his family (wife Jen, son Carson, daughter Whitney and Golden Retriever Kona), traveling, snow skiing, camping and boating around the beautiful Pacific Northwest.

To learn more about Travis Lee and 3D Mail Results and how you can sky-rocket your marketing results with smart, effective 3D Mail, visit: www.3DMailResults.com

CHAPTER 7

SEEING IS BELIEVING

BY BEN PRITCHETT

I didn't need glasses until I was 16 years old. Up until that point, I knew I was colour deficient (the politically correct term for colour blindness these days). When I figured out that I couldn't see the chalkboard properly, that was when I discovered I needed glasses.

Not having needed glasses until then, I hadn't really given much thought to how one got a pair. So, I called the eyeglass store, they arranged for the eye exam, and several decades and many pairs of glasses later, I'm still wearing them.

To this day, I have no idea whether my first eye exam was with an optometrist, an ophthalmologist, or a refracting medical doctor. All I know is that I got glasses, and I saw the chalkboard. Over the years, I've had prescriptions that worked well, and prescriptions that didn't work so well.

I've also owned glasses that, in hindsight, were butt ugly, and some that were pretty good. My criteria for buying glasses was that they had to fit my rather large head, and they had to be relatively cheap. My one luxury was that I bought anti-reflective coatings because I used the computer a lot.

What does all of this have to do with standing apart from the crowd?

Well, in 2001, I met my future wife, and she happened to be an optometrist. Within a year of getting married, in 2002, we owned two optometry offices, and today we have four of them. Our patient databases have the names and medical information of around 70,000 people – considering the fact the Province of Manitoba only has a little over 1.2 million people, that means one out every 17 people in the Province have used one of our offices.

It didn't start out that way, though we did buy practices with a fairly large number of patients, but, the sales weren't there. After 10 years in the business, three of our four practices have grown between 50% and over 100%, while the industry shrank. (The fourth office will soon join them in growth, as it went through a few rough years with a bad partner, but that will need to be a story for another book.)

Consider these points:

1) We accomplished this growth with multiple doctor changes.

2) We've had major turmoil in our industry due to Internet sales.

3) Every major retailer, from Wal-Mart to Costco, feels the need to sell glasses.

4) We have multi-billion dollar international competitors, like Luxottica (which owns and operates LensCrafters, Pearle Vision, Sunglass Hut and other brands), breathing down our necks.

5) We had to survive the worst economy since the Great Depression.

Oh yeah, I almost forgot, a large percentage of the population doesn't even know the difference between an optometrist, an ophthalmologist, or a refracting medical doctor... not to mention the opticians who dispense glasses, but cannot do eye exams.

We have competitors on every side, and online, but we've still been able to grow our business nonetheless, and you can too. We grew by standing apart from the crowd in several ways:

First, we've done a fairly major overhaul of every office that we own, including actually moving two of the offices to larger, more impressive locations. We doubled the size of another, and retrofitted the fourth, because we couldn't find a new space to expand it.

Our offices have colour (some of our competition think a doctor's office has to be white and sterile looking), and modern frame displays. We stand apart from the competition. Does anything say more boring than a plain old white office?

Second, we constantly upgrade and update our equipment. We are, first and foremost, a medically-oriented company that also happens to retail glasses. Some optical offices (they will remain anonymous to protect the guilty) have a doctor there purely to produce prescriptions to facilitate the sale of glasses. Some people have trouble grasping the fact that these two philosophies are different.

Did you know that your optometrist can be your first line of defence for discovering everything from diabetes to high blood pressure or even brain tumours? They can do all of that in addition to discovering serious eye issues, like cataracts, glaucoma and macular degeneration.

We did the equipment purchases because we felt a medical obligation to do so, but we didn't realize how important it was to some customers. Once, while on vacation, we found ourselves sitting in a hot tub with another couple, and during the course of chatting, they commented on the fact that they had left their former optometrist because, after several years, they had seen no new equipment there.

Third, we have worked very hard to differentiate our product selection from that of our competitors. While glasses are an important medical device, they are also a fashion statement. Our patients have to wear glasses in order to see properly, but they want to look good doing it.

We recently went to New York for North America's largest optical tradeshow, and the amount of product that was virtually identical was appalling. Our staff members were given the specific task to find the unusual stuff, the different, and the unique. They found frames in vibrant colours, odd shapes and even rare materials (like hand-made frames manufactured in Italy from Indian Water Buffalo Horn). While we were searching for these special product lines, hundreds of other attendees were lining up to buy the plain vanilla stuff that's just like what everybody else is carrying.

Most optometry offices sell frames almost exclusively to their own patients, while we have literally hundreds, if not thousands of patients who seek out our offices to buy glasses from us, even though another doctor in another office did their eye exam. For example, we recently had a medical doctor from Minneapolis in one of our stores... he had heard about our great service and selection from friends in Winnipeg, and he decided to buy from us. He had to book a flight back just to pick up his glasses, but claims it was well worth the trip!

Fourth, we made a conscious decision to not sell crap. I can't put it any more bluntly than that. Everybody in our industry has a decision to make when they select product... we can choose to sell cheap junk without warranties, and poor optics, or we can sell quality that we can stand behind.

We have online competitors selling three pairs for cheaper than we can produce our cheapest single pair. There are even brick and mortar competitors who sell multiple pairs for ridiculously low prices. It's not that we cannot do it... we choose not to. We would rather explain our price upfront than have to apologize for our quality later.

Fifth, the sale hasn't ended when our patient walks out the door with their purchase. We're always prepared to back what we sell with industry-leading warranties. We're always happy to adjust and repair everything we sell as often as it's necessary.

When people buy a premium product, they sometimes need a little positive reinforcement after the fact. They need to know that they made a good decision. They need to feel special after parting with a lot of their hard-earned dollars. That's as much a part of the marketing process as anything else.

During our trip to New York, we got to meet and spend time with a gentleman named Oliver Goldsmith. He's a third-generation frame designer from England who designed frames worn by royalty like Princess Grace and Princess Diana, actors like Peter Sellers and Michael Caine, and, most identifiable, he was the designer of John Lennon's famous oval frames (in fact, I'm wearing a pair of them as I type this).

He mentioned that, in England, he mails a personal letter to everybody who buys a pair of his glasses, just to welcome them into the Goldsmith family. I asked him if he would be kind enough to give us a copy of that letter to give to our buyers, because we couldn't expect him to pay the postage to send the letter from England. He promised he would do that, if we became his first retailers in Canada. We did, and he has done just that.

We don't tell people about this surprise. Imagine how pleased our patients are when they get a letter all the way from England... from the designer of the frames no less... they've been ecstatic, and refer.

You may have noticed that I haven't discussed marketing yet... at least not the lead generation variety. There is a good reason, because we haven't done much. We have increased our sales significantly without a corresponding increase in advertising dollars. (Of course, the fact that my banker told me a business like ours didn't need marketing and stripped that amount out of our loan application might have had something to do with it. No, that wasn't a joke.)

Of course, we do send recall postcards in the mail to remind people of their eye exams every couple of years. We have done some very basic newspaper advertising. We've got a couple of very general websites and a Facebook fan page, but, that's about it.

Did I mention that one of our offices has doubled its sales over the past decade?

I'm not proud of our lack of marketing, even though I am proud of our results. In the coming year, we plan to roll out a concerted marketing effort that will include a direct mail campaign, websites for all offices, a formalized referral program, and much more. My goal is to double sales again.

Other than some budgetary constraints, there is a reason why I haven't gone wild with my marketing efforts. That reason is that I had to make sure our inside reality would match up with our marketing when we had the budget to do it.

Dan Kennedy (or Bill Glazer) once told a story about the car dealer who wanted better marketing and more leads. It turned out that there was nothing wrong with the lead generation he already had...his salespeople were simply doing a terrible job of selling when potential customers responded.

Have you ever seen a great marketing program, only to go to the business and find mediocrity at best? A restaurant with crappy food or lousy service? A retail operation with dirty floors and terrible selection?

Ambivalent staff? Long waits? No support after the purchase is made? The list of bad buying experiences is endless. That's inside reality. You have to make sure your marketing matches up with what you actually provide. What's your inside reality?

Our offices are all up-to-date, our staff are well-trained, our equipment is some of the best in the industry, our product selection is top notch, we have access to the most advanced lenses money can buy... put simply, we're ready for the next phase of growth. Our inside reality will meet or exceed the image our marketing promotes.

Throughout this chapter, I've only discussed the optical industry, but the principles apply to every business.

People like variety, so, mix it up. If your competitors lack colour in their business, go colourful in yours. If your competitors close at 5:00 pm, open an evening or two. If your competitors have dark and dingy facilities, be bright and airy. Do something different... that's one way to stand apart.

Can you put new technology into your business? Think of something that will set you apart from the competition. When my hometown got its first chocolate/vanilla soft serve ice cream machine, it was in a convenience store and people lined up out the door. No matter what business you're in, there's got to be something new or different to make you stand apart.

Can you differentiate yourself through different products or services? If your industry is going no-frills and cheap, perhaps you should pour on the services and increase your prices. When I moved to Winnipeg, everybody told me that it was the wholesale capital of Canada. I was told that everybody in that City was cheap. Logic would dictate that we go cheap in our product offerings... so much for logic... I moved upscale, and we grew.

Through the so-called Great Recession that started in 2008, we continued to successfully move upscale. Sometimes, the easiest way to stand apart is to zig when others zag. Dan Kennedy writes an entire newsletter about the Mass Affluent, and they're out there. If you listen to what everyone else is saying, consider doing the opposite of what's recommended.

Choose to sell quality. One of my tests, when selecting products to sell, is: "Would I be happy to sell this to my Mother?" (If you don't love your Mom, pick somebody you do, and fill in the blank!) I often ask others that same question when I go to buy something… when I have a massive array of choices, and I'm not on a strict budget, I'll find a sales rep and ask them which one they'd buy for their Mother.

If you wouldn't be proud to sell something to your friends or family, should you be selling it at all? If you've got a restaurant, would you offer your menu in your dining room at home? If you've got a garage business, are those the parts you'd put on your daughter's car?

After the sale is made, don't forget about your customer. You want them to come back again (most of the time anyway). You want them to refer their friends and family. The fastest way to stop me from coming back, or from referring others, is to disrespect me the day that my credit card (or cash) isn't in my hand. It's too easy to fall all over ourselves to service people when they're passing us their money, but it takes more discipline to serve them to the highest degree when you know there's no money coming to you that day.

Provide the highest level of service all of the time, and you'll bank money and goodwill for the future. The old axiom is that a bird in the hand is worth more than two in the bush, but I'd rather lose a sale today to make sure I have two down the road. (Of course, one in the hand AND two in the bush is even better!)

I don't want to oversimplify things here, but, if you take just one thing from the message in this chapter, it is simply this: CHOOSE TO STAND APART!

Look at everything we did to grow our businesses:

- We painted the walls and changed displays.
- We upgraded and added equipment.
- We picked products that differentiated us.
- We chose quality over low cost.
- We take care of our customers, whether they're spending money that day or not.

Nobody made us do any of these things. Many of these choices were not easy. We chose the road less travelled. We chose to stand apart. Now, it's your turn to choose…

About Ben

Ben Pritchett was born and raised in Gander, Newfoundland, Canada where he started his first business at the age of 15, and began his own consulting firm in 1991. For over two decades he has worked with clients in many industries from all over Canada.

Before his involvement in the optometry industry, he worked with clients in industries ranging from restaurants and vacuum cleaner sales to software development and tourism, not to mention dimension stone (granite quarrying and manufacturing) and aviation, and a few others.

Through his varied career he spent a couple of years teaching business management at a private college, owned a business brokerage, a specialty computer company and a sales training business. While not everything was a raging success, he learned a lot about business – both good and bad – along the way. Ben says that, "when things come too easily, you really don't learn much, so appreciate tough times for their learning opportunities, otherwise your time and money was wasted."

Ben's a life-long learner who has plans for a 6,000 book library in his new house (there are already 3,000 in his collection). He tries to attend two to four National business events every year in order to keep up with what's working for other businesses, in other industries, all over the world, and believes that you're moving backwards if you aren't constantly learning.

He describes himself as a serial entrepreneur, consultant and business philosopher who is likely otherwise unemployable. He has a strong independent streak, loves breaking the rules (especially when it leads to greater success for himself and his clients) and hates wearing ties, so you'll rarely find him wearing one!

His main consulting strengths involve finance, marketing and business systemization. He also has a keen interest in copywriting, and would probably spend most of his time doing that if his other services weren't keeping him so busy all of the time. He's also shown a knack for finding the hidden assets in a business and helping its owners to maximize opportunities that were under their noses all along.

He's currently putting the finishing touches on a specialized coaching program for optometrists, but says that it can be used by any entrepreneur wanting to grow their business with less stress along the way. If you'd like to learn more, feel free to contact Ben via email at: ben@benjpritchett.com.

For entrepreneurs happy to learn on their own, Ben and his partners operate a website offering an automatic 52-week training program for business growth at: www. advantagebizconsulting.com, along with: www.advantagebizstartup.com which has training specifically aimed at people just getting into business.

Ben currently lives in Swan River, Manitoba, Canada, with his wife Dawn, daughter Calleigh, and a small pack of Airedale Terriers including Phoenix and Chewie. He plans to add to the pack soon. Ben loves to work from home with his furry "assistants," and can often be found 'burning the midnight oil' on some new project or another.

Despite an already hectic schedule, he takes on select consulting assignments when a project piques his interest, and would welcome the opportunity to work with you if you have a business that you want to grow.

CHAPTER 8

HOW TO STICK OUT LIKE A SORE THUMB AND CRUSH THE COMPETITION

BY BRAD GAINES

When I was a child, the original Nintendo gaming console was the bee's knees. My favorite game was The Legend of Zelda. This game featured a mixture of action, puzzles, adventure/battle gameplay, exploration, and questing. You were frequently rewarded for solving puzzles or exploring hidden areas with helpful items to increase your abilities to rescue the princess at the end of the game. Many items were consistent and appeared many times throughout the game. Items like bombs, which could be used both as weapons and to open blocked or hidden doorways; boomerangs, which could diminish or paralyze enemies, keys for locked doors, magic swords, shields, and bow and arrows to deter the bad guys.

You're probably asking yourself what in the world does this video game have to do with business? The items that appeared for your progress and sustainability with your overall goal – to rescue princess Zelda from Ganondorf the primary antagonist of the game – allowed you to change the game in an instant. Blow open a door; you could proceed! If not, you were stuck. Drink some potion; replenish your life meter; if not, game over. Now, that's what I call changing the game. When it comes to business success, it's all about changing the game. We call this the Legend of Zelda School of Business.

The Legend of Zelda tactic is precisely the concept that should be employed in business: You can change the game you play in an instant, if you're willing to use the tools you have at your disposal, to get you from where you are to where you want to be.

Most companies haven't succeeded in selling more because they simply don't know what ways and tools they can use to create attention and differentiation in the marketplace. Taking a hard realistic view of your product or service, to whom you are selling it, and how you are currently selling it, you must evaluate whether or not your approach is the most efficient and productive way to reach, motivate, and persuade the market to buy from you the first time and each time thereafter. When it comes to selling more, change is the name of the game or better yet –changes. While your competition is stuck on level 1, you can beat the game by arming yourself with more tools to win.

Let's start with the most glaring point: If you're not selling enough, reset the way your business differentiates itself from the competition. It doesn't matter if you're selling software, lumber, clothing or professional services, whether you lead a marketing firm or a temp agency, your business has the obligation for selling your product or service – and selling it perfectly.

I've worked in 117 different industries over my business career. They have all encompassed marketing and sales roles, advisory, and management. I have gone "behind the scenes" and will "peel back the curtain" on my experiences so that you can obtain, in minutes, what took me years to understand. The first is to realize conceptually that your business is no different from any other. There are three main similarities in all aspects of business:

1) Money flows in, money flows out.

2) The pure existence of a business is to sell their product or service for a profit. This is true even with non-profits.

3) Differentiate or disappear.

We're going to spend the rest of this chapter on number 3.

Think about your competition and answer the following questions:

- Can they say they offer great customer service?
- Can they say they have the best people?

- Can they say they have convenient hours?
- Do they have online ordering?
- Do they have warranties?
- Do they have quality products and services?
- Are they price matching?
- Can they say they are the best choice?
- Do they have a money-back guarantee?

Your competition can say virtually anything it wants. It doesn't matter if you think it's true. It only matters if prospective customers will. Would you then agree that your competition CAN say these things? Now, what are you saying that's any different?

In 1933, perhaps one of the most infamous experiments surfaced in behavior psychology. The Von Restorff effect (named after psychiatrist and children's pediatrician Hedwig von Restorff), also called the isolation effect, predicts that an item that stands out like a sore thumb is more likely to be remembered than other items. Simply speaking, the human species has a bias in favor of remembering the unusual and forgetting the usual.

Look at what your competition can claim again. These are the usual statements made by a business and easily forgotten by prospective buyers. Instinctively, you may feel that your business does all these things better than the competition and it's not your fault that prospective buyers don't believe it. It's because they've heard these same things before from so many others. It makes it harder to differentiate because everyone sounds the same. Of equal importance, the examples above that so many businesses claim set them apart from the competition are expected by buyers today. Let's illustrate. Do you know of any companies that say they have terrible customer service? Or, the worst products and services? Or how about the most inconvenient hours? Now, you might be thinking well, Brad that's silly, no one would say that. My point exactly. They say the opposite and so do the majority of businesses in existence. You've got to find other "meat" that is unusual and unlike anything they've ever heard, or you risk going in one ear and out the other in record time.

One of the easiest ways to accomplish this is to create points of difference about your business that you can verbalize to prospects. One of the methods we recommend is to sit down with your management team and answer these two questions:

1. What can you say that no one else can?
2. What do you do that no one else does?

This is not an easy task and may take hours, but the companies who complete this exercise are handsomely rewarded in the future. Plus, you may find some innovation opportunities to further separate from the herd. Articulating your points of difference verbally is a big leg-up over the competition, but to further strengthen your business you need to take it to the next level.

Most sales people give up after the 3rd call. Most marketing messages are self-centered on the company sending it. Many have turned social media into an orgy of bad sales spiels and advertising. Most websites sound cocky and not focused on the buyer and their problems. Don't fall into this trap. Many companies advertise, sell, and market the same way because they look at their competition and do what they're doing. Don't be a copycat. What are some things that you can do to stand out from your competition so that you're seen as different? Are you sending something before your sales call that gets their attention? I mean really gets their attention? Have you ever tried 3-D mail? It's delivered in a 3-D vehicle that doesn't go in an envelope or package. It's delivered as is. You put the stamp on the object itself and mail it out. We've seen great success with 3-D mail.

Think about how many postcards, standard letters, flyers, and coupons you've received in the mail during your lifetime? Hundreds, possibly thousands. Have you ever received a message in a bottle before? Or, a bank bag? How about a prescription pill bottle with the headline – Are you tired of the headaches? Again, the actual bank bag and bottles are not packaged. You can clearly see what it is when you open your mailbox. Many of our clients love the results and feedback they receive from sending odd pieces of mail to get prospective buyers attention, and to stand out from the "me-too" marketing landscape.

Getting attention is important but so is keeping it. Do you then follow up by sending a free report or white paper that will help them with the challenges they face in their business? Do you set up a secret shopper to conduct business there and share the report with your prospective buyer and offer ways to help them improve customer service, bottom line, or efficiencies? How many marketing angles are you really hitting your prospective buyers from? Borrowing a concept from the great change expert Anthony Robbins we often employ the "what have you really done" checklist. Many times we hear from salespeople, marketing managers, owners, and executives that "we've tried everything and nothing is working." Pulling out a sheet of paper we ask them to share what all they have done to obtain business. The list rarely reaches half a page. It may seem like you've done everything, but there's usually 2 to 50 more effective ways to gain attention and attract the business you want. You just have to be willing to be different and creative. Attention is one of the scarcest resources on the planet today and I don't think it will increase ever again. To get the attention you want, you must stand out!

We've all heard the expression walk-the-walk and talk-the-talk. Then why is it when we have a chance to educate a buyer on why to do business with us, we end up sounding just like the last salesperson they spoke with. It boils down to one reason. We don't demonstrate that we are different. The power of demonstration is beyond my justification of words. It's the ultimate, sure-proof way to prove that doing business with you is going to be different. It's not just talked about; it's demonstrated. This a concept overlooked by many businesses.

I've been involved with and observed over 2,000 sales appointments B2B & B2C. Many of them are void of preparation even in the digital age where virtually more than 50% of what you need to know is at your fingertips. I'll never understand, when seconds matter and failure is often the norm, why anyone wouldn't want to be prepared to place themselves in the best position to win. But, I want to be solutions-oriented here and not crass. There's one method – a secret really – that can increase your chances of getting your buyer to understand the value proposition you offer more quickly and succinctly than any sales sheet, brochure, or paper visual ever will. I borrowed this secret from Dr. Oz. Many know his TV show Dr. Oz. There, he is known for his no-nonsense tactics, props and graphic demonstrations to get people to take charge of their health. Because his number one enemy is the person who thinks they know it all, he could talk about constipation until 'the cows come home,' but if he shows you a prop of what constipated poop looks like, it's graphic but it's clear. He knows that by keeping things fun and jovial, people will relax and absorb more information about health.

What can props do for your success while selling your product or service? They create a demonstration whereby you sell your solution using a visual metaphor or analogy that your buyer already has conditioned in their mind. You can then piggyback off the association they already have with the props, and tie in to how your solution is similar, allowing your prospect to make the connection easier. Let's give you a couple of examples.

Kindly imagine you sell advertising. What's the one thing you want people to do when they buy your medium? Buy more than one ad, one issue, one showing of a TV commercial or more than one airing of a radio commercial, right? How can you get that across that to them without having to sell it. Demonstrate! You bring out a hammer, a block of wood, and a nail. You ask the buyer to participate by trying to tap the nail into the wood one time. Then ask if he can pull the nail out of the block with his bare hands. He certainly can. Now, ask him to do the same only this time tap it until he feels it really go down in there good usually 7 or 10 times. Now, you ask him to remove it with his bare hands. He certainly cannot. You'll then make the association, to your prospect, that this is a lot like your marketing. It needs to be repetitive and stick before it can penetrate people's minds. Thus, demonstrating that one ad just won't do. Powerful!

There are many different instances where you can employ this in your sales presentation. Let's say you sell software that functions by sharing information about a problem before your customers even experience it. Perhaps it shares there's a potent virus on the way or speed of system is hampered by whatever. This software notifies their IT Dept. pre-problem so users don't experience a break in usage. Basically it can see into the future. What item do most people equate to seeing in the future? A crystal ball! Now, imagine showing up for an appointment with your usual stuff, but with a crystal ball in your tote as well. It's a great icebreaker and your prospective customers will have fun with it if done properly. Sound cheesy? It sets you apart and it works. We've won many sales presentations with props while the competition brought what was expected—PowerPoint.

I have a personal favorite. In preceding meetings with prospective clients there are often causes for concern or issues that need to be addressed delicately. How do you do that without causing your buyers defenses to go up and to get to the real truth? Ever heard of the expression "elephant in the room." In our meetings there will actually be an elephant in the room. A 3-foot high stuffed elephant that my business partner swiped from his three-year-old. Imagine the looks you get when you're walking through someone's business with that? Simply by having the elephant in the room with us the prospective client brings it up themselves virtually 99% of the time by stating " we've got an elephant in the room" as they laugh and joke about it. It certainly lightens up the mood for the serious discussions ahead. We've had many pose with the elephant and snap a picture or record dancing with it. Elephants are known for having great memories. Your prospective buyers will hardly forget you after that experience.

Other items we've used as props to associate value propositions:

- Rubik's cube to demonstrate solving problems

- Race car to suggest getting off to a fast start

- Hand shovel to show that they are digging their own grave if they don't change

- A velvet bag filled with (fake) diamonds

- A Halliburton briefcase filled with $1,000,000 (it looks real)

The easiest way to determine what props work to demonstrate what you offer is to think about the most salient point you want to get across. Then find a common item that people already equate to doing the same thing.

We all want to be different but do we take the necessary steps to walk the walk and to use the tools around us to advance further? In the commodity world, you can't afford to blend in. With an ADD audience, it's no longer safe to assume that your prospective buyers are thinking about or remembering you when they are making purchase decisions. The most important takeaway of them all is to ask yourself this question: Am I using all the tools I can to create a different brand, different message, and different experience to rescue my princess – the customer? After all, had I not used any of the tools available to me in the video game, it would have never changed. I would be stuck working harder than was necessary on every level. I don't believe you should have to.

About Brad

Brad Gaines is Managing Partner of Reset Strategies. Reset Strategies is a strategic marketing and sales firm that helps businesses grow without advertising.

Reset Strategies' advisors, along with all associates, believe that within all companies, regardless of size or industry, are undiscovered, and at times, instant opportunities for new sales and profits.

By implementing the 12-month RESET system, these opportunities are discovered, leveraged and optimized for A LOT MORE SALES - WITHOUT HAVING TO DEPEND on advertising.

Reset specializes in identifying untapped revenue sources, underperforming activities; overlooked marketing and selling activities that are costing your business $1M or more in LOST revenue and provides the strategy and tactics so that you can grow using the resources you already have – the same effort, same staff, and same budget.

Business Owners and Executives partner with Reset when:

- they want guaranteed ROI

- they want unbiased and proven plans on the best use of marketing dollars

- they've lost market share

- they want to spend less on advertising but sell more

- they want more referrals

- they want focus and attention brought to the most important elements of the business

- they want performance-based strategies

Brad is a 12-year veteran of the sales and marketing industry. He's been recognized internationally for his work with Dale Carnegie's Breakthrough Award program. He's had several sales scripts published by Fortune 500 companies and was awarded salesperson of the year by a Fortune 10 company. He's shattered company sales records and wants to make it easier for people to do the same.

Brad is a sought-out speaker and member of the Kentucky Speakers Association. He also acts as a member of the Harvard Business Review Advisory Council where he stays in touch with the most pertinent business happenings and offers insights and feedback to improve the content subscribers will see.

Best selling author, Jill Konrath of Snap Selling, said Brad had a lot of moxie. New York Times and Best-selling author, Gary Vaynerchuk - *The Thank You Economy* and *Crush It* - has commented on Brad's hustle.

Brad was a collegiate baseball player and received his degree in Business. His firm is available for speaking, marketing, and sales advisory. He resides in the Louisville, KY metro area in Georgetown, IN with his wife Vanessa and daughter Adley.

CHAPTER 9

7 STRATEGIC STEPS TO ROCK STAR COMMUNICATION

BY BILL TWYFORD

My name is Bill Twyford, The Real Estate Rock Star. This chapter will be different than the others as I am a trainer, not a writer. My goal is to give you as much content as possible, these are quick reference tips. You will find yourself coming back to this chapter time and time again to learn. When you make the decision to become a stronger communicator, you will start using this information immediately. That being said, let's get started:

1. ANGLES OF COMMUNICATION

Why is communication so important? Let's start with this, have you ever been to a foreign country and not spoken the language? How did it make you feel? ...Helpless, Out of Control, Frustrated, etc. This is how people feel when you have no regard for their position in the conversation. What do I mean by position? There are three (3) positions in the angles of communication.

(i). You (1st Position):

- This is our favourite position because it is all about what we want out of the conversation.
- We will be selfish.
- We tend not to care about others feelings.

- We know that this position is the most important to us.
- We know how we feel, we use language like "I want," "I feel," "I hear," "I see." We know this because of our past experience.

Downfall to this position:

- Excessive use of this position leads to a lack of understanding of others.
- Very easy to be a controller.
- Bragging is easy in this position.

(ii). Them (2nd Position):

- You look at the situation from the other person's point of view.
- When you put yourself in their shoes, you will have a greater perspective on the whole conversation.
- In this position you are emotional to their views.

Downfall to this position:

- Excessive use of this position causes a loss of self-esteem.
- You will give things away in this position.
- Be careful staying in this position too long, you can get sucked into a manipulator real quick.

(iii). Observer, you looking in (3rd Position):

- You stand back from an outsider's point of view.
- You look at both sides of the conversation.
- You are able to see and hear yourself and the other person as if you were a fly on the wall.
- You will have no emotions in this position.

Downfall to this position:

- Excessive use will lead to a lack of emotion, engagement and detachment from the conversation.

With these three positions in your arsenal, you will be unstoppable. Balancing all three ways will lead to cooperative, assertive behavior, and increased choice and understanding. The best well-rounded and fair decisions are made in the third position. Powerful people always come from the first position; however, if you truly watch the mechanism of their communication patterns and how they process what is being fed to them, you will see them bounce in and out of positions two and three. Become more aware of your conversations.

2. BUILDING AGREEMENT

In communication, if you want people to agree with you...you must agree with them first. No matter what they say...if you are looking to build rapport and accelerate the conversation in your direction, you must agree first.

Talking to your kids...

Your kid says...

"Mom, I don't want to clean my room today, I want to go play instead."

Remember, you are trying to influence the person you are talking to.

How do you handle this?

Start with agreement...you say "I understand, when I was your age I didn't want to clean my room either, I wanted to play too... let's go to your bedroom and let me show you how I solved the problem when my mom or dad wanted me to clean my room." First, let's make a deal. You get everything off of the floor and put it on your bed and make 4 different piles, then you put two piles away now, and the other two before 9 pm tonight after you play, or you can do all four right now... which do you want to do? I will do 2 now... Ok great, now, I'm going to be down here at 9 pm tonight and if it's not all put away then you will not be able to go and play with friends for 2 days...one day for each pile. You might want to do all four now, so you don't have to worry about it later, what do you think?

Now, they are interested in the conversation and also interested in your advice. Remember, kids live day-by-day.

Talking to a homeowner behind in their mortgage payments...

They say, "I don't want to move out of my house."

You say "I totally understand, if I were you, I would not want to move out either...let me ask you this, what has your bank said about your situation so you can stay in your house?"

When you open up with agreement, everyone wants to stay in the conversation with you. You are working to build rapport not tension. When persuading people on your point of view, you must start with agreement first.

The options on building agreement are endless... however practice this.

3. REPEAT, APPROVE AND RESPOND
This alone will connect you with people faster than any other technique. The highest human needs are acceptance, love, and approval. Therefore, when you ask questions, you should always **Repeat** their answer and **Approve** of what they say. When you repeat their answer, they know you heard what they said. When you approve of what they say, now they think you think, they make good decisions. People are compelled to keep talking to you when you do this. If you are talking to someone who you know is listening to you and they think you make good decisions, do you want to stay in that conversation? YES! Always give them enthusiastic approval; great, terrific, fantastic, wonderful, that's exciting and then **Respond** with another question to stay in control of the conversation. Ask open-ended questions like: who, what, where, when, how.

Examples:

- Hello, how can I help you? (I'm just looking.) You're just looking, great! What brings you into our store today?

- I hear what you are saying, how did you get into this situation? (I lost my job.) You lost your job, sorry to hear that. Let me ask you this, have you started applying for other jobs yet? (Yes.) You have, great!

Always Repeat, Approve and Respond.

4. AREA OF COMMUNICATION:
BODY LANGUAGE, TONALITIES, AND WORDS
The first Area of Communication is **Body Language**. Body Language is 55% of communication. Understanding and learning how to read body language will probably be one of the most valuable skills you will ever learn.

When communicating with others is not getting you what you want, the first step is to recognize what it is you want to change and then create some alternatives to achieve your results. Body Language reveals hidden messages, many of which we would rather keep to ourselves. Some people are better at disguising theirs than others. In body language, everyone has various degrees of signals they are not aware of. Most of the time, we are totally unaware of the signals we are giving out. The more aware you become of these signals; the more effective your communication will be.

There are THREE different areas considered in body language:

(i) Voice

(ii) Head and Face

(iii) Body

Examples:

- Facial Expressions (Head and Face)
- Leaning into you when you are speaking to them (Body)
- I hear what you are saying (Voice)
- Arms are crossed (Body)
- That clicks with me (Voice)
- Eye movements (Head and Face)

There are hundreds of ways to read people, so learn all you can about body language.

The second Area of Communication is **Tonalities** which is 38% of your communication. Your tonalities are your tone inflections on what you say. You have heard people say, "It's not what you say, it's how you say it." This is so true. You have FOUR areas of tonalities.

(i) Pace – Rate of Speech

(ii) Tone – Bass and Treble

(iii) Volume – Loud and Soft

(iv) Pitch – Upswings and Downswings

Let's talk about # 4 - Down Swings and Up Swings. When you Upswing on your words you sound as if you have:

- No authority
- No confidence
- Are insecure
- Weak
- Insincere

When you Downswing on your words the opposite happens. You:

- Sound confident
- Sound in control
- Sound commanding
- Sound serious

Command your customer to make a decision ⬎ downswing on the word it follows.

Examples of Down Swings:

- Unless you… feel motivated⬎… you'll never decide to … work with me⬎…which means we will never get you out of this situation⬎… and that's not what you want⬎, is it⬎?

- I can't tell you what to do, I mean, you have to…convince yourself⬎, Robert… to take action⬎… and get the ball rolling. ⬎

- When you…learn this material⬎…you will be able to…use it powerfully⬎…and that will allow you to…feel good⬎…about your increased income, don't you agree⬎? So when you…act now⬎…and…invest in your future today⬎…you'll know you've made the right decision. May I explain⬎?

The third Area of Communication is **Words** which is only 7%. In sales, this is why you should know your scripts and objection handlers when dealing with your customers. When you memorize what you are going to say, you don't have to think about what to say so, you can focus on your customers' body language and their tonalities which, remember, is 93% of communication.

If you think of past conversations you have had with family members or friends, you basically start all the conversations the same way. Pay attention and listen to yourself …that is your script.

5. EMBEDDED COMMANDS

Embedded commands are patterns of language that bypass conscious reasoning and speak directly to the subconscious mind. They influence people at the subconscious level. This allows you to direct people to take specific actions. People will have specific thoughts and will generally do whatever you want them to. The subconscious is in a constant search for patterns. One command is not a pattern. You have to use command after command and basically bombard your customer. Your brain is always analyzing what's going on around you. It's trying to find similar things from your past and trying to line them up. The subconscious has stored millions and millions of conversations with other human beings. These conversations have become so routine that the mind has virtually fallen asleep. Your subconscious mind runs on autopilot.

When using embedded commands correctly, you create unusual patterns of language that force the subconscious mind to wake up and pay attention.

The subconscious has received direct and specific commands that it feels compelled to act upon! When you are in normal everyday conversation with customers, friends or family members; you can influence them to: do as you say, sign the paperwork, go to the store, clean your room, or whatever else you want them to do with absolutely no resistance. Remember, embedded commands bypass conscious reasoning and influence people at the subconscious level. They simply begin to think in their minds that they should do what you have asked them to do all along.

Embedded Commands are 1 to 4 word groups that order you to do something. They make sense on their own. When you use a command you don't instantly see a reaction. When you say a command you plant it in the subconscious mind and it begins to grow into an action. Commands only work in **massive quantities.** The subconscious is looking for patterns and one or two commands is not a pattern. Let's look at some examples:

- You should…*work with me…* so I can help you get what you want.

   Embedded Command is *work with me*

- You must...*take notes*...while I'm speaking. You will learn so much more.

Shall we start now?

Embedded Command is *take notes*

- I don't know when you will begin to...*feel motivated*...you have to *make that decision.*

Embedded Commands are *feel motivated* and *make that decision.*

6. PACING AND LEADING PEOPLE INTO AGREEMENT

Pacing is saying something that is mutually accepted. It is about respecting the state, style, and feelings of others. When you start to match and pace, you build the environment in which to lead. This constitutes influence. Without rapport you have no negotiation. Trust in communication will only exist if it is built on the values of each of the parties involved. People are attached to you because of the values you communicate. Respecting and pacing values is a way of building deep rapport.

Leading is saying what I want you to believe to be true or something I don't want questioned. When leading, you want to script the person you are talking to so you can lead them down the path you want them to go. DON'T take advantage of people when you use these techniques. Learning this makes it easy to manipulate people, so always put their needs first if they are in a distressed situation. If you are negotiating a new car, knock yourself out.

Examples:

- As you are reading this book, (The Pace) you realize this has been the most informational chapter in the book. (The Lead)
- As we sit at the table, (The Pace) you realize you need to work with me. (The Lead)

7. BUILDING SELF-ESTEEM IN OTHERS

When you are trying to sell something: sell yourself at the same time by building self-esteem in others. This is so important when trying to build rapport with someone. Find out what excites them. Find out what gets them talking. Expand on it.

Here are some simple examples of self-esteem builders:

- Bob, you look great...have you lost weight?
- How are you doing, John? Bob told me you come highly recommended. I cannot wait to see how a professional like yourself will handle this situation.
- John, it is so great to meet you.
- Lynn, I cannot wait to work with you. With your experience and attention to detail, my job will get easier.
- I love you.
- You're so awesome.

More complex examples:

- Clearly, Ed, you are sharp...I know you will become aware that after you...take action...you can...shift gears...and focus on the next phase of your life, don't you agree?
- Jim, you're a smart businessman...you need to go ahead and trust your feelings. Intuitively, you can feel that this deal is just what you need to keep the profits flowing into your operation, isn't it?
- I don't need to tell someone like you Bob... that when you... make the decision...the relief you will feel by getting this off your desk will be overwhelming. Don't you agree?
- After you...**make a commitment**...to...work with me...you will **experience** how good it feels to **finally** have someone on your side helping you get past this situation...someone like you, knows this is best.

In Closing, Perception Is Reality.

If people believe you have power, you do. If they think you're an impostor, they're right.

About Bill

Bill Twyford, The Real Estate Rock Star, grew up in a small town in Iowa. His Dad owned a successful industrial painting contracting business. He and his brother, Kevin, worked with their dad as young boys. At the young age of 24, Twyford realized that there were a lot of benefits of working for yourself. In 1982, Twyford started his own industrial painting contracting business in Houston and began his road to financial freedom.

In 1993, he won a bid at Arco Chemical to epoxy-line the inside of a two-million gallon tank. When working in tanks you must pass a respirator test. Twyford failed miserably and his doctor told him that he needed to quit painting immediately and move to a higher altitude to clean out his lungs.

He moved his family to Colorado. He had no idea what to do next. He had some cash and thought he would try retirement. He happened to walk into a real estate office and that is where it all began.

There was a Realtor sitting at his desk with his feet propped up on his desk. Twyford ask him if this is what he did all day. He informed Bill he ate donuts, drank coffee and waited for clients to walk-in from newspaper ads. Twyford asked what is your yearly income as a Realtor? He said he earned $50,000 per year by selling ten properties. Being the assertive person that Bill is, he figured he could do the same thing, but he would sell one hundred houses per year.

His first four years as a Realtor, he sold 574 properties. He was really making a name for himself. Twyford started his real estate career in August of 1994. That month he was exposed to Mike Ferry. Mike had become Twyford's personal mentor.

Bill Twyford, now known as **"The Real Estate Rock Star"** has been an extremely successful real estate investor for over 15 years. He has been involved in the purchase and sale of over 2,000 properties. He is one of the most successful investors in America and he attributes his success to a great work ethic and his strong communication skills.

Bill has been reaching into Corporate America for many years. He specializes in teaching business people **"Strategic Communication Skills"** that their corporation needs to achieve higher success.

As author of the best-seller book, *How to Sell a House When It's Worth Less Than the Mortgage*, Bill has strived to help families in distress throughout his investing career. Bill has written numerous training manuals in the areas of real estate investing, sales techniques, and communication mastery. He is the co-founder of Investors Edge University.

Bill appears regularly on **Colorado & Company,** an NBC Channel 9 show to give homeowners options to foreclosure.

Bill has had the privilege of speaking alongside Donald Trump, Tony Robbins, and Suze Orman. Bill is a heavily sought-after celebrity expert. He was interviewed many times on TV, radio, and print media – including REIP (Real Estate Investor Professionals), Creative Real Estate Magazine, 411Realty, Realty-Trac and Entrepreneur Magazine as an expert in the industry.

Contact Bill Twyford at: www.InvestorsEdgeUniversity.com

Tel: 303-870-8851

CHAPTER 10

1 FINGER FORWARD 3 FINGERS BACK!

BY COLIN SPRAKE

What you will read in this chapter are powerful life-altering concepts that have been detailed and investigated over the past five years and over my life experience. I have spent days, weeks and months documenting very specific examples of how 1 Finger Forward and 3 Fingers Back shows up in our daily lives in every way and form. I'm very excited to share with you these concepts as they relate directly to my own personal life and that of my families, and how we have been able to learn, grow and prosper from really understanding the concepts that you will learn about in this most amazing book.

What I'm really talking about is that as you point one finger forward toward some other person, there will be 3 fingers pointing back at you saying that you should be taking responsibility for part or most of the situation that has arisen, as you point your finger in the direction of that person.

My goal is that really understand that every situation that arises in your life has come about because of your decision, whether consciously or subconsciously, to be involved in that situation. I will walk you through a step-by-step process to really give you clarity on truly how the 1 Finger Forward and 3 Fingers Back shows up in every aspect of your life – whether it be with your children, at work, with family, colleagues, associations in any way, shape or form – one finger forward does result in three fingers pointing back at you in all situations.

GETTING TO KNOW OURSELVES!

1 Finger Forward and 3 Fingers Back is not a new concept, but what you learn as we delve into the details of this concept is that it is quite complex in its understanding – and that's how it is presented to people. My goal is to present it in a simple and easy-to-understand format, that as you read about it you will start to resonate with it and see how it impacts your life every single day.

And I promise you it does show up!

It all starts in childhood. From a very young age we learn to point fingers at other people who have not been good to us or who have done something against us and the blame game begins – this is the essence of one finger forward and three fingers back. The sad part for us as children in our formative years is that we learn all our habits, inborn traits (whether we like them or not), from our parents.

Our parents are only a product of a developed society. The reason why I say a developed society is because in the under-developed world people have very specific tasks that they have to do every single day, and for most of them it's survival looking for food and water - they take responsibility for what needs to be done in their own lives. In developed nations we are surrounded with governments who are deeply in debt, and because of their leadership and mismanagement of funds, the majority of these developed nations have enormous debt situations with their people.

People are living in terrible situations and live in a state of fear wondering how they are going to retire and have enough money to do so. Many people believe that they will win the lottery or sue somebody to have enough funds to live the dream lifestyle. We live in a very litigious society where some people believe that they should take advantage of other people for their actions, by suing people, and not taking responsibility for their involvement in the given situation.

I fully agree that there are situations where legal action is appropriate. The sad part about it is that there are many lawyers around, looking for situations to play the blame game and line their pockets. In fact, society as a whole is deeply embedded in the 1 Finger Forward and

3 Fingers Back blame game. We spend most of our day talking about given situations and blaming other people for things that they did not do or things that they did do! This is the one finger pointing forward!

It has truly got out of hand with people now suing for the sake of suing. In fact, people make up fictitious situations in the hope of blaming somebody else and profiting from it.

A recent example was the one with the lady who wanted to sue the municipality because she tripped on a curb and the curb was not built to exactly the right height. She decided to sue the municipality because she broke her leg. People really need to start taking responsibility for their actions. If you slip on a curb and break your leg you should be asking yourself: What did I learn from this experience and how can I avoid this situation next time? No, we look for all avenues to blame other people whether they are individuals, municipalities, governments, companies, absolutely anybody... other than ourselves! Heaven forbid that we should blame ourselves for a given situation. Sadly, in every situation that arises in our lives that we are part of, it truly is because of our own choices that we have made.

WHAT CONCEPTS ARE INVOLVED?

There are a number of concepts involved in truly understanding 1 Finger Forward and 3 Fingers Back. Some of you may have heard of them as Universal principles, Law of Attraction and most recently in the movie, *The Secret*. I put them all together in a very simple and understandable format, we will go through each one of these to really get you to understand how simple shifts in concepts in your own life can dramatically impact the results that you're achieving.

The first concept I call: <u>What you put out there is what you get!</u> In fact it gets deeper than this, because your thoughts truly do control your destiny. Now you may be asking yourself: What do I mean by this? What you mean by this is that the results that you're achieving in your life right now are directly related to the thoughts that you have every single day. If you're thinking about paying bills, your debt situation, your line of credit or anything that is negative in terms of your financial situation, the more you focus on these and the more you think about them, the more they show up in your life. What this means is the following, if you are focused on thoughts that are about money and the negative situations regarding money, all you will have show-up in your life are negative situations. If you're sitting in front of your computer looking at your bank account and wondering how you ever going to get out of the situation that you're in, and putting all your focus, attention and energy into that debt situation - the universe will only deliver to you what you think about most…more debt!

I cannot stress this enough to you that you really need to be conscious of the thoughts that you have every single minute of the day. We live in a society where for every ten thoughts, one is positive and nine are negative. We are surrounded by negativity and sometimes we wonder how can we be positive when we are drowning in negativity. To be honest at all starts with us, we have to take the first step in drawing ourselves forward and really catching ourselves in active negative thoughts. Negative thoughts truly do not help us, all they do is hinder us!

The most important concept that I teach at our Business Mastery three-day intensive seminar is how to develop a self-observant and self-awareness mindset, so that you can catch yourself in active negative thoughts and switch over to positive thoughts. There is a very set process in this and once it is mastered it is extremely powerful.

I call it: Catching yourself in the act!

The more you can catch yourself in the act of negative thoughts and switch them over to positive thoughts, the quicker the circumstances in your life will shift. Henry Ford said it best, "if you think you can or you think you can't, you are right!" This is a very profound statement because it does say that no matter what you put out there, you will receive. So, if you're living in a situation that you do not want to be in right now, it may be a financial situation, a relationship situation, depression, etc. you're the only one who can take action to get yourself out of that situation. This means that you have to sit back and think about the thoughts that you're having every single day, in fact every single minute know how to switch them over to positive life-enhancing thoughts.

I have developed a system that is very simple for you to understand, and when you get yourself into a negative spiral or you feel negative thoughts coming on, you simply say to the little voice inside your head, "Thank you for sharing that!" and move on to replacing it with something that is more positive and life-enhancing.

For example, when you go out and meet people you often hear people say, "I have trouble remembering people's names." The more you say it, the more you program your mind into believing it, and the more you do not remember names, the worse you actually get! What you should be saying is, "I love remembering names and I'm getting better at it all the time." I hope you see the difference in the above example of how this very simple example can relate to so many other areas of your life. We will get into many of these areas as you start to discuss very in-depth examples of 1 Finger Forward and 3 Fingers Back. As you can see, this concept of 'what you put out there is what you get' is an integral part of understanding why things are showing up in your life according to the situations that you're in.

The second concept that I like to discuss is that everything in life is 100% your choice, especially once you're on this planet. Before you came to this planet you made choices about the family that you want to join to guide you on your path and give you the learning experiences for this life that you are about to lead.

Once you're on this glorious planet called Earth, everything that comes your way in every situation that you get yourself into is 100% because of the choices that you make. Many people believe that the situations they are in are somebody else's responsibility, as you go through the examples later in the book, you'll start to realize that although situations arise, you had choices and you chose to be part of them.

This is extremely enlightening when you start to realize that you have thoughts every single day, and because of these thoughts you make choices and those choices will dictate your future results.

Many people seem to think that the choices that they have made are somebody else's responsibility. They believe that they can blame somebody else for the choices that they have made. They live their lives blaming other people for their situations. The moment they start to realize that their situations are 100% because of their actions and choices, the quicker things will change for them and their lives. It's not about the blame game, it's all about us taking responsibility and realizing that we are part of every single situation, and that we did not get there by chance we got there by choice… Our own choice!

The third and final concept in understanding 1 Finger Forward and 3 Fingers Back is the concept of karma. Karma in simple terms is really stating what you do unto others will be done unto you or if you'd like to put it another way which most people have heard, the wheel turns. Simply put, when you do negative things to people and wonder why negative things are showing up in your life - it's karma. I heard a story recently of a gentleman that was busy robbing a convenience store, the storeowners were able to alert the police who came around and arrested the gentleman in the act. While he was busy being arrested inside the convenience store, somebody else stole the thief's vehicle, which was outside the convenience store. Now, that's karma!

With these three concepts in hand I would've fully described to you 1 Finger Forward and 3 Fingers Back in every aspect of your life through a couple of examples.

CHILDREN

I sometimes hear parents say that their children are a nightmare or disobedient or uncontrollable. This is the 1-Finger point forward. What they really should understand is that the 3 Fingers point back at them are saying, "What are you doing to contribute to the situation?" What are the rules in your house? Are you making rules and sticking to them, or are you breaking the rules and showing your children that it's acceptable to break the rules?

Children that are rude, disobedient or uncontrollable are a product of the environment that they grow up in! This is good food for thought!

EMPLOYEES

Have you ever had a situation where you've had an employee working for you and you say that they are useless or not working out? Guess what? That's the 1 Finger Forward, when you should be really asking yourself the following questions – The 3 Fingers Back:

1. I interviewed the person… Did I choose the right person?

2. Did I hire the right person?

3. Did I train them correctly?

4. Did I give them the tools to be successful – am I hindering their growth?

5. Am I communicating effectively with them?

Remember, you chose them for a reason and need to understand that if employees do not work out, that nearly all the time it is a two-way street and you as the employer have at least 50% responsibility in the situation! You really need to get rid of the blame and take responsibility for putting them in a situation that may have been unrealistic for who they are.

There are countless examples of where the 1 Finger Forward and 3 Fingers Back show-up in every aspect of your LIFE. My goal with this short e-book is to have you thinking more about your actions and getting rid of blame and taking on responsibility.

I believe the sooner the world and each individual in it starts to full take responsibility for every one of their actions, the sooner we will be rid of chaos and live in harmony!

About Colin

Colin H.A. Sprake is a Business Transformation Specialist that fully understands how to build businesses in any kind of economy; this comes from decades of experience in both male and female-dominated markets and having worked in over 70 countries.

Born in South Africa and having both an engineering and business degree, he brought his expertise to North America in 1998 and is now a Canadian citizen and resides in South Surrey, B.C.

Colin is a vibrant speaker that has helped thousands of small businesses and is also a bestselling author of *Entrepreneur Success Recipe.* He captivates his audience by delivering marketing, sales and business strategies and tools in very simple and easy-to-understand formats.

One thing Colin always guarantees his audiences is that you will walk away from his presentations, no matter how long or short, with tools you can use immediately in your life and business.

CHAPTER 11

GOING ROGUE—
HOW TO BE THE HERO
OF YOUR LIFE AND OTHER
IMPORTANT LESSONS
FROM MY DOG

BY TODD LAMB

It was a pleasantly warm summer night that waned uneventfully into the early morning hours. My partner and I responded to a routine disturbance call, which was no different than the thousands of other similar calls we had attended. However, unknown to us, this night would be very different.

As we rounded the corner, a vehicle with its headlights out came racing at full speed in our direction and tried to run us down. We swerved to evade the 2000-pound speeding weapon just in time to see it round a corner. We turned around and carefully negotiated the corner just in time to see a male exiting a vehicle. He saw us, turned and came running full speed in our direction.

The lenses of my eyes flattened as I looked down the wrong end of the barrel of a Glock Model 22 .40 Caliber semi automatic handgun. This was no ordinary situation. My brain was registering a series of very odd facts at light speed, but what really mattered was the undeniable fact that a gun is built for one purpose.

My surroundings became eerily quiet while other sounds were magnified. Rubber soles peeling off warm asphalt echoed as loud as the wheels of a 747 touching down on a hot runway in the Arizona desert. My brain began to process the shooter in tenth of a second intervals... he is running, creating an unstable shooting platform, single hand grip, inexperienced and yelling unintelligible comments. Even the inexperienced can get lucky.

My breathing slowed. I cleared leather in a quarter second to meet my match and even the playing field. I prepped my door for my partner, Police Service Dog Rogue, to deploy.

This was it.

But hang on... A deadly force encounter is not what this story is about.

This story is about you. It is about you being the hero of your own life by "Going Rogue" and setting yourself apart from the pack.

None of this will make any sense unless I give you a quick snapshot of who I am. As I write this, I am a Sergeant in charge of a Tactical Unit (SWAT Team). I also had the incredible pleasure to work as a Canine Handler with my partner Police Service Dog Rogue, who is the inspiration for this chapter. I have spent the last 15 years as a Police Officer, but when I am not doing that, you will find me working on what has become a successful online business. I have an unquenchable entrepreneurial thirst.

I learned many powerful lessons by working with my police dog. I felt bad for him and I often imagined if he could have talked he would have said, "You're a nice kid, but a little thick," as he tried to guide me in so many ways. Many of these lessons are directly responsible for what I have achieved. I am happy to share them in order that you can take a shorter route to achieving success and becoming the hero of your life, as you begin Going Rogue.

FIRST THINGS FIRST - GET STARTED

A dog will track a combination of human scent and ground disturbance. The start of the track is the most difficult and requires laser focus because it is the oldest portion of the track and has suffered from time delay and cross-contamination. As a dog acquires the scent, he or she will move deliberately from footprint to footprint, moving from the oldest scent to the freshest scent, gaining speed and momentum along the way. As this happens, simultaneously there is other corroborating information which will confirm the track, such as a shoe the bad guy has run right out of, a dropped gun, an open gate or other pieces of evidence. Make no mistake, the start is the most important part.

Wouldn't you know it, this is no different than getting started with your idea or business. You require laser focus and once you begin you start to create momentum, and things will begin to move faster toward your goal until you become self-sustaining. The longer you delay, the more cross-contamination will prevent you from moving forward. By cross-contamination, in the business sense, I am referring to all of the useless noise and excuses. Have you made any of these excuses?

- I am not sure about my idea.
- I need to do more research.
- I don't have the money to get started.
- I need more time.

As one of my mentors Craig Ballantyne explained to me, if you continue to wait to bring your product to market, you are preventing someone who desperately needs your solution from finding it. This should not be acceptable to you. Make your plan and get started today, right now.

ELIMINATE SELF-LIMITING DOUBTS

Let's take a look at the Hollywood notion that dogs can't track through water. It was a sunny summer afternoon in July when we were called out from home to attend the scene of stolen vehicle. A car had been dumped by a suspect who was a crystal meth addict and on a crime spree throughout town.

I deployed Rogue and he began tracking toward a fast-flowing creek. The track lead through a wall of blackberry bush three feet thick. Here's a fun fact: blackberry bushes are Mother Nature's equivalent to razor wire, it is unbelievably evil stuff.

We headed through the bushes, getting cut along the way, and down into a creek. The bad guy obviously had seen the same movies as the rest of us, but as Rogue's head snapped left indicating the presence of scent, he began to swim up stream as I waded in the dirty waist deep water behind him. Why didn't he track on the bank? Because it was wall-to-wall blackberries on either side so it was swim or quit, and quit is a word neither of us understood.

Rogue continued to pursue the track through the water, up through a break in the bushes and into a back yard where we were met by three guys enjoying a barbecue and a pint of beer who simply pointed in the direction we were already headed saying, "He went that way," which sadly for us lead back through the blackberries and into the creek. As we navigated up the stream and came out again, the track changed to a trail and Rogue's speed began to pick up.

We were getting close.

Into back yards and over fence after fence, we continued pursuit. I stepped into some old grass clippings piled next to one of the fences, which as luck would have it, was a hornet's nest. Trouble!

To say the hornets were angry is an understatement. I was getting stung multiple times, and they were covering Rogue. We pressed on while my cover officer was literally smashing hornets on my body. Rogue was now at a dead run and closing fast. Over a 6-foot fence he went and there was the suspect, cowering in the backyard of a home, wet, breathing heavy and pale faced. "One in custody," we reported over the radio.

Nobody told Rogue he couldn't track through water. He had no self-limiting beliefs or doubts about his ability to prevent him from succeeding. He simply applied his skills and got the job done. The only thing that changed that day was that he developed an absolute hatred for any flying insects...True story.

The same is true for you. Are you listening to that inner voice telling you to push forward? The voice that has been telling you that idea you have had in your head and causing you to lose sleep will bring value to the world. Set aside your fear of failure and get it out to the world. You possess the ability to succeed. It is up to you and no one else.

THE BATTLE SPACE IS 360°

Rogue and I were tracking a suspect who had fled from a crime scene out in a rural neighborhood. We tracked through a barn full of angry, but thankfully corralled, horses into a wooded area where we encountered a pair of black dress shoes. This guy was now running shoeless and I remember thinking it's only a matter of time. Rogue's pace began to quicken and a short time later he leaped into a small bush and although I couldn't see him, I could feel the tension change in my tracking line. We had our man...or so I thought.

Rogue came out with a shirt in his mouth. I gave him the command to track and he became what I would describe as hectic or frantic, and remained in the area. We cleared every bush in the area, and nothing. I pushed him through the woods into a field and worked at it for 2 hours, still nothing. We had to move on to the next call.

A few hours later I was told the suspect had arrived back at his residence and after being interviewed he revealed he had been up a tree. The very tree right where at the base of which his shirt was located. Rogue was telling me to look up. I just didn't listen. Missing that bad guy still bothers me, but it's a reminder to listen, remain humble and remember that battle space is not linear, it is 360°.

Situational awareness is a critical pillar in your foundation for success. Being linearly focused in business is as much a fatal flaw as entering a room during a tactical deployment and standing in the doorway, it is called the fatal funnel and you're going to get killed. Be aware of everything around you.

The best way to be aware of your surroundings in business is to watch and listen. Doing most of the talking during a first meeting with anyone, whether it's somebody you want to do business with, or get to know on a personal level, is a recipe for a short relationship. Try listening instead. Find out everything you can and figure out a way to add exceptional value to their business. When you add value and take an interest in others, you will separate yourself from the pack. To be interesting, be interested, which is another piece of information Craig Ballantyne shared with me.

Equally important is watching the masters work in person. Observe their actions in a group setting, whether they are speaking or strategically working the room. There is a guy named Rick Kaselj (ExerciseForInjuries. com) who is an absolute master at working the room during marketing events. He makes a list of people he wants to connect with and gets it done. He asks people about their business and works it into a message suitable for his audience. Operating in this manner is very effective and it demonstrates an awareness of your complete surroundings.

The Shortcut

I was a new dog handler and was introduced to a world-renowned dog trainer and judge by the name of Doug Deacon. You know the type. A constantly-furrowed brow, one-word answers and a gravelly voice. He demanded perfection.

On one occasion I was working Rogue in obedience, he gave me a tip and it immediately changed how Rogue responded. It forever changed our performance in obedience and in fact we won two National Police Canine Championships. One exposure to a high level professional literally saved me years of frustration. The stories are endless.

Let's examine my online business which began on eBay. I was selling plans to make a homemade slushee machine for 5 bucks. I made $3k in a month and figured I was on my way to being the next DotCom millionaire.

I put up my first fitness site a short time later and I thought I would do things my own way. That site went nowhere fast, as did the next one, and the one after that. I told myself if I just worked at it, it would come. This was, and remains, categorically false.

Have you ever heard the expression, "It's not about knowing how to turn screws, but rather, knowing which screw to turn." As it turned out, I didn't even have a screwdriver let alone knowing which screw to turn, and it was costing me dearly.

Drawing from my experience as a dog handler and a tactical operator, I sought out the best. Three people have provided me with immeasurable insight. Their slight adjustments to my strategies have produced exponential results.

I was introduced to Craig Ballantyne (he now owns EarlyToRise.com) in 2008 after being laid up as a result of blowing my knee out during a dog track. He has and continues to provide a vast depth of insight into online business systems, personal self discipline related to producing meaningful content and ongoing motivation. Craig is a "switched-on operator." He is like one of my snipers, operating with impeccable precision and providing overwatch.

In a tactical unit, a breacher is responsible for opening doors. That's exactly what Bedros Keuilian does (PTPower.com). He is a master at connecting people and opening doors that would normally stay locked and even barricaded for that matter. His insight into systems is unmatched along with his kindness and willingness to help others succeed. Bedros's story is truly the epitome of the American dream, but it is anchored in a relentless work ethic.

Finally, as with Bedros and Craig, Dave Guindon (ExitSplash.com) taught me the power of innovation and over-delivering value in anything you create. His imagination and ability to provide value to his market place is unmatched. Dave also taught me how to fail forward and how to take away the positives from a venture which did not meet expectations.

The common thread that unites these three and others like them, is their desire to give more and see people achieve success. Learning from these three individuals is similar to having worked with my partner Rogue, he gave everything and asked for nothing in return.

Having a mentor (or mentors in my case) is the only shortcut to success, if in fact one does exist. It is rocket fuel. Feedback from a mentor will enable you to avoid developing bad habits and making critical mistakes in your business. Receiving this insight and playing up a level will be the difference between failing, or alternatively, achieving the success you know is possible.

THE BEGINNING

You are the author of your own story and this could be the beginning. You can accomplish anything. My experiences have served as a valuable teacher, as will yours should you make the choice to be the hero of your own story.

Oh, and as for that little 3-hour hostage-taking incident at the beginning of this chapter...well, lets just say someone has some time on their hands to become a more productive member of society.

Now, it's time for you to take the next step and set yourself apart from the pack by Going Rogue.

About Todd

Todd Lamb grew up on the Canadian prairies and currently lives on the West Coast of Canada. Todd was heavily involved in sports growing up, primarily focusing on football, rugby and hockey.

He attended grade school through College in Alberta. Upon graduation he began commercial diving and ultimately followed his calling to serve his country in the Canadian Armed Forces. He served as part of the Special Service Force in the 1st Battalion Royal Canadian Regiment.

After earning his jump wings he would have gladly continued to take orders from well meaning Sergeant Majors (even the ones with mess tin syndrome - if you've served you know what I mean). However, the storied Canadian Airborne Regiment was disbanded and his military dream of serving in the Airborne and becoming a Pathfinder ended. Disenchanted, he returned to commercial diving on Canada's west coast.

In 1998, he began his policing career and served on the Police Dive Unit, the Canine Unit and the Emergency Response Team (SWAT) of which he is currently the Sergeant and team leader. Todd and his partner Police Service Dog **Rogue** successfully captured 2 Canadian Police Canine Championship titles during their service as a team. Todd also graduated from the University Of Victoria School of Public Administration while working as a police officer.

Along with another team member, he was awarded the medal of Meritorious Service by the Lieutenant Governor of BC for actions taken during a hostage rescue mission. Todd was also awarded the Queen Elizabeth Diamond Jubilee Medal for service to his community with distinction.

Todd is the founder of Rogue Syndication. He seeks out individuals who possess a desire to help people, and grow their business. His partners and clients include Submissions 101, BodyRipped and The White Peony along with a select few others with whom he has worked behind the scenes.

When not working, which is almost never, you can find Todd waterskiing through the placid waters of Lake Cowichan, BC. This is where problems are solved and the real work gets done.

CHAPTER 12

THE BE-A-BESTSELLER MINDSET — UTILIZING THE POWER OF STORYTELLING TO AMPLIFY YOUR BUSINESS AND YOUR LIFE

BY JENNIFER CARLEVATTI ADERHOLD

It's in your moments of decision that your destiny is shaped.
~ Anthony Robbins

A little over a decade ago, my then husband and myself both quit our jobs and moved from Denver, Colorado to Long Beach, California. Jamie was going start an environmental consulting business. I was going to pursue my dream of being an award winning screenwriter and television series creator akin to Lena Dunham – HBO's "Girls" and Diablo Cody - "Juno".

Yes, I actually envisioned walking down the Red Carpet, being on stage holding my award to thunderous applause, and expressing my gratitude to the many people who help me along the way. My vision was crystal clear.

Then, life happened. I have chronic Lyme disease, and in 2002 I relapsed. My symptoms are mainly neurological in nature. So, for months at a time, I would suffer with extreme vertigo while being treated with very high doses of antibiotics that were wreaking havoc on my gut. I couldn't drive. My head was constantly in the clouds. I was exhausted from lack of sleep.

Additionally, at that same time, I began to notice changes in my father. You can read about my Dad's story on www.jenniferaderhold.com. It tells you about my family's journey with dad's diagnosis of frontal temporal lobe dementia.

Needless to stay, my crystal clear writing vision was a very distant memory. Feeling like a failure, I retreated, and shut down one of the most important aspects of my life – my writing.

This is when, however, I learned how the power of a supportive community can hold you up, believe in you, and cheer you on even in your darkest hours.

Fast forward to 2005. Arm in arm with a dear writer friend, I went to a writers' conference hosted by my mentor Larry Brody. Being away from this world for 3 years, I was shaking in my boots knowing that the first question most people ask you at a writing conference is - "What are you writing?"

Lo and behold, the first person I ran into was another one of my mentors, the Executive Director of the Southern California Writers' Conference, Michael Steven Gregory. And, you guessed it. The first words out of his mouth were, "So, Jen, what are you writing these days." Flush with embarrassment, I stuttered, "Just sentences."

Michael hesitated before he answered me. In that moment of hesitation, my mind was reeling, "He thinks, I'm a joke. Why did I come here? Oh my god, I'm mortified."

When he did respond, what came out of his mouth changed the course of my writing career. Stroking his beard with his fore finger and thumb, he said, "Jen, I bet if you went back and compiled those sentences, you just might find a theme there."

Because of that advice, my screenplay "Oasis For The Soul" was born. And, with my renewed writing vision, I took a leap of faith, and submitted my screenplay in the 2012 Spec Scriptacular competition.

Months later, an email arrived in my inbox with the subject line, "18th Annual SPEC SCRIPTACULAR WINNERS."

Holding my breath, I opened the email. I let out an audible gasp as I read – The 2012 Grand Prize Winner in 18th Annual Spec Scriptacular competition is Jennifer Carlevatti Aderhold for the screenplay 'OASIS FOR THE SOUL.'

I know I wasn't on a stage being given a standing ovation, but it felt just as good. It was my Sally Fields moment, "You like me. You really, really like me!"

So, what does that story have to do with the Be-A-Bestseller mindset? I'm so glad you asked ☺.

As a storyteller we use the element of suspension of disbelief to draw our readers in, get them to sacrifice realism, then thrust them into a fanciful new world for their enjoyment. E.L. James and her "50 Shades" success is a good example of how to do this effectively.

Being able to take giant leaps of faith with your storytelling is THE core element of the Be A Bestseller Mindset. But don't just take my word for it. Let's take a look at the science of storytelling and how our brain is wired to read/listen to stories.

Ever since the first caveman drew a bison on a cave wall to the latest tweet on Twitter or viral video viewed on our iPhone, storytelling is in our human DNA.

In a recent interview, Cognitive Neuroscientist Michael Gazzaniga explains why the left hemisphere of the brain is always trying to make sense of past thoughts and experiences through storytelling.

"I think the human as a storytelling animal, as some people put it, is because this system is continually trying to keep the story coherent and, even though these actions may be coming from processors going on outside, initially, of conscious awareness, an action is produced and then you might want to explain that action to be part of your coherence and your story, your narrative."
[http://bigthink.com/videos/your-storytelling-brain]

Currently, in the business world, utilizing the power storytelling to sell a product or services is all the rage. Enter the world of neuromarketing.

Neuromarketing is the process of researching the brain patterns of consumers to reveal their responses to particular advertisements and products before developing new advertising campaigns and branding techniques.

Christopher Morin, one of the pioneers of neuromarketing, over the past ten years has collected a vast amount of empirical evidence showing how the brain is responsible for all our consumer behaviors. This fascinating statistical information includes:

- The brain is only 2% of our body mass, but burns nearly 20% of our energy.
- 80% of our brain energy is needed to sustain our rest state or default mode.
- We only use about 20% of our brain consciously.

Therefore, our brain spends most of its time in survival mode known widely as the reptilian brain.

Author and noted neuroscientist, Antonio Damasio, sums up this phenomenon well: *"We are not thinking machines that feel, we are feeling machines that think."*

So, how does all this scientific mumbo jumbo translate, for us, the storytellers, in amplifying our business and life pursuits? Let's first begin by dissecting what the elements are that make a good story.

In the excellent book *Resonate*, Nancy Duarte shares this definition of story pattern:

"The most simplistic way to describe the structure of a story is situation, complication, and resolution. From mythical adventures to recollections shared around the dinner table, all stories follow this pattern."

There are many ways to structure your story. I personally use Syd Field's Paradigm method whenever I set out to tell a story. Field's Paradigm is the classic three-act story structure that most movies that we watch follow. This illustration gives a clear breakdown of each element

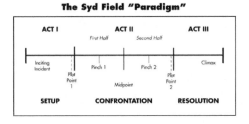

As you can see, every story must have a clear beginning, middle and end. Let's use the classic movie, *Casablanca*, to show how this story structure comes to life.

1. THE INCITING INCIDENT

Ugarte (Peter Lorre) comes to Rick's Café Américain, a nightclub owned by American expatriate Rick Blaine (Humphrey Bogart). Ugarte gives Rick letters of transit he obtained by killing two German couriers.

The papers allow the holder to travel freely around German-controlled Europe. Ugarte plans to sell the documents to the highest bidder but leaves the letters with Rick for safekeeping.

2. PLOT POINT 1

Ugarte is captured by Captain Louis Renault (Claude Rains), a corrupt police official accommodating the Nazis, before he can sell the letters of transit to Victor Laszlo (Paul Henreid), an infamous Czech Resistance leader.

Rick waivers on keeping letters of transit papers until Ilsa (Ingrid Bergman), Victor's wife and Rick's past lover in Paris, walks into the Café Américain.

3. MIDPOINT

Laszlo and Ilsa seek out Signor Ferrari (Sydney Greenstreet), one of Rick's competitor's and owner of a club called The Blue Parrot to obtain transit papers for him and Isla to leave Casablanca.

Ferrari, however, is only able to secure one exit visa for Ilsa, explaining that "it would take a miracle" to get Laszlo out of Casablanca. Ferrari hints that Rick has possession of Ugarte's letters of transit.

4. PLOT POINT 2

Ilsa confronts Rick in the deserted café, holding a gun on him in a desperate attempt to retrieve the letters of transit. Rick dares her to shoot. Unable to pull the trigger, Ilsa confesses that she still loves him. After hearing Ilsa's confession Rick decide to help Laszlo escape Casablanca, leading Ilsa to believe that she will stay behind with Rick when Laszlo leaves.

5. CLIMAX

Laszlo is jailed on a minor charge. Rick talks Renault into releasing Laszlo, promising to set him up for a much more serious crime of possession of the letters of transit.

Rick double crosses Renault, forcing him at gunpoint to assist in the escape of Laszlo.

6. RESOLUTION

At the last moment, Rick makes Ilsa get on the plane to Lisbon with her husband.

Oh, how I love that movie!

Now that we know the proper structure of a story the fun part begins – *creating* our personal stories that deeply connect our readers/listeners with the message we want to share.

The first step is to know "WHY" you are sharing this story.

In determining your "WHY" start by asking yourself the following questions:

- Why did you decide you wanted to share this story?
- What kind of impact do you want to make on the world through this story?
- What special gift do you offer to others by sharing this story?

Step two: You need to understand your "WHO."

Who do you think will benefit the most from what you have to offer as a brand, a product/service or a person? Questions to ask in regard to finding your "Perfect Person" (PP) include, but are not limited to:

- What is the gender of your PP?

- What is the age of your PP?
- What kind of environment does your PP live in?
- What does your PP do in his or her spare time?

The goal here is to drill down deep. The more you know about your "Perfect Person" the better you can connect with them.

Lastly, direct your PP to take ACTION to receive the maximum benefits from your story.

Calls to Action can include:

- Buy this widget
- Share this story
- Click to gain access to…

Right now, I know in my heart, that every person who has read to this point has a Be A Bestseller Mindset and is destined to become a Bestselling author.

How do I know that? I know that because you took a leap of faith and joined me as I shared with you how utilizing your powerful stories will impact the world for good.

I am so passionate about this topic that I created www.BeABestseller.com, a website dedicated to assisting entrepreneurial minded writers to elevate their storytelling craft to a career.

BeABestseller.com is a community of liked-minded storytellers who are dedicated to your success. I may be the facilitator of the community, but it is the collective voices of us all that will raise the level, and the impact, of entrepreneurial authors around the world.

The mission of Be-A-Bestseller is for each member to:

- Gain clarity of your unique vision
- Be held accountable for your writing career pursuits
- Share and receive tangible tips and resources
- Achieve connectedness as a community

We can do this by:

- Sharing personal experiences – both challenges and successes
- Learning from leading experts in writing, publishing, and platform building
- Networking with other members to form strategic alliances, accountability buddies

So, with the Be-A-Bestseller community, it is my mission to create ongoing, action-packed, page-turners filled with insightful stories, interesting characters, and lively dialogue.

Together, let's engage to create a dynamic, interactive story together. I look forward to having you be a part of this exciting journey!

About Jennifer

Jennifer Carlevatti Aderhold is the Founder and CEO of BeABestseller. com, a website and inbox magazine dedicated to elevating the voices of entrepreneurial authors around the world.

Prior to founding BAB, Jennifer worked in a variety of industries ranging from the Fortune 500 to small entrepreneurial ventures. Most recently, as a digital marketing consultant, Jennifer created a water monitoring training video for C.I.Agent® Storm·Water Solutions, whose water monitoring program was utilized during the Deepwater Horizon oil spill in the gulf. This video is currently being utilized for trainings worldwide.

Additionally, Jennifer has received several literary recognitions for her writing. Her accomplishments include being the Grand Prize Winner in the 2012 Spec Scriptacular competition for the screenplay *OASIS FOR THE SOUL*, a Finalist in the People's Pilot competition for the educational series premise *JEFFREY BEAN*, a Finalist in the Acclaim TV Writing competition for the spec script *POPULAR – Let the Games Begin*, and a Semi-Finalist in the North American Poetry contest for the poem *SOUL CAMPING*.

Jennifer holds both a Master in Business Administration degree from Suffolk University, Boston, Massachusetts and a Bachelor of Science Degree in Speech Communication from Syracuse University. She has also completed extensive course work in online marketing and social media from noted industry leaders including MaryEllen Tribby, Ryan Deiss, Perry Belcher, Frank Kern and Brendon Burchard.

From her knowledge of being the primary caregiver for her father who was diagnosed with Alzheimer's ten years ago, Jennifer is currently working on a book advocating for the rights of the elderly in their twilight years.

Jennifer resides in Los Angeles, CA. She is an avid reader as well as a student of filmmaking with the intent of producing her own film projects.

CHAPTER 13

IMPROVE YOUR LIFE WITH FENG SHUI!

BY ANGELICA SANDSTROM

We begin to see the importance of selecting our environment with the greatest of care, because environment is the mental feeding ground out of which the food that goes into our mind is extracted.
~ Napoleon Hill

Whatever success is for you, Feng Shui can help you reach it by showing you how to select and design the most conducive and healthy environment to work and live in. This will help you to enhance your vitality so you can perform on a higher level and create more abundance for yourself and others.

You experience your outer environment through your inner environment and vice versa, and like positive emotions, happy thoughts that nourish your mind and body; it also nourishes you as a soul. Like Feng Shui, these are things you can't see or touch but you can definitely feel and experience the effects of it!

Let´s say you have a big dream you want to accomplish, you want to make your world a better place for living in. Then, whether its about strengthening your health or your relationships, creating and succeeding in your business, becoming wealthy or feeling more joy in life, the scientific system of Feng Shui is your key.

My journey of acknowledging this art of placement, time and self-knowledge began when I searched for a solution to my health challenges in a marvelous place, the rainforest, and under rare circumstances got introduced to something that became a mentor and inspirational source in my life – Feng Shui! It gives you guidelines you can take to reach your dream.

I've bet you have a dream, a dream in your mind that you want to materialise.

Imagine this picture in your mind, can you see it?

How do you feel when you visualize this dream right in front of your eyes?

Do you feel alive? I'd guess that!

Do you think you can get there? I know you can!

How can I be so sure about that? Well! I had a dream once, a dream of living in total health and I materialised it!

Among different circumstances in life, I went through the hardest of them, showing myself that I could achieve what I had in mind. Today, I am living my dream. Even if the road that led to it was narrow and full of challenges, there was one particular thing about life that I learned to appreciate the most, and that most people take for granted. Still today, its presence gives me a feeling of deep humbleness.

As long as you can BREATHE, you can do, be, have, achieve and succeed with whatever you want!

MY STORY

Imagine you are sitting here in the green grass with me, the sky is clear heavenly blue, and you are basking in the radiance from the sun, smelling the fresh clean air and holding the most beautiful red flower in your right hand. You are enjoying life to the fullest!

The birds are singing in the trees and you are looking at a big yellow butterfly who has landed in your left palm, it reminds you of how joyful life really is. Now it tries to tell you something but you can't grasp it, because it feels like the air suddenly is running out of you, you become dizzy, and you struggle to get air. You can see your grandpa running towards you before everything around you appears in bright white light and you pass out.

Surrounded by your parents and other loving relatives you wake up, lying in this hospital bed in the same place where you eight months earlier descended to this earth and where you looked into your parent's eyes for the first time. A man with white clothes enters the room and clarifies the problem:

"You have severe Asthma, it seems to be very dangerous when breathing attacks can emerge at any time due to the severe allergies you also seem to have. We are afraid that you will have to live with this for the rest of your life. You will not be able to have a normal life with daily physical activities. Also, you will have to take our prescriptions seriously even though they can give you side effects, and this includes inhaling medicines everyday for the rest of your life!"

This was to be my reality during the next twenty years.

I went to the hospital each week for my breathing problems. Because of all the medication, my immune system was very weak at the time, and my vital energy was absent. I was close to death several times, but in those moments when my lips were blue and I struggled to get air, I had other things in mind than to die. I remember I was so focused on my dream of becoming healthy and balanced again, I almost forgot these severe attacks – as fast as they appeared.

FINDING MY GOLDEN SOLUTION - FENG SHUI

I was so grateful to live that I became a fighter through the tough moments of not being able to consume the air and I kept being persistent to my dream. The older I got, the more I refused to accept that I was sick. I started to get more conscious about how my body functioned, and when I found my Golden Solution the pieces of the puzzle came together.

I started to learn how my inner environment affects my outer environment and *vice versa*. I learned how important it is to have clean air, clean water and organic food, and how my mind and thoughts are integrated and how they affect the whole spirit.

I came to gain knowledge throughout the years, but it was not until I traveled to the rainforest to detoxify myself and my then heavily medicated (polluted) body that I first came to hear about it.

It was on my transformational travel to the Mayan culture in Central America that I was introduced to this Golden Solution through indigenous wise Mayan people, who discussed an ancient art of time and placement called Wind and Water, Feng Shui, which could strengthen your health and vitality.

In the following years, I studied and practice the classical version of Feng Shui and absorbed everything that I came across according to it. I became a licensed consultant, and I discovered a whole new world of solutions that presented opportunities to live happily, healthy and wealthy!

If you want to find the secrets of the Universe,
think energy, frequency and vibration.
~ Nikola Tesla

A MULTIDIMENSIONAL WORLD

Since you are living in a fantastic multidimensional world of vibrations, colors and lights, a world full of chi, life prana, where this invisible electromagnetic energy radiates in particular patterns from objects, of all sizes and shapes and in the nature around your dwelling, you can benefit from applying Feng Shui unselfishly into your life and business in order to reach success.

You along with other celebrities, billionaires and business owners can learn to place matter in a right manner on a physical level – accordingly to the constant flow of energy that penetrates both time and space to gain wealth.

So, no surprise that many business magnates along with the world's largest companies embrace Feng Shui.

YOUR FIRST STEP TO TAKE

Before you start applying Feng Shui it is important that you:

DE-CLUTTER YOUR SPACE!

As long as the energy around you and in your body flows freely, you feel good, you are energized and creative. If there is a blockage in either your surroundings or in your emotional, mental or physical body, it affects you in a certain way and it can drain you out of energy.

Clutter comes in many forms, not only from your collected objects that you have, don´t use or don´t like, or your unfinished tasks on your work desk, you can also count toxins from the food you eat as clutter, from what you drink and from negative emotions you feel. They all create a blockage in some way.

When you first de-clutter yourself and your space and then apply the old science of Feng Shui, it will create a harmonious place for you to be in, where the life prana flows freely and gives you the vital energy you need to succeed.

A SYSTEM OF SOLUTIONS

Feng Shui is a system full of solutions from which you can diagnose an imbalance and then positively affect the health of your home or business environment.

Broadly described, this system combines astrology, cosmology and geomancy based on detailed observations of our living world and the way in which earth energy, along with universal energy, affects all of our daily lives.

When it comes to diagnosing the energy flow in your outer environment, your house or office, you divide your architectural map of that space into different compass directions using an energy map called The Bagua, and a special compass Lou Pan, which shows you how to balance and enhance these different directions.

The compass locations, their connected aspirations and some examples of what you can use to enhance each area:

EAST stands for Health: Place something here that represents health and vitality for you.

SOUTH stands for Fame: Place your diplomas, award-winning prizes, a painting of you when you succeed or that represents fame for you.

SOUTHWEST stands for Relationships/Romance: A beautiful picture of you and your loved one or a photo of a happy couple, or a photo that represents satisfied people if you have a business (your customers).

WEST stands for Creativity: Place something here that reminds you of your creativity. It might be a note on a goal you´re working towards.

NORTHWEST stands for Helpful people and Travels: Here you can place pictures of mentors, your best friends or places you want to travel to.

NORTH stands for Career: What's your dream job? Dream position? Put a picture of it here.

NORTHEAST stands for Personal development: Here you can store all of your books, your library if you have one or other objects that remind you of what you want to reach in the field of personal development.

SOUTHEAST stands for Wealth: Place a water fountain and a vase or a pot with a light on it full of money here.

THE CENTER OF YOUR HOME stands for Inner peace: What reminds you of Inner peace? A painting of a tranquil landscape, a candle, stones, crystals, a statue?

POWERFUL GUIDELINES FOR YOU TO IMPLEMENT WHICH ALSO HELPED ME ON MY JOURNEY

The Air!

Fresh clean air helps you to detoxify your lungs. Whenever you have free time to spend, spend it outside for at least three hours at once. It takes some time to renew the air in your lungs. You can go for a walk, play a sport or game, or have a lovely picnic with family and friends.

On a daily basis you absorb toxins from inks, plastics and other surface materials from inside your home and office. So if you are sitting inside quite a lot, buy yourself some fresh plants such as:

Tulips, English Ivy, King of Hearts or a Peace Lily. They are all good poison eaters and will help create a greater natural energy around you.

The gentle wind does move, silently, invisibly
~ William Blake

The Sun!

Try to be in the sun as much as you can. You are biologically designed to live outside. The sun contains all the colors of the spectrum and triggers production of serotonin, a neuro-chemical that helps you induce good feelings and make you feel optimistic.

Clean Water and energizing Food!

Our human race stands alone in having a complex system for retrieving and storing information. You insert, intercede and extrapolate information in a part of the brain called the neocortex. This neocortex is involved in higher functions such as sensory perception, spatial reasoning, language, conscious thoughts, behavior, art, creative expression and your intuition.

To keep the balance in this region it is very important to eat and drink as clean water and organic food as possible, because whatever goes into your mouth affects your whole body in different ways as well as your neocortex. Your beautiful and intelligent body deserves the best!

Living Food!

Try to eat as natural food as you possibly can, raw organic unprocessed food is something to consider. It tastes good, gives you energy, helps your body clean itself and overall, it can assist you to restore your health.

Living Water!

Mountain spring water: look for a spring near you at: www.findaspring. com. Spring water is some of the healthiest water on the planet because it classifies as "living water." Living water, like living food is in its raw, natural state the way nature intended it to be. So consume the best spring water you can find and drink a lot of it; it will help you stay hydrated at the same time and it's good for your memory.

Water increases vitality and you feel energized!

Coconut water: This is an excellent source of fresh, pure water and electrolytes. Coconuts are also rich in Lauric Acid, which is known for its immune-boosting as well as its antiviral, antibacterial and antifungal properties, so it's an ideal choice when you want to boost yourself!

<u>Nature!</u>

For your vitality, it's important that you make a strong connection with nature. Plan a trip to a waterfall in an attractive location.

Even if you are living in a beautiful home in the city, your internal environment there is bound to be somewhat artificial. It's easier to live more naturally if you live in the countryside or have a garden. The alternative to this is to design your interior. Use natural materials such as bamboo, ecological cotton, silk or canvas. Invest in green plants. Moreover, use full spectrum lights, water features like water fountains, and ambient music that connects you with nature.

FINAL WORDS

Who is THE most important person in your life?

I can tell you!

The most important person in your life is YOU! Now it is time to create the healthy and wealthy life you deserve by using this ancient knowledge of time and placement. Remember, as long as you can breathe you can act! When you act, the life of your dreams is one step closer to you. When you unselfishly apply Feng Shui in your life and business, you will start to become more, and from this state you can give more and serve more.

You are important!

About Angelica

ANGELICA is your inspirational Feng Shui expert who instructs you as an entrepreneur, business owner or any form of leader with an open heart how to design your life and business for growth and success by using the well known ancient science of Feng Shui.

She is a multi-faceted blooming entrepreneur who travels around internationally in her working sphere. She has experienced indigenous cultures that always understood that we are not separate from our planet, our homes or one another, and that Feng Shui brings together our internal and external surroundings by creating peaceful, balanced environments whose occupants can develop health and happiness in.

Her traveling and work has taken her from Acupuncture masters in China to the Bedouin people in Africa. She has walked the pilgrimage to Santiago de Compostela in Spain and lived self-sufficiently out in the jungle with the Mayan People. She learned their universal wisdom about planet earth, to work with the forces and spirits of nature and how to show gratitude and compassion for them.

When it comes to instructing and guiding you to develop higher consciousness and success through the principles of Feng Shui, *she is the one!*

Her recipe on how to create your own reality and live the life of your dreams, is to start knowing yourself, think big, believe in yourself, act on and stay persistent to your big dream!

She has experienced herself and this planet we all are walking on in the most comprehensive way there is. From early years, she learned how to grow with challenges – using a strong mind and consciousness about the Universal Laws. She has always been eager to learn the importance of getting to know matter as well as energy in its natural state.

When she instructs you how to design your life and business according to Feng Shui principles, you will stand out from the multitude. It will increase your energy, vitality and productivity and besides from expressing yourself and your creativity to the fullest, it will also strengthen your relationships and give you the opportunity to gain more wealth. It will make you stand apart! Are you ready for Feng Shui?

I have not eaten enough of the Tree of Knowledge, though in my profession I am obliged to feed on it regularly.
~ Albert Einstein

www.fengshuiedge.com

CHAPTER 14

ACCOUNTING 101?
— NOT AT THIS OFFICE

BY DIANE GARDNER

What makes an accountant stand apart? Is it the level of service provided, the amount of knowledge or experience the accountant has, marketing, or something else?

There are three areas that make my accounting practice stand apart from other accountants. These areas are:

1. Personal touch
2. Pro-active tax planning
3. My growth strategy

I feel that personal touch in dealing with clients is extremely important. One of the biggest reasons clients seek a new accountant is because their old accountant didn't return phone calls, made them feel unimportant, didn't stay in close contact with them, etc.

We have several ways that we use personal touch to make our clients feel important. When a new prospective client comes into the office for their first appointment, we have a small gift bag sitting on the conference table. Attached to this bag is a card that says, "Welcome to our office!".

We want their first experience with us to be a positive one. After the initial appointment, we send out a "shock and awe" package that consists of: a welcome letter, a brochure, information about the days and hours we are open, an introduction to our staff members, and a copy of my short book, *Don't Overpay Your Taxes: Why New & Existing Businesses in the Pacific Northwest Overpay Their Taxes.*

Once the prospect has become a client we send out a box of cookies with a hand-signed card that welcomes them to our company. This always gathers a positive response from new clients!

In addition to the little touches we give to our new clients, we have a weekly emailed article or blog called, *Talk It Up.* These articles cover a wide variety of topics such as: tax law changes, business success tips, marketing information, tax deductions, etc.

All of our clients receive birthday cards signed by each staff member. In addition to birthday cards, we send get well, sympathy, congratulations for new babies, etc. We feel it is important to have the personal touch of hand-signed cards. We also send out hand-signed Thanksgiving and Christmas cards (about 600 of them) each year.

Another way we touch our clients is through our monthly print newsletter. We mail out a monthly newsletter that is filled with articles about health, nutrition, seasonal tips, business tips, senior living tips, famous quotes, trivia, recipes, community events, and even jokes.

In our newsletter, we feature a client's business each month. The client is interviewed and a story is written. The article includes a picture of the client and encourages people to patronize this client. This is a popular feature each month.

The second way my accounting office stands apart from other accountants is through pro-active tax planning services. What is pro-active tax planning? It is the preparation of a plan that saves a business owner income tax year after year.

Pro-active tax planning utilizes time tested, IRS-approved tax saving strategies. These strategies determine when and how personal and business transactions should be conducted to reduce or eliminate tax liability.

Many accountants are not familiar with true tax planning. Some accountants prepare tax projections throughout the year and call this "tax planning." Others come up with a tax savings suggestion or two during the income tax preparation process. They generally don't take it any further than that.

I like to ask new prospects - When was the last time your accountant told you about a tax saving strategy? They usually just look at me and say nothing!

What is the difference between pro-active tax planning and tax preparation? Tax preparation is the processing of a stack of documents and then recording the items correctly on the tax return. The tax return is prepared and filed and the job is considered complete. Tax preparation is an incomplete service for business owners who are paying too much income tax.

Pro-active tax planning is quite different as it takes time-tested, IRS-approved tax strategies and implements the strategies that work best for your business. A good tax plan requires action to be performed before year-end in order to set up and implement the various strategies. These strategies will save you money by reducing the amount of tax that is paid.

Many business owners ignore tax planning. They don't even think about taxes until the annual meeting with their accountant at tax time. The IRS estimates that 80% of people overpay their taxes. The numbers are even higher for business owners.

Pro-active tax planning is an ongoing process, therefore it is important to develop a good relationship between the client and the accountant. We prepare financial statements for our clients so they can review their income and expenses monthly or quarterly. This allows us to monitor taxable income so our clients pay the least amount of tax legally possible.

I like to meet with my clients twice a year to enable them to take full advantage of the provisions, credits, and deductions that are legally available to them as a business owner. I keep my clients apprised of tax law changes and how these changes affect their businesses.

Recently I met with a new tax client to talk about their tax return. After analyzing the tax return, I determined the client could benefit from a retirement plan and they were using the wrong entity type for their business. The client was thrilled when I came back with a tax plan that was estimated to save them $30,000 on their 2012 tax return.

This particular client was able to skip two of their estimated tax payments. At tax time, they received a $38,300 refund. When I called the client with the outcome, they said, "I didn't think you could really do it. I'm amazed at what a difference tax planning made in our tax situation!"

We went one step further and walked them through the implementation of the plan. This assistance was important to the client as they didn't know how to implement the tax-saving strategies from their plan.

What is the difference between tax planning and tax evasion? Tax planning gives you concepts and strategies which allow you to minimize your taxes legally. Tax evasion is the reduction of tax through deceit or concealment.

We all know that tax rates are going to increase over the next few years. If you are like most business owners, you aren't satisfied with the taxes you pay year after year. You may not be taking advantage of every legal deduction, credit, loophole, and strategy. You may also be frustrated because your accountant isn't giving you pro-active strategies and concepts to save tax.

The good news is, you don't have to feel that way! You just need a better plan. Pro-active tax planning is the key to beating the IRS legally. It doesn't matter how good your accountant is with a stack of receipts on April 15th if you don't have a plan. Pro-active tax planning gives you the concepts and strategies you need to minimize your taxes without intimidating spreadsheets or endless projections that change every time Congress decides to change the law.

The key to your financial defense is pro-active tax planning. As a business owner, you have two ways to put cash in your pocket: Make more money or spend less money. Taxes are probably your biggest single expense. It makes sense to focus your financial defense where you spend the most money.

Pro-active tax planning guarantees results. You can spend all sorts of time, effort, and money promoting your business. But that can't guarantee results. Or, you can implement a time-tested, IRS approved tax strategy and guarantee tax savings year after year.

With proper tax planning, you may be able to lower or even skip your next estimated tax payment. What will you do with the extra money? Will you take a vacation, pay for your daughter's wedding, buy a new car, or maybe even remodel your house?

I feel intense satisfaction when I call a client and tell them they don't need to make the rest of their estimated tax payments for the year. It's even better when I can tell them, in addition to not making the estimated tax payments, they have a $30,000 refund for the year! The phone usually gets quiet for a minute or two but then the client gets excited about the great news they just heard!

The third way my accounting practice stands apart from other accountants is the growth strategy we have implemented. In 2008, my business was hit pretty hard due to the many construction and real estate-related clients we had that went out of business. This caused us to have a very high accounts receivable number and eventually we ended up writing off a large amount of it as bad debt. I was also having difficulty in attracting and retaining qualified staff.

I took some time to explore my options. In 2007 I had just purchased the office building where our office is located. Due to the decrease in property values, I couldn't sell the building and get enough money to pay it off so I realized I had only two options:

- Close the doors and try to rent out the building, or
- Learn everything I could about marketing.

I chose the second option and began the marketing journey.

I began to seek out marketing classes, books, seminars, and webinars. I quickly realized we needed a website so potential clients could learn more about my business before they ever contacted us for an initial consultation. As I learned more about marketing, I realized that I really didn't know anything about marketing. The one marketing class I took in college was totally useless to me when the economy was crashing down around me.

I worked with two different marketing coaches to get my business back on the growth track. This entailed developing systems in our business. After reading Michael Gerber's *E-Myth Accountant*, I got to work and started developing systems. I quickly found out that everything we did in the office was kept in my head instead of on paper.

My staff worked diligently to record the steps of the various tasks and duties they were working on. Over the course of the next year and a half, we developed systems for every task in our office. I've teased my staff over the last couple of years by saying, "I'm working my way out of a job."

It's so important to be able to work on your business, not just in your business. Now I spend time each week working on various marketing campaigns and on projects which lead to increased client satisfaction and retention.

Eventually, I found my way to Bill Glazer's and Dan Kennedy's marketing information. Along the way I also found Jim Palmer's newsletter information, Mike Capuzzi's information about copy enhancements (Copy Doodles), and Travis Lee's 3D marketing information. Now I am proud to say that I am one of many who have "drunk the Kool Aide" of direct response marketing. What a difference this has made in my business!

What is direct response marketing? Direct response marketing is a type of marketing designed to generate an immediate response from consumers, where each consumer response (and purchase) can be measured, and attributed to individual advertisements. This form of marketing is differentiated from other marketing approaches, primarily because there are no intermediaries such as retailers between the buyer and seller, and therefore the buyer must contact the seller directly to purchase products or services.

Direct response marketing is delivered through a wide variety of media, including TV, radio, mail, print advertising, telemarketing, catalogs, and the Internet. It is marketing that has measurable results which allows you to calculate your return on investment on every campaign.

Direct response marketing includes sales letters, ads, websites, landing pages, blogs, newsletters, social media posts, TV or radio commercials, flyers, etc. It is marketing that uses incentives to ask potential customers or clients to "raise their hand" and identify themselves. Once we have obtained a prospect's contact information, we can utilize a "drip" marketing campaign.

Drip marketing is a multi-step marketing system which allows us to email or mail information to the prospect. After a few contacts, the prospect will receive enough information to know, like, and trust us. Once this has been accomplished, there is a very good chance the prospect will become a customer or client.

Drip marketing allows prospects to enter my sales funnel by taking advantage of various special offers, special reports and books. Once they get to know me and my business, they usually become a client.

As a result of utilizing direct response marketing, my business has now exceeded our highest previous annual sales level and is on target for a strong 20% growth rate for this year. It is exciting to see a steady growth rate for the past 3 years in spite of the troubled economy we have been operating in.

Most business owners expect to pay somewhere between $1,000 and $2,000 each year to their accountant. Our clients spend between $3,000 and $10,000 per year because of the additional services that make us stand apart. These business owners realize that by using an accountant that gives personal service, watches for tax-saving strategies, and shares marketing and growth ideas, they are investing in the future of their business.

In addition to marketing projects, we have also implemented client retention projects. One of these projects is our annual Client Appreciation event that is held each summer. My office is located in a small town so finding a location that can seat between 100 – 150 people is quite challenging. We solve this problem by reserving one of our local parks.

Each summer we host an annual outdoor event that consists of great food, music, prizes, special awards and lots of fun for our clients. We present awards for:

- Tax client of the year
- Business client of the year
- Most improved client
- Most prompt client
- Most organized client

Our clients are presented with a plaque and a certificate that can be displayed in their office. This gives us the chance to be seen by other people who visit the client's office. In addition to the awards, we give away prizes throughout the evening.

This year we will be adding two new features to the event. We will be introducing our "community partners" and have them speak about their business for a few minutes. These businesses are the ones we refer our clients to for key services such as legal services, retirement planning, printing, graphic design, etc.

I will also be talking briefly about Obamacare at our event this summer. We plan to put on seminars around our local area to explain how Obamacare will affect individuals and businesses. This will answer many of the questions people have about this complicated new set of laws.

So as you can see, we really do stand apart from other accounting firms.

About Diane

Diane Gardner, the Entrepreneur's Choice for Your Financial Future, is a native of Idaho. She has been working in the accounting field with small businesses since 1982. She is the founder of Adept Business Solutions and Tax Pro Solutions which meet the needs of her clients by providing accounting and tax planning services.

Diane is a graduate of San Jose University where she majored in accounting. She is a licensed Enrolled Agent (EA) which allows her to prepare income tax returns in all 50 states. Diane is also a QuickBooks Pro-advisor, an Accredited Tax Preparer (ATP) and a Certified Tax Coach (CTC). Certified Tax Coaches are an elite group of professionals who focus on helping businesses and individuals pay the least amount of tax that is legally possible.

Diane has worked hard to make her businesses stand apart from other accounting and tax professionals by utilizing personal touch in her client communications. She wants each of her clients to feel they are important to her and to her staff. This has greatly increased her retention rate.

Her clients also benefit from her knowledge of marketing which she shares freely. She writes articles, presents seminars, and offers coaching services so her clients can benefit from this information.

One of her main goals is to be sure her clients are paying the least amount of tax they can legally pay. This is accomplished through pro-active tax planning. Her clients generally realize an average tax savings between $5,000 and $50,000/year.

Why does she do all of this for her clients? Because she cares about people! She feels it is rewarding to grow her own business, share that information with other businesses, and then watch them grow too.

Diane is currently working on her second book which should be released in the spring of 2014. This book will be titled *Grow Your Business in the New Economy* and will contain bonus information about the effect of Obamacare on individuals and businesses. There is nothing affordable about the *Patient Protection and Affordable Care Act*, commonly referred to as Obamacare. Its impact will be felt by everyone, not just business owners.

For more information about any of the concepts Diane has presented, you may reach her by calling (800) 841-0212 or (208) 687-0508 or by going to her websites: www.adeptbusiness.biz or www.tax-prosolutions.com. You may also email her at: diane@adeptbusiness.biz.

Diane is married, has a daughter and one grandchild. She enjoys reading, camping, picnics in the woods with her husband, Dutch oven cooking, and spending time with her family. She is active in her church and serves on the board of the Twin Lakes Friends Camp. She is also active in the Rathdrum Chamber of Commerce where she chairs the Economic Development Committee and the Spirit Lake Chamber of Commerce where she holds the office of Treasurer.

CHAPTER 15

SELLING BRILLIANTLY

BY DAVID TRAUB

Like many, when I started college I had no clue what career I wanted. I considered and tried many things: Electrical Engineering, Creative Advertising, Philosophy, Sociology and Political Science. The one thing that I knew for sure though is that I didn't want to go into sales. In my mind, I had bought into some of the primary stereotypes about salesman... that only "good talkers" do well in sales, that they have to be overly aggressive, that it's just about the numbers and that a career in sales would be boring and unfulfilling. I also bought into some of the stigma around salesman. I believed that salesman were fake, fast-talking, pushy and insincere. All that meant that the only thing I new about my career was that I did not want to be in sales.

I also hadn't made the connection yet in my own mind that I had already started my sales career many years ago (more than I'd care to admit). It was my own company and I was ten. It was New Years evening and my parents took me to a fancy party with hundreds of people. It was a company party and there were people from various offices of my Dad's company, their families, some customers and vendors attended at well. The tables were decked out and at the center of each one was a colorful flower arrangement with balloons floating from each one.

When I noticed how much people seemed to be enjoying the centerpieces, I realized there was a great opportunity there. I wandered the room and removed the balloons from a few of the centerpieces and then started approaching prospects offering my wares. I managed to make several sales before upper management (my parents) decided that this market was not one in which they wanted to participate.

A couple of years later I decided to open a new market. My parents had me attending mid-week religious school classes. Class ran from 4:00 to 6:30. There were no vending machines or snacks on campus and it was a frequent complaint of the other students that they'd be hungry. There were often conversations of how great it would be to have various candy bars or snack food during breaks. Once again I saw the opportunity and opened up shop. On Wednesdays as soon as I got home from school I'd jump on my bicycle and head over to the local convenience store and invest my entire allowance into an inventory of candy and snack food before rushing home. I'd then dump everything into my backpack and wait for my mom to take me to the office (religious school).

This time my business lasted three profitable months before school officials asked my upper management to have me withdraw from the market. A couple years later I took on another in-school sales position that ultimately led to another request from management to find a new market. Despite my repeated entries into the sales profession, I still was reluctant to consider it a career throughout college. After college however, I ended up taking a sales position thinking it would get me good business experience before going back for law school. It turns out that I found out how wrong the stereotypes were. Sales is all I've done throughout my career and I can't envision doing anything else.

Many though, have let these stereotypes get in the way of them doing what it takes to actually be successful in generating the most revenue possible from their businesses, and from standing apart from others in their field, whatever that may be. If you run your own business you make think about yourself as a lawyer, a doctor, therapist, veterinarian or tradesman, but you've still got to sell your services if you want to be successful.

In sales, people often say there is no formula for success. They say that it can be elusive, that it can't be predicted. They point to the example of when a new and inexperienced rep comes on board who barely knows what he (or she) is doing, somehow comes away with a large contract, or closing a customer that everyone has tried to close before as evidence.

158

The truth is that it's not all that difficult to stand apart from the others in the field.

Success in selling comes from three distinct aspects of your salesmanship. There is a formula for it. You can get success in sales from **SmEQ**.

Sales Success = SmEQ = Brilliance

- **Sm = Smarts** or What you **KNOW**
- **E = Effort** or What you **DO**
- **Q = Quality** or How **WELL** you do it

Following this formula will ensure your success and that you stand apart from others in this field.

The three components of SmEQ (Smarts, Effort and Quality) are not an either/or proposition. If you want to stand apart, you need to master all three areas. To be truly successful in selling you need to be Brilliant. You need to DO the right things, do them WELL and have impressive KNOWledge of your market, your competition, selling and a variety of other topics.

When I traveled to teach and coach, I'd frequently be asked what are the keys to each? There are no magic answers, but I can share with you some core principals.

The Six Key Aspects to SMeQ, that you need to be great at if you want to outsell everyone else. Every top seller I have met, every seller that stands apart ... those getting outstanding results... that stand beyond the rest of their peers... who have loyal customers that love them invariably do different and better than everyone else. As you learn new sales concepts and ideas, ask yourself which of these will help you do better.

Focus on mastering these and you'll find your sales skyrocketing. Don't try to master everything at once. Focus on truly improving 1 to 3 specific things at once. That approach will get you consistent and dramatic improvements. Many will be little things that you can change or master quickly. Others will take you a lifetime to master.

Sellers that stand apart from others, those that embody SmEQ always:

1. CLOSE MORE BUSINESS FASTER – They execute their sales plans better. They ask better questions, they overcome objections better, and they are great at finding every opportunity to shorten the sales cycle. The end result is that their skills allow them to shorten the average time to close; letting them move on and focus on the next deal while others are still trying to get the decision maker to return their call when they "check in."

One great way to close more business faster and ensure you keep momentum going on each dial is to schedule a specific date and time for your next conversation. Too often sellers end conversations and set the next step to be to talk tomorrow, next week, next month or the like. When reaching out to your decision maker they find that they don't connect with them and next week quickly turns into next quarter by the time you connect. Every time I have gotten out of the habit of scheduling each next conversation I've found my numbers fall. When I've corrected course, they climb back up.

2. **HIGHER AVERAGE DEAL SIZE** – Top producers get a higher average deal size. They do this because they build value up front for their clients making them less prone to try to negotiate. The higher average deal size also comes from the confidence their customers have in them and as a result they are asked to help clients with larger projects.

3. **GET RID OF THE JUNK FASTER** – if you have been selling for more than a couple weeks, you probably have active deals working that have gone nowhere. You HOPE that will change, but for now they continue to go nowhere and the customer gives you no real evidence that they are ever going to buy from you. Most sales people keep working these deals. They pour their soul into them, they deliver proposals, do more research, provide lots of free consulting and yet the business still doesn't start pouring in. One reason top producers get more business is that they learn to recognize the junk much faster and don't put time into chasing it. You need to do the same. Top producers spend more time with customers who are likely to buy. Remember your time is valuable! Top producers get their customers to earn their effort.

4. **ALWAYS BE PROSPECTING** – This seems obvious, but way too many salespeople do not spend enough prospecting time. No matter how WELL you approach your business, you need to actually DO the things that let your skills shine. Unless you are regularly in front of every possible person who can influence a

decision to buy from you in every company that could possibly buy from you, then you haven't gotten in front of enough prospects.

Think the top guy in your office doesn't prospect? Think again. First of all, he's probably been there way longer than you and has many more established clients... clients he got from focused prospecting. Secondly, the more established reps may seem like they are not prospecting, but if you look closely you will see they still do it. It's probably a bit different than yours, because with their established and happy customers they are ASKING FOR and receiving referrals regularly and they prospect those leads. Think you don't need to prospect because your company provides you with leads? How's that working out for you? Are you making as much as can be made from those leads alone? The best always work their own leads in addition to what the company provides.

5. **HAVE A HIGHER CLOSING RATE** – This is all about skill. When you close a higher percentage of your deals you get more business. Learn to ask better questions; to qualify prospects quicker; to recognize the signs that something's not right faster. Get just 5% better at this and your annual income will go up by 60%.

6. **SPEND YOUR TIME BRILLIANTLY** – I can't even begin to count how many times I've visited a client and half or more of their sales team are working on proposals, sending correspondence, or doing research in the middle of the day! I've even been guilty of it myself. You've got to use your time wisely. All of your high reward activities (the things you actually get paid to do) have to do with speaking with and being in front of prospects and clients. There are limited hours in the day that you can do this. Don't use potential selling time for your non-priority tasks. How should your time be broken up? Most of the Brilliant Sellers I know spend 40-50% of their time protecting and penetrating their base, 40% prospecting for NEW business, and the remaining time analyzing their business.

As a free bonus, here are two other things that the Brilliant Sellers do that most of the others don't:

(a). INVEST IN YOURSELF FIRST – This is simple… You must invest in making yourself better. Invest time, invest money, and invest your own effort. To be a brilliant seller, you must always perform at your best, and your best must always get better. First of all, constantly work on improving your skills. To do this you must learn, and you must practice. It's not just about books, tapes and seminars (although there are several great ones and you should partake), but it's about doing. As David Sandler puts it in the title of his book *You Can't Teach a Kid to Ride a Bike at a Seminar*. You need to practice, you need to invest time, and you need to seek ideas and information outside your immediate circle. Are you in a mastermind group? You should be. Do you brainstorm with others on a regular basis? Are they only from your company or industry? You should, and they shouldn't. When was the last time you read a book? In 2006, one in four people did not read any. Yet some of the richest people in America read as many as 75 books a year. Just as important, what did you do about the information you learned? You cannot just read a book and assume that your life or sales will get better. Selling is a skill and an art form. You can't get better at either without investing your own time.

(b). KNOW YOUR MARKET – This one seems obvious, but I'm constantly surprised at how many sales reps don't really know their market. Do you know your top competitors in your market? The average ones? Do you know what you offer that they don't? Do you know what you do better than you? Do you know the names of their top and most reputable reps? The insights you gain from knowing all this will allow you to sell your strong points against the competition on each deal.

About David

David is fiercely committed to helping great sellers become Brilliant ones. He's not years removed from his craft, he practices it every day working as a full time seller.

As a frequent President's Club Member, he has personally closed tens of millions of dollars of product and services sales, seven-figure dollar deals, and has set several sales records (at least one still stands from over 15 years ago). As a sales manager and coach, his teams have repeatedly reached previously unprecedented levels. He has traveled to over 25 states and 2 countries teaching others his sales and management insights.

If you are looking for actionable ideas and concepts from a proven professional that helps you:

- Sell more, faster
- Spend less time with prospects who don't buy
- Dramatically increase your income
- Or do any of that for your sales team

…then David can help.

After spending years working with hundreds of sales professionals with similar worries and concerns, and guiding them to achieve remarkable success, David's mission and commitment is to help you Sell Brilliantly. His path to become an expert salesman and leader became clear to him accidently.

When starting college, David had no idea what he wanted to do. He did know one thing however… <u>that he did not want to go into sales.</u> While still in school, he fell into an opportunity to work for IBM on campus, selling computers to students, faculty and staff. His manager, Vince, was and is an amazing professional, mentor and expert sales manager, who helped him realize this was what he was meant to do.

Now David spends time helping others hone their craft. What lights him up about this work is knowing that when he has helped a sales professional improve their results, it extends well beyond their professional lives. You can get three actionable reports designed to help you improve each aspect of the SmEQ success formula and grow your income. You'll learn to improve: (1). What You Do, (2). How well you do it, and (3). What you know.

To get your 3 SmEQ reports, to learn more about David and how to smash quota by becoming a Brilliant Seller, visit:

www.SellingBrilliantly.com/StandApart

CHAPTER 16

THE 3 FUNDAMENTALS FOR GETTING ON BASE – *IN THE GAME OF BUSINESS*

BY DOUG FRIESEN

SAVA!

1. Self-Awareness, (*the warm up*)

2. Vision, (*stepping up to the plate*)

3. Action, (*the swing*)

Approximately 750,000 new businesses are started each year in North America. 90% of them will fail. This is disturbing! Many great ideas and many great people, despite their tremendous efforts and great intentions, never manage to get off the bench and on base in the game of business.

Although fueled with great ideas, energy and ambition, without a good understanding of the three fundamentals, they too are headed for the 90% majority. Most often these new business start-ups are created by the: "*I can do betters.*" These are the people that either don't like the company they work for, don't like their boss, or simply think they "can do better."

This is most often what sits at the base of new business start-ups. Not that this is a wrong reason to start a business, but what *is* wrong is starting a business on that emotion without equipping yourself with an understanding of the three fundamentals.

Start applying the three fundamentals for getting on base, *in the game of business* and you too can join the 10% success club! Live the life you want, get the success you want and be in control of your future. Put your business on base, in scoring position and get set to hit the celebrity status home run!

FUNDAMENTAL #1- SELF-AWARENESS
(...the warm up)

Every newbie shows up to training camp with excitement and eagerness. In their mind they are going to be an All-Star! Full of enthusiasm they eagerly jump into every exercise with vim and vigor. Often there is a bullheadedness about charging forward, head down and not realizing what is about to happen. *They don't know what they don't know.*

You have decided to come down from the grand stands and switch from spectator to participant in the game of business. You also must go to training camp. To think that you can go straight into league play without going through some kind of training is naïve – and a recipe for disaster.

The first fundamental, Self-Awareness, is the most important of the three. Spend some quality time right here. "Know thyself and see what others see."

For a ball player to be considered for the big leagues, he is scouted. He goes through a personal assessment, is scrutinized by the Team management, coach and the other players. For the new player to make the Team there are more factors than just his skill level taken into account. How does he act under pressure? Can he follow instruction and rules? Does he have the stamina to carry on when things get tough?

Consider for a moment that starting a business means that you are about to be the owner, manager, head coach and probably the player in the early stages. You may be thinking, "I know it will be hard work, but I can do it." *You don't know what you don't know!*

Become aware of how you act in social environments, at work or with family and friends. Be brutally honest – you need to understand yourself! Search for your authentic self and yet also understand your adapted self. This process is not easy and should not be underestimated. You must go at this fundamental with an open mind, an open heart and be ready for a rough ride. You may not be the person you think you are. That is very hard for some to accept.

A great step towards building your self-awareness is to start by doing a personality test. TTi, also known as the D.I.S.C. system, is the format I am familiar with. It is extremely thorough and after witnessing the results of this test many times, I can say that I have seen it change lives. It opens the door to understanding yourself.

It is imperative that if you are going to start a new business you be clear on what your strengths are, what your weaknesses are, what lights you up, what it is that you do not want to do and most importantly, what you should not do. You need to position yourself on the team in the most sensible position to achieve maximum results. Give yourself the maximum opportunity percentage for getting on base.

Realize that developing self-awareness is a life-long event. You must be dedicated to the growth process. You should determine through this exercise what your core values are. These core values will be imperative to your business and set the parameters for hiring, firing, promoting and qualifying vendors and clients.

Included in the self-awareness process should be your story. Step back in time as far as you can remember and work through the understanding of what made you the person you are today. Although this will likely be an emotional journey, it should guide you to an understanding of your "why." Why is it that you want to start a business? Why is it that you want to start this *type* of business? This part may take several months and possibly years, but it is well worth the effort. I am not suggesting that you do not proceed until you have your "why" determined, but don't let this requirement disappear.

My "why" took several months to figure out. My wife Janice can attest that I was notably excited when I finally arrived at it. I was trapped in a condo in the Bahamas for three days due to a torrential downpour. That was exactly what I needed to complete this process. I was working through my "why" by reading the book "Start With Why" by Simon Sinek. After months of traveling on this journey, I all of a sudden found myself getting a grip on the reasons why I have always started service companies. My life story will be a story for another time.

My "why" is now our company "why" and at the core of everything we do. Here it is:

"To enthusiastically serve with heart and soul to create a higher standard."

This is why my company exists. Everyone on the team must understand and accept this statement as our purpose and reason for existence.

After working through a personality assessment, searching for your "why" and really paying attention to how you function, you should be well on your way to a greater level of self-awareness. With a better understanding of who you are, you are ready to set your sights on a vision.

FUNDAMENTAL #2 – VISION
(...stepping up to the plate)

No vision = chaos!

A company without a vision is like a ship without a rudder. Show me a company without a vision and I promise you their business life span will be far exceeded by a competitor that has a clear vision. The blurry-eyed company may get by for a while, but they will never get out of the junior league. Be a business optometrist and create clear vision!

What if a ball player stepped up to the plate with no idea where he was going to hit the ball? T-ball players, ok. Recreational players just hoping to hit the ball, ok. All professional ball players know before they step up to the plate where they are supposed to hit the ball to get on base, advance another runner or perform an RBI, Run Brought In. They have a clear vision of hitting the ball and where it should land. It may not always work out but they always start with the vision. Start with a vision, take action, and adjust. Vision, action, adjust & repeat.

Most businesses unfortunately start with either no vision or a very short-sighted vision. If you are an "I can do better" person, your vision is likely simply filling the gaps that you saw your previous employer create or miss. They don't do this or that well. So, your business is focused on those items. The next thing you know you haven't got a runner on base in several games, definitely haven't scored a run and whoops, you're out of money. What you had wasn't a vision it was a *bunt*. A bunt can be very useful when used strategically, but you cannot win a game by bunting every time. The defense will figure your game out quickly and you will be out of the game before you know it.

This vision is what fuels the plan. You must set a clear vision that is written out, formulated and crystal clear in your mind. Don't worry about all the details of "how" you are going to get there just yet. Just become clear on where you want to end up. Determine your BHAG-*Big Hairy Audacious Goal.* This saying was coined by Jim Collins back in 1994. Set your sights high but know that to get to the World Series you have a lot of work to do. People will play a huge role in whether you get there or not. The subject of people, (EXTREMELY IMPORTANT!), is a topic that could fill an entire book.

Once your business grows and you add employees, your business may change direction slightly. But to attract the right people onto your team and keep them, you should already have a clear vision and share it with them before they are hired – to ensure they believe in the vision, get excited about it and can support the effort required to get there.

If you want the reward and fame of a World Series title and all the glory that comes with that accomplishment, you must see it clearly in your mind, document it, get others to believe, support it and step up to the plate and get ready to take action!

FUNDAMENTAL #3 – ACTION
(...the swing).

Swing and miss! What should you do? Swing and miss! What should you do? Swing and miss! *NOW* what should you do? In the game of baseball, you're out! In business the decision you make at this point will be proof of your level of Self-Awareness and how clear your vision is.

If you have really warmed up, (worked into your self-awareness) and you understand that although this *out* is upsetting, it is not going to stop you from stepping up to the plate again, you have the PHD – Passion, Hunger & Drive – to push forward. You *believe* in your clear vision.

Remember you will hit some foul balls and strike out every once in a while. Do not be discouraged. These are special learning opportunities that will make you better each time. There is hope for you!

Taking action is obviously important to get on base. You could hang out and wait for a walk but that is not sustainable and clearly not ambitious. You don't get into business to leave things to chance. You have to take a swing! Make a decision and go for it! If things don't work exactly as you hoped, you reassess and swing again. Each time you should be correcting the things that need to be corrected. Don't be the example of insanity, doing the same thing over and over again and expecting different results.

If you long to be an entrepreneur, you should constantly be taking action. If you can't hit the ball right-handed, hit left-handed. Do not be afraid to step outside your comfort zone and challenge the person you think you are by taking action in different ways than you ever first imagined. Hire someone to take a look at your swing and provide you with professional feedback. Keep your elbow up, put your hips into it, follow through, etc. Be humble and ask for help if that's what it takes. Don't just take action but take the *right* action.

If you have others on your Team, get one of them to swing the bat if you suck at it. Stick with your strengths and place people around you that will support your vision. Remember that it is up to you to take action. If your strength for taking action is managing people then do that. Let others swing the bat, catch the ball or dance the dance.

The important thing is that your business must take action. If you aren't taking action rest assured, your competitors are! What are you going to do if you are on a losing streak (for example, the market is soft)? Go sit on a beach and say, "there is nothing I can do, I might as well take some time to relax." If you agree with that statement, you my friend, are not an entrepreneur and should sell before things get worse.

Take action! Ensure that all your decisions are aligned with your core values and your company culture will emerge. You may make some decisions that become *learning opportunities,* but at least you are making decisions and taking swings at the ball. Be sure to learn from each swing and improve. It will happen that you start connecting with the ball. You may hit some foul balls, but soon you will start making base hits, hitting doubles, triples and then..........A home run!!

SUMMARY

The professional ball player doesn't just walk into the big leagues without ever playing the game before. He will be assessed, have vision and take action. Through practice after practice his skills will progress and eventually he will attain pro status. Even then he must continue to work on all three fundamentals. The moment he decides that he is complete and doesn't have to progress any further on his learning, he is done and the junior players will pass him. He will be sitting on the pine!

You should put extreme effort into your self-awareness and keep the learning process progressing constantly. Ask friends and family to assist you with constructive feedback.

 Be realistic with a vision but challenge yourself and search for a vision that is unique to your industry. Employees, clients and vendors love to attach and support a great vision. My company TAK Logistics Inc has an aggressive and sexy vision – 10 cities in 10 years. The objective is to open 10 locations in 10 years. People love this vision and can easily visualize it. Make sure your vision is easy for others to see.

Finally take action. Action, action, action! Potential great companies never make it because action wasn't taken. Take calculated steps, but don't be so over paranoid that you never make a decision or take action. Employees will become frustrated if they see no action toward the vision. Even when you think you are taking action, others will wonder why things are moving so slowly, and why you are not taking action.

Communicate the action steps and include everyone in them. Remember that the average person needs to hear something seven times before they remember it. Keep the vision prominent in your company and repeat, repeat, repeat.

Follow the three fundamentals of getting on base in the game of business and move out of the junior league into the majors. This is where the pro's (real business), hang out!

Enjoy the game!

About Doug

Doug Friesen, also known as "The SAVA Guy", is a successful entrepreneur and business builder. He is a visionary expert driven to keep his eye on the target and has an exceptional ability to provide effective solutions to get over, around or through the challenges along the way.

Doug has effectively built multiple businesses from scratch, turning each of them into multi-million dollar companies. In the truest form of entrepreneurship, Doug has built some companies with very little start-up funding and found creative ways to get from zero to millions!

His newest venture, "The Sava Guys" allows Doug to bring his expertise to companies looking for a clear vision. Passionate about supporting the entrepreneur to grow their businesses and prosper, Doug is dedicated to the SAVA process. With the SAVA process recognized as the true 3 Fundamentals of business, Doug is a pioneer in simplifying the success process. Are you currently an entrepreneur with a business that has no vision of where you want to take it? Or perhaps you have a vision and need support to road-map the journey.

The SAVA process will:

- Improve your _Self-Awareness_ (and that of your Team).
- Determine a crystal clear _Vision_ for your company (and you personally).
- Create the road map and determine the _Action_ required for getting there.

Through years of working with entrepreneurs, business owners and corporations, Doug has developed the SAVA process through hands-on experience. "I continually see business owners wondering why their company isn't growing or moving in the direction they want it to and why they are not making the income they desire," says The SAVA Guy.

Doug has performed many SWOT analyses on businesses and been afforded the opportunity to look into many companies to see their inner structure. Through these opportunities it became clear to Doug that the 3 Fundamentals are required before anything else.

The SAVA process will elucidate:

- the role of the business owner and the other teammates
- the marketing that is required to support the vision

- the operations that are required to reach the vision

Doug is a man of integrity and lives by a set of unwavering core values. The SAVA Guy has even assisted churches in developing their vision! He is a family man married for 30 years, with 3 children and 3 grandchildren. As founder, CEO and President of TAK Logistics Inc., Doug brought his 3 children, one sister and a nephew into the company. His supportive approach to life is summarized in his "why" – *"To enthusiastically serve with heart and soul to create a higher standard."*

Doug is an example of work hard, play hard. He is an accomplished vocalist, musician, writer and performer. Doug even applies the SAVA process to his personal life and comments, "I see the SAVA process also as a life application." The SAVA process will enhance your personal relationships, make your family stronger and allow you to enjoy life to its full potential!

To learn more about Doug Friesen, the SAVA Guy, and the SAVA Cycle, please visit: www.thesavaguys.com.

CHAPTER 17

EMERGENCE OF THE KUNDALINI RISING SUN.

BY DAMIEN GODKIN

I was walking the streets of Wexford, where I was born. It's a small working class town situated in the South-East of Ireland. A lady in her mid-forties came running up to me calling my name.

"Damien," she says. "I have been meaning to tell you this for years, but after seeing you on television the other night it just all makes sense."

I ask Ann to tell me what's on her mind, and she enquires if I remember when I was a little boy no more than four, being outside our local church. I replied that I do not recall. Ann says she has never forgotten that image of me, tapping her on the shoulder and asking her, "Is this where God lives?" This story hits me hard in my heart and we shed a tear together on the street.

I have seen many films but "the Champ" is one film I cannot watch easily. I looked liked the little boy in this film, and like him, I was sensitive and loved my parents, but was so in need of their acceptance.

I had been asked by our national broadcasting authority, RTE to be interviewed as part of a documentary called: "Moment Of Truth." In Ireland, many people are dying by suicide: young and old, particularly those who feel isolated. As someone who had tried to end my own life on more than one occasion, I was asked to tell my story. Thankfully, I was unsuccessful, and I am now living a happy, contented and peaceful life. Blathnaid, the interviewer for my TV appearance, feels my story is one of hope. Maybe some, who heard my story, will have learned to reach out and begin the process of recovery.

Bo Eason, whom I had the good fortune to hear speak at a Make Market Launch IT conference held in May 2013 in San Diego, speaks about making a list when he was nine years old. What is powerful is that it was a wish list, which came true for him, at the exact time that he wished for. Maybe as the child, Bo caught a glimpse into his adult soul, writing down what was important for him to remember. Was it a type of time travel, the power of intention, or plain good old luck?

It moves me when I hear Bo speak about this list, compelling me to reflect on another image from my own childhood: At the age of only eleven, I was staring into my mother's eyes, vowing from the depths of my heart, that I would never give her the power to hurt me again. I had been in survival mode for most of my childhood. Maybe the reader will now have some understanding of the four-year-old boy who was looking for where God lives.

I was born the youngest of six, with four brothers and one sister. By the time I was old enough to remember, my father had probably passed the invisible line into alcoholic drinking. He was untreated. My Mam was in survival mode, trying to keep enough food on the table for her hungry children. As an adult, I want to say how blessed I feel to have had the parents and family I had. From my soul's perspective, they have been the family I needed to help me carry out my mission. As children, however, our needs are different and the eleven-year-old boy could not have understood.

When I was growing up, I witnessed more violence than I should have: the anger between our parents was like a warzone. I remember feeling like I did not belong: I asked my twin brothers, who were next to me in age, if I was adopted. They said I was. They were teasing me, in fun, but I held onto this. My soul was so sensitive. As a young boy, I was absolutely terrified of the dark. We lived on a tough street, so I had to hide my secret fear. Come bedtime, I would sit on the stairs and hear my family in the sitting room talking and listening to the TV. I was the youngest, so I went to bed alone, terrified in the darkness.

My parents and I rowed endlessly: it took so much out of me. I guess

I would not back down, especially when I felt someone needed to be protected or something needed to be said. My sister tells me today of how she would sit upstairs in terror, holding her ears tight, hoping I would give in for the sake of peace. I guess it is not in my blueprint to give in, but I have learned the art of the side step over the years. To my sister, I say sorry for adding to her pain. She learned to hate confrontation, and as an adult she still does what she can to avoid it. This is not always a good thing: we should strive for balance if at all possible.

So at the ripe old age of 11, I guess my quest to find my place on this earth begins; my wish to experience the love I feel I deserve, and to find my soul family begins. If I had known what was ahead, I may never have started the journey. I was about to walk into a darker, more sinister world than the one I was leaving behind.

I leave my home place, which is strict and full of rules, to live in another home, which has no rules. I can watch what I want on TV, I can select what I want to eat, I can stay away from school, and I can drink alcohol and take drugs. The mother of the house is grooming me, and I mistook it for love. Interestingly, in Ireland up to the year 2005, women were not recognized by law to be capable of abuse. In other words, men were capable of perpetrating sexual abuse but women were not; my story and journey helped bring some balance into this sorry situation. This has helped me a great deal in coming to terms with my life and in becoming the person I am in this world.

I believe the core feeling we are all running from is the fear of rejection. That is why so many of us wear masks. Our belief is that if we were to show ourselves as we truly are, we would somehow be rejected. Take my life and the conditioning from my parents, passed from generation to generation: you can imagine the inner dialogue or mirror was not too healthy. So when my first love came along at the age of sweet sixteen, the loving energy that channeled through her was too beautiful for me to handle. I floated on air when I kissed her, or spent time talking in the alley by her home. I remember leaving to walk home on evenings and it was as if I floated from her; this love was too pure for my dark background and I was unable to stay in the relationship. I rejected her love and broke her heart; her love was too powerful for me to accept. I felt unworthy of such energy.

Drink and drugs filled the next nine years with self-destruction, fueled by a sense of self-loathing and anger. I was slowly disconnecting from life and people; I would put out cigarettes on my body, testing myself to see if I was capable of feelings. I would leave cryptic clues, expecting people to understand. I would eventually try to end my life by taking pills and trying to crash my car. Two years before my moment of truth, in November 1999, I lost my ability to speak; I lost my voice. Yes, I could act out, shouting and screaming. But I lost my voice and my ability to reach out to people. I was voiceless but making plenty of noise.

Universal truth: Finding one's voice and its frequency, whatever that may be, is a key function to the path of freedom and empowerment. But the voice needs to be one's own voice and not the voice of the conditioner. When meditating with Source, Truth says it is not by fighting these other voices that we find freedom, but in accepting these voices as a part of us. It is the key to finding our authentic selves. The ancient art of acceptance will always make an unwanted voice smaller. Young souls will attempt to fight it, or run away from it, but what we accept becomes smaller and what we fight becomes bigger.

The morning of November 10th 1999 is burned into my memory. For about twenty seconds, I had an epiphany of sorts: a spiritual awakening, a moment of sanity. It was like a razor thin light of the Great Spirit cutting through my walls. These walls had taken years, even generations to build. I was lifted from my body and was given the gift of insight, foresight and objectivity all at once. The blame game had to end; I was 25 now and had to take responsibility. This was the dawning of real humility and an end to the silence, which was destroying my life. Hope lived once more, and I was worth saving.

I was introduced to a 12-step program and fellowship. I found no one was judging my actions or me. This was a fundamental key in my recovery. I was given space to make sense of my life, and over time, it gave me the opportunity to show myself as I was truly was to another human being. The masks or fear of rejection were beginning to crack, and I was able to show God my true self.

When on the spiritual path, mistakes are absolutely essential to help us grow. If we truly understand the lessons hidden under each leaf and rock, we realize that it is in our darkest moments that we are loved most.

The trick is to become aware of this universal truth.

The most important breakdown or breakthrough for me, depending on how you wish to view one's soul journey, happened at the time of my father's death.

Dad, around mid January 2004, was given the news by his Doctor that he had Cancer of the lungs and that it would be fatal. Smoking and spraying cars without any safety equipment had finally caught up with him. The bravery and acceptance of his death was not of this world. My Dad would normally fight over the slightest of things, but a peace fell over him in the last nine weeks of his life. He was at home being nursed by my Mam and family, as was his wish.

The Irish way is to make fun or joke at a time of sadness, to save people from what is the bleak truth. However, as I watched this powerful man wither away in front of me, I became very angry and insecure. I realized I had no happy memories of the two of us together; others in my family had. At the time, I was in a relationship, which was breaking up. I was also seeing a counselor, who was bringing me to a place in my childhood, which was recognizing what had happened to me: the abuse.

My counselor advised me to speak to my Dad about how I was feeling. The following day, I went into his room and asked everybody to leave. I held my father's hand, and as I looked at him, I saw his soul leave his body. To my amazement, just over my shoulder my father's parents' presence filled the room. I tell you, I could not feel angry with my father during his passing to the other side. But I did feel a universal love filling me from head to toe. I asked my father, as my own soul opened in front of me, to protect me, as I knew I was in trouble mentally and emotionally. From the bottom of my heart, I took full responsibility for my own actions. I said sorry that I had not been a better son. I told him that Granny and Granddad were here to take him over to the other side. I asked him not to forget to help me if he could. In the spirit world today, I dare anybody to mess me about intentionally: my father has been, and continues to be, a tremendous guide and protector.

This was the day that my soul school lessons began, my travel inwards to the deepest part of myself and beyond. On this day my spiritual guide and teacher became visible to me. His name is Maitreya. He is sometimes fondly known as the universal Christ Magician.

179

He teaches micro balance and truth, which in turn translates to macro healing and empowerment. We live in a world which depends on evidence, but I gently say that teachings of the soul will not always be evidence-based. The human mind can trick us, and the human heart can be broken and unable to try to love again. The answers to empowerment and healing lie in understanding the heart, mind and soul. They cannot exist individually, so to fully understand the human being, all three must be understood together, as having a relationship with each other. I ask you, when have you ever heard or seen a universal truth that just resonates in the soul like a seed? It cannot be denied. Under the right conditions, it grows like a flower into gained knowledge and empowerment. No evidence base is needed; it just is.

The American natives speak of a time of great balance between the way of the cougar and the way of the eagle. There exists a balance between science and mother earth, and the Kundalini Rising Sun represents that balance here on earth: balance between man-made laws, universal laws and animal instincts.

I have being given my name, Damien Godkin, by my parents of birth. I joke about this: it's got both the Devil (Damien the Omen) and God in it, so I am well balanced!

The name Maitreya is to be shared with all who believe and ask for his\her magic. The Kundalini Rising Sun, given to me during my right of passage, will also be used. It represents the new and the old healing energy that is sometimes referred to as the spark of all life. The Kundalini is a dormant energy within most people, but under certain circumstances, the Kundalini energy awakens and rises through the body and the universe.

I have been trained as a master in healing energy attuned to the IET ray; alongside this – Maitreya has trained me as a medicine man.

The Kundalini Rising Sun is the new healing energy experience by all who work closely with him. I believe that in time, many witnesses will bare fruit to the healing powers and magic of Maitreya. This chapter represents the emergence of the Kundalini Rising Sun. If I were to pass anything onto the reader, it would be this: keep it simple, believe in blind faith, and remember always that the Universal Truth sets us free.

About Damien

Damien Godkin also known as Kundalini Rising Sun has been channeling Master Maitreya teachings, healing and magic energy since the passing of his own father John in May 2004. He is not only a respected life coach but he also, during his recovery, has managed to train Irish Boxing Teams at International events.

Damien is a master in Integrated Energy Therapy since 2006, and Maitreya has been training him as a medicine man since 2004.

Damien is in recovery from what seemed to be a hopeless state of body, mind and soul since the 10th November 1999. He is hugely sought after back home by the Irish Government, Mental Health Commission, HSE and Media. Damien is widely and fondly known as an expert by experience in relation to real recovery and empowerment.

Damien is a Mental Health Advocate and teaches Nurses, Doctors and all other Mental Health Service Providers about recovery and empowerment from the service user and family member perspective, which in turn translate to policy changes and direction in relation to Mental Health Law and Policy for the Irish Government.

He has also trained as a Legal Executive and his Journey has helped change the Law as can be read in his chapter. His current work will help bring much needed balance and fairness, in relation to employment law and also family law in Ireland.

Damien is a proud single father to Tadhg Dia Mc Cabe Godkin.

If you would like to connect with the New Healing Energy, or go on an empowering and healing Journey with the Kundalini Rising Sun and Maitreya, please visit: www.kundalinirisingsun.com

Damien would like to sincerely thank all that have helped and supported him over the years to get him to this point, especially his neighbors and friends in Cromwell's Fort Ave where he lives.

He would like to thank his Mam and Dad, Brothers and Sister, in-laws and out-laws for their help and love over the years, especially in helping him on his soul mission. He would also like to thank his universal family and teachers you should know whom you are by now.

On this particular project he would like to thank James his universal bro, Shirley his universal sis, Laura for the brill web design: alphalaura@gmail.com, Anne for the proofreading, pat_sheridan@eircom.net for the photo shoot, Bobby from DNA for the advice, and last but not least, Chasity from MakeMarketLaunchIT for believing.

I owe everything to Maitreya the Universal Christ Magician for saving a wreck like me, so it is fitting I think, to finish with a piece of an Indian Prayer which was given to me on my medicine man journey with him.

"O' Great Spirit, whose voice I hear in the winds

And whose breath gives life to everyone, hear me.

I come to you as one of your many children.

I am weak, I am small, I need your wisdom and your strength."

(Healing & Training is developed from this universal Indian prayer)

CHAPTER 18

HEALING AFTER HEARTBREAK:
SEVEN SECRETS OF HOW TO RECOVER FROM DIVORCE

BY DENISE NABINGER

I ran out of the church service because I knew I was going to start crying - and ended up in the parking lot sobbing uncontrollably. The floodgates opened and I bawled like there was no tomorrow on top of the hood of the nearest car. I didn't care about how much noise I made. I didn't care how much of a spectacle I was to anyone passing by. All I cared about was the pain I felt inside that wouldn't go away.

When you finally realize the life you thought you had is over, when you stop holding back everything you've been desperately keeping inside, appearances no longer matter. All that *does* matter is your personal agony - and you can't help but be shaken to your core. That's where I was at that moment in my life.

And, if you marry or are married, there's a 50-50 chance you may go through that exact kind of soul-shattering moment.

Statistics don't lie – and they show that 41 percent of first marriages, 60 percent of second marriages and 73 percent of third marriages end in divorce, averaging out to roughly an overall 50% divorce rate. Here in the U.S., there is one divorce every 13 seconds. That adds up to 6,646 divorces per day, and 46,523 divorces per *week*.

That's why I know a great many of you reading this have experienced or will experience the end of your marriage. Yes, it's not a pleasant subject to contemplate – but you *can* "stand apart" and come out of the trauma stronger and more resilient than ever before.

My own divorce was extremely difficult. In this chapter, you'll hear about that terrible time in my life. More importantly, you'll learn how to handle this kind of situation, should you have the misfortune to go through your own marital split. I want to share with you seven important secrets I discovered about how best to deal with your divorce - and emerge from it intact.

A Marriage in Name Only

Like most people who enter into marriage, I expected it to work out. We had been planning our future together since we were teenagers and I sincerely believed we were meant to be together. When we eventually had children, I considered them gifts from God and I took my roles as wife and mother very seriously. I also expected my dreams for the future to be fulfilled.

Those dreams consisted of:

- Having a loving, appreciative, supportive and compassionate husband.
- Raising our children to be outstanding citizens in a stable community.
- Having their father be completely involved in the kids' upbringing.
- Continuing to have a wonderful and happy family right through our planned-for financially-secure retirement, when we would enjoy spending time with our grandchildren.

To me, these were beautiful dreams. But this was the reality I woke up to:

- A move every two years for the 23 years we were together, due to my husband loving to change jobs and relocating with alarming regularity.
- A workaholic husband who was always on the computer and/or the cell phone and regularly verbally abused me.

- An unwillingness to give the children and me a proper living budget. Despite his executive-level salaries, I bought my clothes at the Salvation Army and I was known as the "coupon queen" at the grocery stores.

- Having to assume total responsibility for the kids, the house and our family life. He couldn't be bothered.

Why did this happen? Because I let it happen. My father treated my mother the way my husband treated me – badly, so I grew up thinking this was the norm and accepted it in my own marriage.

Still, I knew this wasn't what I really wanted. Every year, I would start to cry while choosing a Valentine's Day card for my husband. None of the flowery sentiments applied to my marriage – and I wondered if they actually applied to *any* marriage. I just had no idea if there was anything better out there for me. One of my friends used to say, "Once in awhile your husband throws you a bone. Why is that enough for you?"

So I dug in even harder, trying to be the best wife and mom any man could imagine. I read volumes of books written to help people like me who wanted to improve their marriages. I jumped through hoops to try and please him, but was lucky if I got a cursory hug or kiss as recognition for my efforts.

Not only that, but, while the kids and I were forced to make do with little money, he lived like a king on his business trips. He stayed at the best hotels and ate at the best restaurants. His idea of a big night out for us was a trip to Taco Bell, and even there, we would share meals and sodas, rather than be allowed to have our own individual orders. Making life even more difficult was the fact that I had severe health problems throughout our marriage, and had to undergo at least one surgery every year.

THE SHOCK OF SEPARATION

Despite all that I was enduring, it was still nothing compared to what happened after separation papers were first delivered. I was totally unprepared to deal with the ramifications of our break-up.

As with my marriage, my divorce didn't go the way I thought it would. The proceedings lasted a grueling three years, and a lot of money disappeared into the attorneys' pockets. The outcome seemed to favor my now ex-husband. He ended up in our family home in northern California with his twenty-three-year-old girlfriend and my two older sons. As for myself, I moved to southern California with our youngest son to find an affordable home. Although he helped pay for the boys' college tuition and cars, my own personal dreams of a financially-secure future were shattered – and so were my insides.

Because I was completely unprepared for divorce, I literally lost several years of my life. Besides losing my home and two of my sons, I felt like I had lost myself. I no longer knew who I was; the marriage and the divorce had completely crushed my self-esteem and I was left bitter and angry about everything that had happened to me. Worst of all, because I had been a stay-at-home Mom, I had no outside career to speak of and little money-making potential. He had also kept control of all the family finances, so I was unprepared for that responsibility. In a way, I felt like I was a teenager thrown out into the world to make it on her own!

Yes, I made it to the happy, successful person I am today – but it wasn't easy. For many people like me, divorce can be an ultimate shock to the system. Even in best-case divorce scenarios, there is always some pain and anger that must be dealt with. Today, my passion is to help other women who find themselves dealing with destructive emotions as a result of divorce – women who want to begin a new and fulfilling life!

THE SEVEN SECRETS I LEARNED WHILE RECOVERING FROM DIVORCE

You don't have to suffer as I did, if you're open to learning from my experience, which, as you can tell, was a very traumatic one. You can start by taking a look at these seven important secrets that I discovered were important to my healing process.

SECRET #1: ACCEPT THAT YOUR LIFE WILL NEVER BE THE SAME AGAIN

This can be an overwhelming concept to accept. I wanted to be married to one man my entire life; I wanted to grow old with him and enjoy our grandchildren together. All that was, of course, completely gone and holidays went from being the most joyous times of the year to the most difficult. I felt overwhelmed and confused for a long time.

It wasn't until I let go of my old dreams that I could embrace new ones. I began to look at the advantages of my new situation. Being alone meant I didn't have the stress of preparing huge meals, doing all the laundry and taking care of everybody all by myself. I never got a break from my children, because we seldom hired babysitters. When I considered all the chores I no longer had to do, it suddenly felt like a huge weight was lifted – I actually had the time and energy to do new things on my own.

SECRET #2: EMBRACE YOUR NEW FREEDOM

As I mentioned, my responsibilities when I was married seemed endless. After my divorce, I finally had the opportunity to spend time on myself. I discovered ballroom dancing, along with other new interests, because I finally had the time to figure out what I actually liked to do in my spare time. I started to feel alive, instead of going through the motions of life as I did during most of the years of my marriage, when I felt lonely, unappreciated and controlled.

SECRET #3: LET GOD TAKE CONTROL

As a religious person, my faith was tested to the max when the divorce happened. I couldn't understand why God would allow this to happen to one of His faithful servants and I was actually angry at Him for allowing me to lose so much in the court proceedings. I felt like God had abandoned me. After the divorce, I was faced with events that required me to get down on my knees more often and pray with more fervor than at any other time in my life. My spiritual life became more powerful, because I had no option other than to let go and let God take over. My faith became stronger than ever – and I saw that good things came out of some of the events that happened after the divorce.

SECRET #4: GET IN TOUCH WITH WHO YOU REALLY ARE

I had always been an independent woman before I met my husband – but, because I was married to someone who was a control freak, I was forced to shut that part of myself down completely. I mean, I wasn't even allowed to buy lemonade at a fair, unless he said it was okay! Now, I could make my own decisions and do things the way I wanted to do them.

The divorce forced me to search deep inside and figure out who I really was. Even though I was forced into it, this was a remarkable time of recovery and self-discovery that I would otherwise have never experienced. If I hadn't taken that journey, I would not have been able to function. I had to learn how to be open to healing so I could go through the necessary personal growth that would carry me through to a new and rewarding life.

SECRET #4: DON'T MAKE THE SAME MISTAKES IN A NEW RELATIONSHIP

After being married for 23 years, entering the world of dating was, of course, a huge challenge. But again, I learned more about myself by doing it – as well as what constituted a healthy relationship and what boundaries needed to be observed. Yes, I made a lot of mistakes – but I also saw that I was repeating many of the same patterns that I had played out in my marriage. After some heartache, I learned to avoid those patterns. Finally, I learned that it was preferable to not have a relationship rather than pursue an unhealthy one.

SECRET #5: HELP YOUR CHILDREN LEARN FROM YOUR DIVORCE

One of the positives that can come from a divorce is your children can learn the consequences of an unhealthy marriage. They can see for themselves that a successful marriage requires two committed people who are willing to do what it takes to make it work. That will hopefully make them consider carefully any commitment they're thinking about making to someone else. They won't want to put their children through the pain of a divorce – and they will hopefully be careful in terms of whom they choose to build a family with.

SECRET #6: YOU CAN'T BE RESPONSIBLE FOR WHAT OTHER PEOPLE DO

As I said, I do believe God is in control – and I had to learn that I am not. I thought for those twenty-three years, I was doing everything I could to make sure my children grew up in a stable family that would always be there for them. The lesson I learned was that I could never really guarantee that – for them or anyone else. The unexpected is always around the corner. Not only that, but everyone has a free will and they end up making their own decisions that may conflict with what we think is best for them. We can only take responsibility for our own actions and we have to allow others to control their own destinies as they see fit.

SECRET #7: MAKE THE MOST OF THE MOMENT

There is a natural urge when you undergo a divorce (or any tragedy, for that matter) to constantly revisit the past and obsess on what you've lost. There can also be an extreme fear of what will happen to you in the future as you begin an entirely new life.

Speaking for myself, when I spent too much time looking back at my old life, it prevented me from moving forward. And when I was overwhelmed with anxiety about what might happen with my new life, it kept me from enjoying the present.

That's why I had to learn how to appreciate life in the "now," despite my circumstances, and enjoy my new freedom. By living fully in the moment and building towards a happier and more successful future, I could be more at peace with myself and my environment.

I hope these "Seven Secrets" are of help to you or anyone you know involved in a divorce - and I want to share one last thought with you. It's a saying I have hanging on my wall that consoles me whenever things get tough – and I hope it will have the same positive effect on you.

> *"Just when the caterpillar thought the world was over,*
> *it became a butterfly!"* ~ Unknown author

I wish you all the best. And if you'd like more information on Divorce Recovery, I invite you to visit my two websites:

www.DoneLickingDivorceWounds.com and
www.DivorceRecoveryforWomen.com.

About Denise

Denise Nabinger is known as the woman who took too long being "done licking divorce wounds" – and is now passionate about helping other women recover from divorce. Because her divorce recovery lasted many years longer than expected due to many surprising turns of events, she is eager to help other divorced women and save them from "wasted years and way too many tears!"

Divorce left her without two of her sons and her family home. Even her friends and church members betrayed her. Nobody understood the agony, guilt, despair, and self-esteem issues that plagued her. Sometimes she even asked the question, "Why am I even alive?" in her own head.

Because she's gone through so much, she can tell you the "Do's and Don'ts" of recovery from divorce. You can also feel confident knowing that Denise "has your back." Her expertise comes from living in the trenches, dealing with the unexpected and the devastating, and rising above it all against the odds!

Denise will share quality information, strategies for success, book recommendations and reviews, interviews with experts in the field of divorce recovery, "lessons learned the hard way" and proven strategies to overcome the effects of divorce.

Denise loves to read, learn from experts and attend seminars. Her children are grown and she doesn't have any grandchildren as of yet. So let her do the work for you. Let her invest her time and energy finding the most helpful information to assist you in your recovery from one of the most painful events in your life. Nothing has prepared you for what you will experience. Denise believes you are a valuable, worthwhile woman – and most importantly, she wants you to know that your life is not over because of a divorce.

Even though your entire life has been turned upside down... there is still hope! You name it, she's "been there done that." Be ready to become who you were meant to be and accomplish what you were meant to accomplish – no matter what your circumstances are! She can help you not only thrive, but overcome.

An Elementary School Teacher, and later a volunteer and advocate for other Teachers, Denise is an independent entrepreneur. Being a Stay-at-Home-Mom led her to home-based businesses such as: Discovery Toys, Stampin'Up, Creative Memories, Avon, Premier Design's Jewelry and Nu-Skin Enterprises.

She raised three gifted and talented ADHD sons (also two ADHD foster children for a time) and was married to an ADHD executive. She has lived in New York, Texas, Georgia, Illinois, Mississippi and California.

Always lending a listening ear, even strangers feel comfortable telling Denise their life story. She's a "stop and smell the roses" kind of woman, known for suddenly slamming on the brakes for a garage sale or a thrift store. Her nickname is "Sidetrack Sally," due to her many interests.

Nothing will stop Denise's devotion to something - including fibromyalgia, chronic fatigue, several surgeries and years of health problems! She even continues dancing despite blisters on her feet and a partial knee replacement!

Contact information:
www.DoneLickingDivorceWounds.com
www.DivorceRecoveryforWomen.com

CHAPTER 19

"KATRINA WAS NO LADY" OR **HOW I LEARNED TO STOP WORRYING AND LOVE SMALL BUSINESS CACA**

BY ED TOUPS

Starting a business is super *EASY*…pretty much anyone can do it.

When I was five years old, my sisters and I opened one. On hot Louisiana summer afternoons, we sold frozen Kool-Aid cups to the neighborhood kids out of our garage for a quarter. The kids loved them.

But we were lousy business owners back then. The freezee pop stand was a complete financial disaster. We drove the business straight into the ground…utter mismanagement. We literally ate the profits, the operation capital, and the seed money. If it weren't for our investors we would have been destitute…living on the streets with nothing.

But I guess that's what moms and dads are for…picking up the pieces and keeping their kids out of bankruptcy court. Yeah, opening a business is *easy*…**mastering a successful one you *truly enjoy* is the challenge.** Eventually, dreamy-eyed entrepreneurs have to grow up too, and when we do, the stakes are real. Our livelihoods, the security of our families, and even our reputations as competent people are on the line.

Few give their trust or their hard-earned cash to "perceived failures."

It's not as if providing an awesome product or service will automatically make adoring patrons hunt you down, throw money at your feet, and praise you for a job well done either.

People demand more. **An exemplary product or service is simply the price of admission...from there, the real work begins.**

In this chapter, I'm going to give you tools that can be like Miracle-Gro for your business. I'm going to show you shortcuts you can use to dramatically reduce your learning curve and exponentially increase your success rate. I've condensed them into nine of the most important lessons I've learned to build, grow, and ultimately sustain my businesses.

These tools didn't come cheap or easy. They were honed during my relationship with a heartless, ruthless, and very unforgiving "Lady." I had to lose nearly everything to get them...

Surviving her aftermath taught me **you don't have to be smarter, work more hours, or work harder than everyone else to get what you want**...no, you just have to work smarter and make wiser decisions.

Before we get into all that I think it's important for you to know how I went from a green as grass, not knowing a damn thing, clueless new business owner to sharing the pages of this business book with marketing legends like Dan Kennedy.

I wasn't born with small business super powers or anything. I'm just a regular guy wading through the same endless swamp of small business caca as you. **Competition, failure, and complete ruin lurk around EVERY corner for me too.** No free pass, privilege, or favoritism here. I have to study, practice, and experiment like everyone else...

I'm continually waist-deep in figuring out how to squeeze the most out of websites, mobile websites, Facebook, Twitter, online reputation, video, long sales copy, short sales copy, lead capture pages, money magnets, email systems, auto responders, sales funnels, text ads, mobile apps, Google Places (or whatever they're calling them these days), order pages, subject lines, Google ads, SEO, Facebook ads, pod casts, Google Hangouts, Skype, backlinks, YouTube, blogs, articles, screen capture video, upsells, down sells, direct mail campaigns, list management, post cards and on and on and on...

And the above is just marketing basics of a modern-day small business. This doesn't include operations, financials, sales, people management, or traditional advertising...which each have a laundry list of their own. Nor does it include the actual knowledge and knowhow that goes into product or service creation, construction, fulfillment, and delivery.

There really isn't anything *small* about a small business, is there? We don't have the "simply buy an expert to make it go away" luxury of larger businesses and corporations either.

Nope.

It's up to us to figure out a solution on our own. So how did I make it into a major book as a co-author? About a month ago, my soon-to-be agent, Bobby, called to let me know I was selected to write a chapter in a book alongside marketing legend Dan Kennedy and longtime Tony Robbins right hand "man," Pam Hendrickson.

Whoa...that's a big deal. I was blown away.

He felt I overcame some unique challenges in my business path that you could benefit from reading about, while pointing out I'm still a relatively small fry, digging, scratching, and clawing my way through the small business trenches. He also thought my experience working and consulting with entrepreneurs brought an interesting perspective to small business development. After all, Dan and the other guys are multimillionaires, and as great as they are, they have been long removed from the everyday reality of entrepreneurs like you and me.

In the summer of 2005, after months of planning, financing, selecting, building, painting, furnishing and all the rest that goes into launching a new business, I was all set and ready to open the doors two weeks later. Then *she* came along...you know the despicable "lady" I mentioned earlier.

It was a Friday afternoon when I heard she might be coming to town. I went out for drinks with a friend that night. It was just like any another hot summertime evening in New Orleans...sweaty beers and good times.

Two days later, my city, my community, and my business were completely wiped out...Destroyed!

Early Monday morning, Hurricane Katrina sauntered through New Orleans and sliced through the ill-prepared levees like a sharp knife through warm butter.

Lake Pontchartrain and the Gulf of Mexico poured in and washed away entire neighborhoods...people and all. By Tuesday, New Orleans was gone...a wasteland.

My city was all but dead... I wasn't going to open in two weeks. I wasn't going to open in two years. Hell, I, along with about 1 million others, was homeless.

The New Orleans economy (and a big swath of the Gulf Coast) dropped nearly 100% in one day and stayed that way for months. It was at a complete standstill. There was talk New Orleans would never come back...that it should return whence it came...a swamp.

There were few people living in town...even fewer in my Bayou St. John, Mid-City and Faubourg Jackson neighborhoods. We spent the next months helping family and friends put each other's homes back together again. Someone scrawled, "*Katrina was no lady*" in big sketchy black letters along the side of a flooded out house down the street from me. I read those words nearly everyday on my way home for months and months, maybe years. Katrina definitely was no lady, but she was one hell of a *motivator*.

Slowly but surely the city came alive again. And so did I. Nearly two years after the storm, I opened a teeny tiny stripped-down version of my original business plan.

Over six and a half years have passed since that day. I'm extremely grateful and amazed to be able to pay the bills, let alone reflect on all that I've achieved and remember all the entrepreneurs and businesses I've been able to help along the way. However, at times, I feel I've spent my thirties surviving that storm, and that I'm somehow behind schedule in my entrepreneurial career.

I find myself wondering where I would be *if...*

But every time that creeps into my mind, I realize the storm didn't impede my development…**it MAGNIFIED business for me like nothing else could.** I was fighting for the survival of my city, my family and my culture. Everything mattered more. Everything counted more. Everything was at stake. One misstep and it was over. There was no safety net. Everyone was in precarious situations… family, friends, other businesses, even the banks. There were no second chances or bailouts we take for granted in "normal" times. There was no fall back job. You learn to learn FAST in that sort of experience.

Here are nine lessons I pulled from the Katrina furnace. They're forged like steel in my mind…second nature. Some may sound familiar to you but don't overlook the context of where they come from and the value they can bring to you:

LESSON 1: KNOW YOUR "WHY"

Dreams are delicate things…you've got to protect them. There are a lot of dream snatchers out there. Some lurk within family, friends and even employees, but the most dangerous are the ones that live inside our own minds.

Knowing the deep down reason *why* you do what you do is what keeps you on track to getting what you want. Your "why" is fundamental to everything you're building.

LESSON 2: HAVE A "GET MORE GUARANTEE"

Forget Even-Steven. Aim to have every deal end in your clients' favor. Shoot to deliver 10 times more value than the money they're giving you. If the investment for your services is $100, deliver $1000 worth of value.

When you do, your clients will happily pay you more. Why wouldn't they? You're a bargain. But like beauty, value is in the eye of the beholder…so see the world from your clients' perspective. Time savings, convenience, exclusivity and done-for-them service are great value boosters. There are many more.

LESSON 3: PLAY "FIND THE NEEDLE IN THE <u>NEEDLE</u> STACK"

Your time is precious. Your energy is precious. Your will is precious. A poorly matched client will suck all of these resources away from you and more. Not everyone is a match. When a mismatch is a mismatch, no one is happy. It's ten times easier for everyone when they're spotted and avoided BEFORE they're a client.

Finding great clients can feel like finding a needle in a haystack... frustrating, time consuming, and costly. When you get clear on who your ideal clients are, the game becomes much easier...it's like finding a needle in a needle stack...a no lose game!

I created a simple and HUGELY effective exercise to determine and identify your ideal clients and help avoid the not-so-ideal. Simply go to: www.EdToups.com/book and click the: "How to Find My Perfect Clients Who Happily Pay Me More" exercise button.

LESSON 4: REINVENT FASTER THAN *THEY* CAN COPY

Ray Kroc from McDonald's had it right when he said something like, "They can copy me all they want...because I can invent faster than they can copy."

If your ideas are good (and maybe even if they are not so good), people are going to borrow, copy or downright steal them...this holds true for your web copy, marketing pieces, products and services, and even your business model. Take precautions. Do what you need to do to protect yourself, and when a situation arises, hand it over to your legal team **and move on.**

Don't let this distract and slow you down...you have things to invent!

LESSON 5: LIVE SENSIBLY...SO YOU CAN REIGN LIKE A KING!

When you live paycheck-to-paycheck in your personal life or with your business, you're screwed. You're one chance event away from game over. That's no good for you, your family, or your clients.

Live *way* below your means. A financial cushion gives you the absolute power to make sound business decisions and the authority to negotiate from strength.

LESSON 6: BUILD A TIME MACHINE

Once upon a time, I freelanced for a parcel company and drove the bayous of south Louisiana delivering packages. It was a tough gig. I was pretty much always lost…and late. I was paid by the day — days that would start at 5 a.m. and wouldn't end until all the packages were delivered… for me 10 or 11 p.m. (5 or 6 hours AFTER most everyone else). Exhausting.

Each day I'd have between 70 to 120 stops. I learned MINUTES matter. If each stop took only 3 extra minutes, by the end of the day I could be as much as 6 hours late. A few seconds saved here and there meant hours by the end of the day. This lesson has been with me ever since…I fine-tuned and honed it during my post Katrina days.

I've literally saved YEARS of extra time. It doesn't take much to do…5 minutes here and 10 minutes there add up quickly. When you scrape together **just one hour a day, this equals over six full 40 hour work weeks over the course of a 50-week work year.** Email, phone calls, Internet, texts and meetings…build systems around these and you'll easily gain more than an hour per day.

I created a simple and HUGELY effective exercise to shave hours off your workweek. Simply go to: www.EdToups.com/book and click the "How to Build a Time Machine In Your Business So You Have Over 6 Weeks of EXTRA Vacation Every Year."

LESSON 7: DAVID VS. GOLIATH

There are bigger, faster, and stronger Goliaths out there who are ready to stomp you into the ground. It's nothing personal…just be prepared. Just last week I was made an offer to sell one of my niche businesses. It's a very lowball offer. I know it and I'm sure they know it too.

In no uncertain terms they made it clear they were coming into the market full force. They intend to squish me into the ground and take the market away from me. They may or may not be able to do that. If they have enough money and resources, which it appears they do, they will make things difficult for me.

Business is not for the meek. Be ready. Stay focused. Game on.

LESSON 8: BUILD A LEAN, MEAN, FIGHTING MACHINE

One of your biggest assets is your ability to adapt quickly to opportunity. Build your business to be as easily changeable and alterable as possible. For example, your website can (and should) be one of your biggest marketing assets and testing ground for all your marketing materials.

Headlines, font color, copy, and layouts can be changed with the click of a button…in real-time you know if you have a winner or loser. You're then able to deploy PROVEN successes into every aspect of your business. You can't buy that sort of pinpoint knowledge…and you get it free.

But, you can only do this if you build an easily changeable website that YOU control.

You don't need anything fancy…a simple ugly site can make you a lot of money. I've been instrumental in helping sites reach Alexa.com rankings as high as the top 3,395 most trafficked sites in the United States and top 15,149 in the world with simple sites.

Your message is what matters…if you need help with this, contact me.

LESSON 9: BE A KUNG FU MASTER, NOT THE KARATE KID

I studied Kung Fu for a VERY brief period. One thing that stuck in my mind was every movement can and should have multiple purposes. With Kung Fu, you don't block a punch and then strike like you would in Karate; rather, you direct your opponent's energy in a slightly different direction and counter by using that energy as a springboard to unleash your attack.

This is a very elegant and effective way to run your business too.

Hint: Make it your goal to have EVERYTHING have at least two results…one should always be marketing.

About Ed

Ed Toups is a Best Selling Author, founder of New Orleans entrepreneurs' #1 office and collaboration space, Office Ready LLC, and is regarded as one of the world's leading experts in business consulting for small business owners, Internet entrepreneurs and solo professionals.

Ed was named New Orleans Urban Legend of the year in 2012 for entrepreneurship, and was recognized with a prestigious New Orleans City Council Proclamation in 2013 for his charitable contributions to the Back to School kids programs. In addition to his local business, Ed has become known for his ability to get big results from online marketing. **He is instrumental in achieving top 3,395 most trafficked website in the United States and top 15,149 most trafficked in the world with over 20 million page views and over 3.5 million visits a month as determined by industry authorities Alexa.com and Google.com respectively.**

Ed is also recognized for his skill in converting site visitors into active followers... building lists of several thousand to over 76,000 responsive, engaged and interested prospects. He does this by building highly effective multistep email and marketing campaigns readers love to receive – that are written with his casual downhome appeal.

It's easy to get lost and overwhelmed in the technical jungle of a modern-day business, but Ed has the uncanny ability to bridge the gap between this fairly technical experience and his local small business owner and online niche entrepreneurial roots.

Early on, Ed discovered most people need only a few tweaks here and there to have the lifestyle and business success they dreamed of. **Ed's laid-back style combined with his knack for seeing the path of least resistance along with his no-nonsense approach for seizing and executing "low hanging fruit" opportunities have helped him and his clients get the results they want quickly.** Ed makes things simple for clients who feel "stuck" and are not getting the results they expect, but are ready and anxious to make a LEAP forward in their business careers.

When consulting with small business and online entrepreneurs, Ed collaborates with them to create the most effective offline and online plan of action and outlines the step-by-step tactics and strategies needed to get the profits and results they want.

Ed learned firsthand in the Small Business and Internet marketing trenches that you don't have to be wealthier, work more hours, work harder, or even be smarter than everyone else to have success in the modern world...you just need the foresight to know where you want to be and simply make the wise decisions that lead you there.

To learn more about Ed Toups and his Short Cut to Success VIP Days, finding Internet marketing gold in your business, packaging your ideas into online info-products, list building and communication programs and more on his business consulting, visit: www.EdToups.com/book or call 504-272-2221.

CHAPTER 20

THE EXPERT EQUATION:
FIVE STRATEGIES OF TODAY'S CELEBRITY EXPERTS THAT STAND ALONE AT THE TOP

BY GREG ROLLETT

Have you ever been in a room with a professional athlete or celebrity? There is a certain aura around them. People's eyes light up. We hang onto every single word that comes out of their mouth as if it was the gospel itself. We get timid, sweaty and shaky with the thought of asking them a question or saying hello.

It's an interesting and fascinating concept. After all, these athletes and celebrities are just like you are me. They put their pants on one leg at a time. They eat food, exercise, talk and even Tweet - sometimes too much.

But the magnetic attraction they have is something that has fascinated me since I was a little boy seeking autographs at spring training. Me and my friends would sit by the bullpen and wait for the pitchers and catchers to toss a few balls our way and maybe break out the sharpie to sign one of our programs. It was an incredible feeling for a kid to meet their hero and someone they aspired to be or be like.

And now, as an entrepreneur, I look to fascinate my clients in much the same way. In order to stand apart in what has quickly become a crowded marketplace, you need to be seen as more than just somebody with a business card. You need to become both an expert in your trade and the celebrity within your field, …known as much for the media you create, the commotion you are involved in and the results that your products and services require.

An expert by Wikipedia definition is someone with: *"extensive knowledge or ability based on research, experience, or occupation and in a particular area of study. An expert can be, by virtue of credential, training, education, profession, publication or experience, believed to have special knowledge of a subject beyond that of the average person, sufficient that others may officially (and legally) rely upon the individual's opinion."*

I want you to take that definition to a whole new level in your life and in your business. In effect, I want you to become the Celebrity Expert® — *The known expert in your field.* The one who's marketing, story, positioning, pricing, media and results speak volumes about what you can do to help others achieve what they desire from their lives.

Today I am going to share five strategies that Celebrity Experts exhibit that enable them to not just stand apart, but stand alone at the top:

1. CELEBRITY EXPERTS HAVE A DEFINITIVE CHARACTER

I am drawn into comic book heroes like many testosterone-driven males today. From Iron Man to Superman, Batman and the X-Men, these super heroes allow us to live out some of our very own fantasies. They let us see strength, heroism, freedom and justice for what is right.

But they are also vulnerable. They have more human characteristics than one might first observe. For if every super hero were perfect, then there wouldn't be much story, would there?

Batman is the character derived from Bruce Wayne, the billionaire running a mega-conglomerate in the biggest city in the world - Gotham City. His parents were murdered in cold blood right in from of him. That suppressed anger that built inside of him allowed him to create Batman and help others get justice and sleep well at night.

And I bet many of you reading this right now can describe the origin stories of the super heroes listed above. We know these stories because they have been told, time and time again. They have become part of our pop culture. They are powerful and incite emotions within us.

This is the story you need to have for your own character. How did you come to be? Where did your magic powers come from? What mountains have you climbed to get where you are today?

You need to create and piece together your own story and then share it with the world - just as the comic book heroes have. They have been glamorized in comic books, TV shows, movies, toys, newspapers, blogs and nearly every type of media you can think of.

Find ways to tell your story so others in your influential circle know your story as if it was part of their pop culture. Share it on radio interviews, Podcasts, blog posts, books, special reports, videos, TV interviews, documentaries, marketing pieces, advertisements and wherever else you can share your story.

Once you create your story, you need to shift how you think about your business to...

2. MARKETING FIRST, TRADE SECOND

Celebrity Experts know that marketing is the lifeblood of their existence. They are the best in the world at what they do, but they know without marketing, they can never display their skills and help others.

Imagine if Dan Kennedy never did any marketing. His penmanship would not have impacted millions of entrepreneurs that read his books and newsletters, have copy written by him or been moved to become Renegade Millionaires themselves.

Instead, he has a marketing first mentality. And he lets his marketing display his expertise. His newsletters are full of useful information and always have a hint of "here's how I can help you more." He utilizes different media and combines them beautifully. From direct mail sales letters and postcards to email marketing, sales letters, product launches, content videos, information products, newsletters and more - you cannot escape the marketing from GKIC or Planet Dan once you enter that world.

The key is to use education to continue to advance the sale. Add value in your marketing. We do this by giving away valuable media pieces in our lead generation process. From giving away copies of our Best-Selling books, to sending off DVD's of our documentary that was aired in the Bio Channel, to special reports, videos, CD's and more. Every marketing piece is designed to showcase our expertise along with the marketing message to pull people into our services.

One of the biggest lessons I have learned from Dan Kennedy over the years, and that I now pass onto clients is that "you are not in the _____ business. You are in the marketing of the _____ business."

Therefore if you are a dentist, you are not in the dental business. You are in the marketing of dental services business. I am not a copywriter or a marketer, but I am in the marketing of marketing services business.

Without a constant and consistent stream of people showing up at your door, you are not going to be able to have the impact of a true Celebrity Expert. Now that you have your mindset intact, it time to share...

3. THE CELEBRITY EXPERT'S TOOL BOX

Celebrity Experts see the world as their playground and media as the stadium to showcase their stories and talents. Today's Celebrity Experts are not waiting for the media to come to them. Not by a long shot. They are making so much noise through their own media that major media cannot wait to come knocking on their doors for the story.

The first tool from a Celebrity Expert's tool box is to have a book that displays their expertise. And it needs to be a hard copy, physical, in the flesh book. Not an eBook or a Kindle book. While those may be valuable and have their place in your overall marketing strategy, nothing says expert like thumping down a hard cover copy of all the things that you know that can help to improve the lives of others.

After the book, you then need to continue to create media that positions you as the trusted expert and the Celebrity in your marketplace. This can start with media that you run and own. Start with your blog and create daily or weekly commentary, opinions of authority and articles that are at the forefront of your market. Be sure to show off your personality, infuse story telling, and fascinate others with your words.

Building on media that you own and control are videos and Podcasts. Leveraging two of the largest platforms in the world, your videos can be placed on YouTube, and your Podcasts on iTunes, opening you up to a virtually unlimited and captive audience.

Creating pieces like story and personality-driven catalogs, special reports, CD's, DVD's, sales letters and other tangible media helps to further bring your story into the lives of those around you. This indoctrinates them into your way of thinking, your philosophy and ultimately to do more business with you.

Constantly be using these tools, always creating and always starring your story and expertise. Once people begin to see you everywhere they look and you deliver on your promises, you begin to have the ability to…

4. CHARGE CELEBRITY EXPERT FEES

In a market where everyone is competing on price, you want to stay far, far away. The lowest common denominator generally goes out of business first, unless you are Wal-Mart, which you presumably are not.

In the expert space, we want to be at the top of the food chain – being paid more for who we are than what we do. Try to get an hour with Dr. Phil. You are not paying for credentials or letters that follow his name. You are paying his sky high fees because he is a Celebrity Expert. This is how you should strive to compensate yourself in your own business.

If you have correctly told your story, are doing a good job of marketing your business first using the tools in your tool kit, you should begin to see an inbound selection of leads that are coming to you for your expertise. They are looking to you for answers. They want one thing and one thing only - the guy who can solve their problem. If you are that guy, your fee becomes irrelevant.

But you must do the marketing; you must be seen in your sphere as the expert and display your magical powers in order to sit at the top of the food chain. The clients are also better clients. They respect your decisions and processes. They might even put up with your demands on them if they are so privileged as to work with you.

Now this doesn't happen overnight, but I am betting that you can raise your prices overnight and business will still keep coming in. The wrong clients and customers will leave. But if you are taking care of their needs, sharing your story with them and truly giving them an experience, they will stay with you forever.

The other luxury of having higher fees is higher profits – your take home. This also means that you can reinvest into your marketing and spend where your competitors cannot…Full page ads…Extravagant direct mail pieces…Shock-and-awe style packages…Extensive follow up programs.

As a Celebrity Expert, you are able to find the pick of the litter to work with and spend whatever it takes to get them into your office. That is true power. Once you have begun performing at this high level, having put in the work, it's time to…

5. LIVE THE LIFESTYLE OF A CELEBRITY EXPERT

There is a big canvas in our office that reads:

"A master in the art of living draws no sharp distinction between his work and his play, his mind and his body, his education and his recreation. He hardly knows which is which. He simply pursues his vision or excellence through whatever he is doing and leaves others to determine whether he is working or playing. To himself, he always seems to be doing both."

It was written by James Michener and it has become the motto of the Celebrity Expert. When you rise to the top of your field, work with clients who you love and who love the work you provide, work becomes less work. It doesn't mean the long days and hours stop. Or that you won't have to do a few things that are irritating or make you a Mister Rogers, an always smiling, always looking-on-the-bright-side person.

It means that you now have the ability to dictate how you do business and in turn how you run your life. It is how I run my own life. Structuring my writing, client meetings and events around the local or international surf report. It means bringing clients with me as I travel the world for events that add value to their lives while continuing to provide for the lifestyle I desire. In the past few years we have taken clients to the Kentucky Derby, to the Grammy's, to Wine Country, Bermuda and more. …All to grow their businesses and have a good time in the process.

208

This is the ultimate desire of many entrepreneurs and business owners. To do business on their terms. In essence, you become the celebrity... The person others want to be around...The one that people get excited, sweaty and shaky to spend a few minutes talking to...The one who enters the room like a professional athlete or a movie star – only you get to skip the paparazzi, the Hollywood antics and the Beverly Hills tax code.

About Greg

Greg Rollett, @gregrollett, is a Best-Selling Author and Marketing Expert who works with experts, authors and entrepreneurs all over the world. He utilizes the power of new media, direct response and personality-driven marketing to attract more clients and to create more freedom in the businesses and lives of his clients.

After creating a successful string of his own educational products and businesses, Greg began helping others in the production and marketing of their own products and services. He now helps his clients through 2 distinct companies, Celebrity Expert Marketing and the ProductPros.

Greg has written for Mashable, Fast Company, Inc.com, the Huffington Post, AOL, AMEX's Open Forum and others, and continues to share his message helping experts and entrepreneurs grow their business through marketing.

Greg's client list includes Michael Gerber, Brian Tracy, Tom Hopkins, Coca-Cola, Miller Lite and Warner Brothers, along with thousands of entrepreneurs and small-business owners across the world. Greg's work has been featured on FOX News, ABC, NBC, CBS, CNN, *USA Today, Inc Magazine, The Wall Street Journal*, the *Daily Buzz* and more.

Greg loves to challenge the current business environment that constrains people to working 12-hour days during the best portions of their lives. By teaching them to leverage marketing and the power of information, Greg loves to help others create freedom in their businesses that allow them to generate income, make the world a better place, and live a radically-ambitious lifestyle in the process.

A former touring musician, Greg is highly sought after as a speaker, who has spoken all over the world on the subjects of marketing and business building.

If you would like to learn more about Greg and how he can help your business, please contact him directly at: greg@dnagency.com or by calling his office at 877.897.4611.

CHAPTER 21

STAND OUT BY REVERSING YOUR PROSPECTS RISK!

BY KEN HARDISON

It's not unusual for businesses to double or even triple their sales once they use the marketing strategy of "Risk Reversal." It's one of the easiest strategies to test and one of the fastest ways to grow your business.

A new prospect will make a decision to buy your product or purchase your services based on two factors:

1. The extent to which they believe that your product or service will solve their problem(s).

2. The level of risk (monetary commitment, likelihood of getting their desired results, ease of use, level of satisfaction, etc.) associated with purchasing your product or services.

Does your product or service provide all the answers they're looking for? Will it solve their problem(s)? Well, this is the first part of the equation and it all hinges on how well you articulate your marketing message. Are you telling them what they want to hear? What they need to hear? Why you? Why your product or service?

Do your prospects:

• Know you?

• Like you?

• Trust you?

Have you conquered the goals of your message? Once you accomplish this goal and make the desire for your product or service palpable, you're ready to move on to the second factor…making them an offer they can't refuse.

This is where the role of Risk Reversal enters the picture. If you can reduce or totally eliminate the risk of doing business with you, then converting your prospects into buyers is exponentially easier. When you make it easy for them to say yes and hard for them to say no, your sales and conversions will skyrocket!

THREE WAYS TO REDUCE RISK

1. Money Back Guarantee: The most common form of this type of guarantee is the 30 day money back guarantee. The stronger the guarantee (for example, 1 year as opposed to just 30 days) the higher the increase in your sales and conversions.

I am the owner and founder of PILMMA - Personal Injury Lawyers Marketing and Management Association (www.pilmma.org), the first and only marketing and management association exclusively for contingency-based law firms. We use Risk Reversal in all our sales and it works.

We feel it's our duty to see that our members get results from the knowledge we provide them. If not, we don't deserve to have them as members. This point of view is what led us to develop our newest guarantee. If at anytime during a new member's first year of membership, they become dissatisfied for any reason – we will refund every cent of monthly dues they have paid, even if we have to go back eleven months. This has dramatically increased new memberships because all the risk has been on PILMMA to either satisfy the new members' expectations or lose them. Each new member had no risk the first 12 months of his or her membership. We completely eliminated it!

The stronger your guarantee when compared to your competitors – the more you will dominate the market and succeed in making your competition irrelevant.

2. Better Than Money Back Guarantee: This means that if you are not completely satisfied with your purchase, not only will you get your money back but you will also be given something extra for your

212

trouble or inconvenience.

At PILMMA we use this type of Risk Reversal to sell tickets to our Annual Super Summits. The following is the Ironclad Guarantee we offer to all attendees:

KEN HARDISON'S PERSONAL 100% IRONCLAD MONEY-BACK GUARANTEE

If after the first day you have not captured enough immediately profitable strategies and ideas to have made your attendance worthwhile, you can bail out and ask for and immediately receive a full 100% refund of your registration fee, PLUS, up to $500 in travel reimbursements based upon your documented costs. No hard feelings. No questions asked. – *Ken Hardison*

Thus, we not only refund their price of admission, but we also reimburse them up to $500.00 in travel expenses…this is much more than the usual money back guarantee. By the way, we have been offering this for five years now and not one lawyer has asked for their money back!

This Better Than Money Back guarantee is most commonly seen in infomercials offering products you can try for 60 days and then return if you aren't completely satisfied, but yet you still get to keep the free gift that accompanied your order - *free knife set anyone?*

Why do you think they make these types of offers? It's simple. They do it because, just as it does for PILMMA, it works!

The increase we, and others who use this tactic, see in sales, more than compensates for any customer who actually takes advantage of the guarantee.

CAVEAT: If you offer such a guarantee, your product or service MUST work and deliver as promised; otherwise everyone is going to cash in on your guarantee – rendering it and you irrelevant.

3. Emotional Guarantee: This works when it might not be practical to guarantee results with a money back guarantee (an advertisement for a medical professional, lawyer, or consultant for example).

In a case such as this, you may want to offer a free audit or assessment in lieu of a traditional guarantee.

The goal is to reduce the prospect's fear of doing business with you and increase their confidence in you. You must remember this when you are crafting your message. With my former law firm, Hardison & Cochran, we offered the emotional guarantee set out below.

No lawyer can ethically promise or guarantee results of the outcome of your case and neither can we. But, our firm is so committed to quality work, personal attention and client satisfaction that we will give you Our Personal Guarantee. If you are not 100% completely satisfied with the way we treat you and your claim, during the first 30 days after hiring our firm, you may take your file, no attorney fees and no questions asked.

Other lawyers thought I was crazy. They said people would take advantage of me and leave in droves. Here are the facts: In seven years we lost two clients to the above guarantee. Compare that to the hundreds of new cases we converted because we took away the fear of dealing with lawyers and staff they had never met and you have a winner. The two clients weren't even a drop in the bucket compared to the rainfall of clients we signed up simply because we took away the risk of hiring us. It's simple, when you make them feel like they have nothing to lose, you have everything to gain.

I know that Risk Reversal can sound a little intimidating, but my experience and studies have shown that time and time again, reducing or eliminating your prospects' risk increases your sales and conversions so significantly and beyond any payouts you might experience in refunds, that the intimidation factor is a moot point.

More importantly, Risk Reversal is a clear way to stand out from your competitors. Most are just too scared or lack confidence in their product or service to reverse the risk and take it on themselves.

Aren't you glad?

Their fear gives you the golden opportunity to "STAND OUT" from your competition, maximize your sales and conversions, and dominate your market!

<u>Bottom line: – Risk Reversal works. No matter what form it takes, it's a risk worth taking.</u>

About Ken

Ken Hardison practiced injury and disability law for over 32 years, and built one of the largest Personal Injury Law Firms in the state of North Carolina. He still actively participates and consults with his former partner Ben Cochran regarding the marketing of the firm. Go to: www.LawyerNC.com to learn more about the law firm Ken helped build.

Ken is the founder and president of PILMMA (Personal Injury Lawyers Marketing and Management Association). PILMMA is the only legal marketing and management association exclusively for injury and disability lawyers. It's all they do, and they do it better than anyone else in the country. For more information, visit: www.PILMMA.org.

Ken was chosen as Glazer Kennedy's Inner Circle's Diamond Coaching Contest Winner for 2010. His cutting-edge submission focused on the promotion of PILMMA's Marketing and Management Summits. His breakthrough, cost-free marketing technique promoting PILMMA's Fall 2010 Summit at the Wynn in Las Vegas, more than doubled the Summit's attendance.

He is also the author of *How to Effectively Market Your Personal Injury Law Practice in the 21st Century* and numerous articles on marketing and managing injury and disability practices. He frequently addresses other lawyers and professional organizations focusing on marketing and managing contingency-based law firms.

CHAPTER 22

STOP IT! YOU'RE SCARING ME! — OR HOW APPLE COMPUTER LAUNCHED OUR BUSINESS

BY KEVIN O'SHEA & STEPHEN BOSCH

"THIS IS CRAZY!" That was the thought we both had as we sat in the slightly intimidating, high tech waiting area of *Apple Computer.* We were preparing to pitch a new service that was fundamentally sound but untested on a brand of this magnitude. Back then (2002), Apple was a notoriously hard client to break into, even for the most seasoned of vendors, but we had *boldness* on our side and a (fool-hardy?) notion that if presented with the "better mousetrap", large brands would quickly embrace it and our business would take off like a rocket! That notion turned out to be a bit overly optimistic, but the events that followed were none-the-less magical and the resulting eleven-plus years since, none-the-less rewarding.

We had begun our company "BrandTruth®" as a way of exploiting the collective talents of three very different corporate retail veterans. Our combined 70 years of experience working for and managing large apparel, experiential and consumer-packaged goods companies led us to believe that we could offer great value to those manufacturers looking to get an edge in business. We had a single service to sell…called *Visual Share™*. A company's *Visual Share* is a quantification of its overall presence in the marketplace. Our early test projects had indicated that a company's *Visual Share* closely aligned to its *market share*. The working theory was that if you could identify Visual Share and then work towards increasing your own (visual) share, the corresponding market share would also increase. Our Unique Selling Proposition (USP) was that we could obtain this information *in stealth*. In other words, we would visit, measure, AND report on findings before any authorized study could even get started!

Apple in 2002 was less than a year into the live operation of its <u>Apple Store</u> chain rollout. Great care had been taken in every aspect of the design, layout, location and staffing of these early locations. Steve Jobs and Ron Johnson had even built a mockup location in a warehouse, close to the corporate HQ in Cupertino to test consumer-facing concepts. While never directly stated, the need for *real-life* shopper behavior data and interaction was apparently needed. A single phone call and follow-up email resulted in an almost immediate response from Apple; *"We like your backgrounds and were wondering how quickly you could do a national survey of one (1) store group with a couple of hundred stores?"* the resulting voicemail queried. Flights were quickly booked to San Francisco for an in-person meeting with Apple.

We met with the (then) head of *Worldwide Retail Marketing* and quickly learned that while he found our service offer "interesting," he had a whole other project in mind…He wondered if we could start immediately and have the project completed in a ridiculously short amount of time. Traditionally, a drawn out process of applying for and (hopefully) getting authorization from the targeted store group would have killed this project before it even began. Our *Stealth Immersion™* techniques (as they would later be known) were the solution to this dilemma. As we began to describe the process and how we envisioned the investigation unfolding, our Apple champion suddenly arose from his chair and shouted *"Stop it! You're scaring me!"* and theatrically stormed out of the room (for the first of several dramatic exits during the life of our relationship). Moments later he returned composed and ready to talk business…but we were first instructed, in no uncertain terms, never to speak of our "techniques" again and overtly told to never bring our Dell presentation PC (referred to contemptuously as "that thing") with us to a meeting at Apple again either! Ultimately we were tasked with studying the 238 store CompUSA chain located in the continental U.S. We had been hired not for our proprietary brand-presence measuring ability, but for the fact that we could do high quality work *undercover*, and the fact that we were all ex-retail and brand executives helped to seal the deal.

Why? You might ask, would a company pay extra money (over the millions already invested) to get a *seemingly* redundant read on the *live* consumer. The question holds the answer: Live Consumers (people) who are unaware they are being interviewed give truthful replies and opinions. Consumers (people) who are aware of the fact that they are in a study can no longer be considered subjective and tend to alter their responses due to subconscious factors such as self-expectation and self-image. *As much as we would like to believe that the conscious mind is the driver of all consumer decisions, the truth is that we are many times driven by more subtle factors and these factors are not always easily divined by traditional research methods.*

This last statement was the "Aha!" moment derived from our first Apple project. From this realization, a new business model was born. While we still consult large brand marketers on how their products and services should be physically represented, we now focus predominantly on studying and reporting on *natural human behavior and preferences in the marketplace* and what really drives buying choices across categories and channels. All aspects of the consumer experience are taken into account, including personal biases, need states (personal drivers on any particular day) and reaction to employees and brand representatives. We have been successful in converting some of the most prominent brands on the planet into our way of thinking…that **systematically collecting and interpreting naturally-derived consumer behavior and attitudes data is a major key to on-going success.**

We have been able to further develop our marketplace approaches and have been blessed to add the likes of HP, NIKE, Coca Cola, Nintendo and Columbia Sportswear to name a handful of our past and present clients. Our **natural elicitation**™ techniques have uncovered deeper consumer information and supported subsequent selling strategies for our clients. We owe a debt of gratitude to Apple Computer (now Apple Inc.) and the spectacularly unpredictable unfolding of events that propelled our company and our careers.

The Apple experience armed us with a business concept and maybe more importantly, a philosophy. It has helped us and our present day clients to flourish. Undoubtedly, Apple could have stopped short of "going this extra mile" and STILL have been phenomenally successful, but by insisting on doing the unconventional, they confirmed to us a powerful maxim that is timeless and is present in all success stories, large and small: *truly elite[1] companies do the extra things that other "successful" companies are unwilling or uninspired to do....*

It has been our experience that many brands today pay lip service to the idea of true service and commitment to their customer. Even the term "Customer Service" usually denotes a standard that barely passes any practical test of satisfaction and rarely, if ever, inspires the customer to more favorably consider that same brand's products or services in the future. The practice of *doing what everyone else does* is rampant and leads to mundane and undifferentiated outcomes.

Consumers today have become conditioned to expect and (unfortunately) be satisfied (?) with these incredibly low standards. Superior products and services are seemingly only available to the select few willing to pay a premium for them. A dive to the bottom line or "bean-counting" approach to sales and marketing has possessed a great many brands today. As we encounter consumers across all categories, we are hard-pressed to find brands that consistently delight (not merely "service") their clientele. As we interview consumers in the marketplace, we unfailingly uncover attitudes and opinions ranging from tolerance to downright disdain for some brands.

Fortune 500 companies and sole-proprietors alike can create personal and passionate relationships with their customers, but it invariably takes **strong authentic leadership and adherence to strong branding rules and realities**. Brands, and by extension brand leadership, must be authentically concerned with each end user's ultimate experience and relationship with the brand. This dedication must be echoed from the top down, not merely another workforce mandate or company memo.

Through years of working for and observing hundreds of global brands,

---

1. BrandTruth's definition of "elite" is a fairly demanding one. Financial success is not enough....a brand must continue to recreate itself to match the ever-changing world and consumer. An elite brand is looked to as a trusted friend and resource and is financially successful as a bi-product of its relationship with its customer, never in spite of it.

we have found that by honestly assessing your brand against the following **five (5) criteria,** you may begin to determine whether you are moving towards or away from **elite brand** status. These criteria are constants in all the great brands we have encountered:

I. Do you (as a company leader) lead from the front? – A defining and almost universal trait of an elite brand is the powerful effect that leadership has on top-to- bottom brand identity. Whether you are the CEO of a Fortune 100 company, a divisional president or a startup entrepreneur, you are ultimately tasked with taking a lead position that produces outstanding results. The business landscape is replete with figurehead leaders and cost-cutting masters. While those types of leadership models may retain the current status quo, they may also forecast your extinction as the next wave of change and disruptive events (read new or stronger competition) inevitably arise. A shared trait among the legendary business leaders of the last half decade is the ability to create a vision that transcends the day-to-day operation of the business. Leaders like Steve Jobs, Richard Branson and Phil Knight are legends, but equally impressive to us are the up-and-coming leaders of **In-N-Out Burger** (Lynsi Torres), **Chipotle** (Steve Els) and **Under Armour** (Kevin Plank). These leaders entered or expanded into seemingly mature markets and created powerful presences. Aspiring (elite) business leaders would do well to study these operations and uncover the non-typical approaches that these brands use to separate themselves from the competition and create differentiation in the minds of their customers.

II. Is your brandpromise powerfully authentic? – Is the energy and intention of your brand palpable as your customers interact with your product? *This is a gut check here.* We are not talking mission statements and other such aspirational statements or manifestos. We are talking about a tangible quality of experience that extends to and from your customers. When we speak directly and casually to elite brand customers, words like "love", " trust", "friend" and the like are often used and deeper connection alluded to than brands would normally provoke. Like most intimate relationships, these loyalties are earned over time. Trust and expectation are established and consciously built upon…this trust is sacred and every opportunity to reinforce this strength capitalized upon. Do your current customers tell tales of delight and evangelize your brand, or are you and your services considered "functional"? (Functional, even "good" brands are quickly relegated to price-comparison utility and thereby threatened by the next disruptive or better – not necessarily best – mousetrap.) The emotive brand promises of **Subaru** and the **Ritz-Carlton** separate them from their closest competition. The Ritz does it by what it calls "anticipatory service." Everyone involved with the brand is charged with elevating and enhancing relationships on a daily basis. Although a premium hotelier, this added value does not appear to add appreciably to the operation costs of the chain, but is part of the reason that many people choose the Ritz over its closest competitors. How do you systematically elevate your brand promise daily?

III. **Does your brand promise permeate your organization? Do your employees represent your brand at its finest?** - This may be the single most important question you ask yourself as you attempt to separate your brand from the pack. We work daily with clients who struggle to offset the effects of less-than-optimized employees. We have witnessed multi-million dollar launches under-perform expectations due to poor associate training. Many companies pour scores of money into product or service R&D and marketing…only to be derailed by the employee at the end of the product/service chain. Many selling programs utilized by brands today rely too much on either personal impetus, OR rote, unimaginative scripts and training. *Employees left to their own devices will usually revert to personal biases and may ultimately represent a less-than-desirable face to your product or service. Additionally, "canned" customer engagement approaches that we see in too many organizations today are viewed as inauthentic and gratuitous by customers.* Juxtapose this to say, **_Trader Joe's_**, whose sometimes quirky clerks engage most shoppers in genuine conversation and banter that at least feels authentic. We are not saying that you can just plug in a system and suddenly have super-motivated, super-engaged employees. These results are imitable, but the culture must first be fostered and the mandate must be shared and be authentic.

IV. **Measure, adjust …repeat!** - It's not "how well did we do?" but rather, "How well _COULD WE HAVE_ done?" It is critical to determine ways to accurately read customer attitudes and trends relating to your products or services. ***You manage that which you*** *measure.* This truism has been recited by many respected individuals (from Lord Kelvin to Albert Einstein to Tom Peters and Bill Hewlett of HP fame). *Another defining trait of an elite brand is on-going quantification and a commitment to continuous improvement.* Bars are meant to be set and then methods devised for raising them. Elite brands find ways to measure the seemingly "un-measurable." A century ago, U.S. merchant and civic leader John Wanamaker famously stated, *"I know that half of my advertising doesn't work. The problem is...I don't know which half."*...**today's elite brands find creative ways to measure the seemingly immeasurable.**

V. Fail Forward Fast - This is a (controversial?) strategy that we endorse and recommend to our clients. In today's marketplace, ***Action*** trumps analysis-paralysis! The rate at which consumers are adapting new technologies and by extension, new behavioral patterns, dictates that brands be willing to make errors and quickly adjust rather than wait on the traditional "data dump" models of the past to dictate action and direction. Many of our biggest clients bemoan the fact that much of their consumer data is too dated to use effectively...even within 6 months! The prize these days goes to the swift.

As we reflect back on the seminal request by Apple to us to ***"Stop it! You're scaring me!",*** perhaps the take-away is that innovation and expansion should be a little bit scary. Playing it completely safe is herd behavior and herds eventually get led to the slaughter. You're not learning and advancing if it feels completely safe...don't get us wrong, we don't advocate high-risk behavior for our clients, but we do encourage pushing to the point of healthy discomfort. Each of the five (5) above-mentioned criteria is meant to cause a little discomfort if honestly assessed and internalized. We look forward to hearing of the evolution of your elite brand.

About Kevin

Kevin O'Shea is a co-founder of BrandTruth and he has a long and varied retail, branding and qualitative research background. Kevin's management career spans 25+ years, allowing exposure to all levels of retail branding and product/service execution. Starting his career in the grocery and FMCG arena, he was eventually recruited by San Francisco branding pioneer ESPRIT and became an integral part of their management team. As a director and 10-year corporate officer for the trendy apparel brand, he was responsible for developing and supporting multiple programs and brand initiatives for such major retail accounts as Federated Department Stores (Now Macy's Inc.), May Company, Dillard's, Saks Inc., Kohl's and Nordstrom.

During this period, marketing, merchandising and fulfillment successes were tempered with losses as "best guess" forecasts, and ineffectual primary research methods were all that was available to marketers of the day. We figured that there had to be a better way...**what if a brand could actively and consistently monitor its relationship with the buying public in real time? What if high-level executives and business owners could reach out (even by proxy) and interact with their customers and products in the marketplace and get immediate and uncorrupted feedback...and then ADJUST their programs accordingly?**

This was the promise and value born out of the BrandTruth formation. To speak with Kevin directly and discuss how BrandTruth might be able to help you and your brand maximize your go-to-market spend, please call 650.269.3434 or email: koshea@ brandtruth.com.To read more about BrandTruth and to access the expanded version of _Five (5) Criteria for Elite Brands,_ visit: www.brandtruthcom

About Stephen

Stephen Bosch is the president and Managing Partner of BrandTruth. He co-founded the company in 2002 as a way of more powerfully applying his 30+ years of experience in appraising how some of world's largest and most iconic brands (including P&G, NIKE, Coca-Cola, Adidas, Microsoft, HP, Apple, Nintendo, and others) connect or disconnect with their customers.

"We ultimately started BrandTruth because being corporate and brand insiders ourselves, we recognized that leaders of companies were basing critical decisions on partial or incomplete information about the consumer and marketplace conditions in which their products and services lived."

Stephen is one of the key architects of BrandTruth's proprietary "Stealth Immersion" methodology – which was created to provide brand leadership teams rich information very quickly. Mr. Bosch says *"To boil it down; we tell them what they missed… how many sales they didn't get and why…. What competitors made and missed and why… what consumers are truly doing and saying and what that all ultimately means to their brand and bottom line"*

To speak with Stephen directly and discuss how BrandTruth might be able help you and your brand maximize your go-to-market spend, please call 206.310.1622 or email: stephenbosch@brandtruth.com. To read more about BrandTruth and to access the expanded version of *Five (5) Criteria for Elite Brands*, visit: www.brandtruthcom.

CHAPTER 23

DEVELOP YOUR PERSONAL VALUE

BY JORGE OLSON

STAND APART WITH YOUR PRODUCT OR SERVICE, BUSINESS AND WITH YOURSELF

It was late Sunday night when I got a call from Andreas Johansson, "Let's announce the Dennis Rodman Vodka tomorrow," he said. "Tomorrow?" I answered in a bit of a panic with twenty things going through my mind. "Why tomorrow? I need at least a week to work with my team and plan a strategy." "Dennis Rodman will be on the cover of Sports Illustrated this week and I want to announce the product the same week," he said.

He's talking about Bad Boy Vodka with Dennis Rodman, the basketball player that has been on the news recently for his trip to North Korea to meet Kim Jong-un. The trip made national news and placed the athlete on top of the media relevance radar. After his trip he made it to almost every single print, radio and even TV news organization in the country. The entire media super frenzy culminated with an entire segment on HBO's "Vice", an interview with George Stephanopoulos on ABC's "This Week" and with Piers Morgan on CNN's "Piers Morgan Tonight."

In your own marketing life, you'll be faced every single day with branding decisions. "Should you market yourself, should you market your products or your company?" The answer is simple, market yourself. The most important thing to remember in your daily marketing is to focus on yourself. Remember, people want to do business with people, not with objects. Don't focus on your product, service, or company, focus on <u>yourself</u>. In the Vodka example, you'll see how I used Personal Branding to accomplish the positioning and achieving the launch of an entire organization in one campaign - Marketing Dennis Rodman, the owner of the product, Andreas, his company, his Vodka product, and even myself and my company as I'm in most media stories.

"Yes Jorge, please send a press release and get some publicity this week," he said. It was Sunday night, I didn't have anything prepared, and I was tired, but I said "sure, we can do it."

Now I only had a few hours to strategize and do the launch for one of my major customers, and I had to do it on my own, without the help of my team. Usually this process takes at least one week and several brainstorming meetings with six members of my marketing team. Now I had a couple of hours, at most, and I was already tired on a Sunday night.

Sometimes you have to rely on your years of experience and your ten thousand hours of practice to make a decision in a blink of an eye, as Malcolm Gladwell explains in his books: *Blink: The Power of Thinking Without Thinking* and *Outliers*. This was the case for this marketing conundrum.

My initial thoughts and feelings told me to call him back and tell him I couldn't do it. After all, I couldn't put out a mediocre product or campaign, my reputation was on the line here. After taking five deep breaths I filed those thoughts and feelings in the "excuses" column and decided that he was right. Sometimes branding and Standing Apart is about timing and opportunity, not just planning and strategy. Now it was time to get all the doubts out of my mind and do the work.

When faced with these types of situations, you have to rely on your gut feeling and experience. In Gladwell's books he explains this is achieved through a long process of practice, study and experience. When you're ultimately faced with an opportunity, or problem (sometimes they are the same), all this knowledge and experience will work together without you knowing it. Your decisions will be fast and clear, even if you can't explain how or why you came up with these decisions. This "gut feeling" is what allows experts to make decisions on the fly, without weeks of research, without reading thousands of pages or browsing for hours through the Internet. What we have to realize is they already did the research, the reading, and the browsing. They did it many times over many, many years, maybe more than ten thousand hours' worth of practice as Gladwell states in his book *Outliers*.

What happened with the Vodka? I followed my gut feeling and prepared a quick branding campaign (a one-day campaign for starters). That one-day campaign placed the product, story, and photo in every major news organization including ABC, CBS, NBC and Fox affiliates, CNN, The Wall Street Journal, Reuters, LA Times, USA Today, Time, ESPN affiliates, as well as the beverage trade magazines and local newspapers, radio and television channels.

HOW TO STAND APART –
START WITH YOUR PERSONAL BRANDING

If you're not in a position to just "Blink" and come up with your entire personal branding and self-promotion or marketing strategy, don't worry. In this chapter you'll learn the secret to creating an incredible personal brand that you will be able to keep for the rest of your life. You'll apply it in your personal and in your professional life; you'll use it for economic gain and to influence, to position yourself as an expert and to make the phone ring.

In the example of the Vodka, we're branding several things for several people, and it has a lot of moving parts to the branding campaign. We're branding the Vodka, the CEO and entrepreneur behind the Vodka, Andreas Johansson, and by default, Dennis Rodman. That's not all; my company is also involved in this process, so we're branding my company, my services (beverage development, branding, sales and distribution) and myself as I appear on most of the media coverage.

The first thing you have to do when creating your own brand is start with YOU. Your brand has to start with a Personal Brand and then move outward from there; it can be a Company or it can be a Product or Service. The first step is to know what you want, in other words, your goal.

I know, in business, in seminars and in personal development, you've heard it more than a hundred times, "you must have goals." This is repeated over and over again in everything from books to self-help audios. Now listen, this is particularly important in marketing and branding because if you don't have goals you can go in so many directions you'll lose a lot of time and you will lose a lot of money.

There are three big strategies for you to Stand Apart from competitors and for you to Stand Apart all together regardless of competitors. The strategies are a combination of classic-proven marketing techniques and a personal branding approach that crosses over into your **personal philosophy** and vision of business, life, and the world. Yes, it's a personal view, not just a business view. After all, if it's just a business or corporate view you will be like everyone else, and what we're talking about here is not about being like everyone else, it's about Standing Apart.

YOUR THREE STAND APART BRANDING STEPS

1. Your Personal Philosophy Starts at Home
2. Start with the Finish Line
3. Develop your Unique Value Proposition (UVP)

To Stand Apart you don't need to work double the hours, you don't need to spend double the money, you just need to think differently, and then act differently. This difference in the way you think and behave comes from your personal beliefs. This is why we call it personal branding, because it's personal. Thinking and acting differently is the definition of standing apart. Start applying it to your daily life. When everyone else gets mad you will be understanding, if people scream you will be calm and speak in a soft voice, if an employee screws up you'll mentor them instead of scolding them; the same at home with your spouse, your kids and your entire family. After all, if you can't do it at home, how will you be able to do it anywhere else? You have to be able to influence and attract attention, love and respect from all of your friends and family before taking it outside those familiar walls into the business world.

Step 1: <u>Your Personal Philosophy Starts At Home</u>

"To stand apart you first need to stand together."

"But Wait! You mentioned personal philosophy, what does branding have to do with philosophy and with standing apart?" This is what a client asked me after exploring his personal branding campaign in a strategy meeting. "What were you expecting, some social media advice?" I said. "Yes," he answered, "That's what everyone else tells me."

Guess what? If everyone gives you the same technique it means two things. The first one is that they are probably right, you probably need it. The second is that everyone else has the same technique, so they don't stand apart.

If your goal is to Stand Apart you need to work on your personal branding. Personal branding is not about social media, it's not about backlinks or any type of SEO. It's about your personal philosophy. Remember, you don't focus on the strategy; you focus on the person, on you.

What is a personal philosophy anyway? Philosophy is the study of everything that is important. Your personal philosophy is everything that is important to you. This includes your values, your dreams, your family, your goals, and your view of the world, religion, the economy, and your business. Notice your business is just one of the things in your personal philosophy.

It's important for you to analyze and meditate on your personal philosophy because this is what you'll communicate in your personal branding. People want to know about you, they will judge you on your personality, your views and your character, not your product or your company. Make sure your personal goals are in line with your philosophy and then do the same for your products and for your business.

Step 2: <u>Start With the Finish Line</u>

"Let's get our hands dirty! You'll go over the best techniques to make you stand apart in business and in life."

Here is a golden tip, always start your marketing in reverse, start at the Finish Line. I call it reverse engineering marketing. It is a simple formula that I personally use for myself and all of my clients. I use it when selling my own services, with my personal branding, in developing beverages and other products and for companies and institutions.

Start this exercise by imagining the finish line. This is where you would like to be, where you would like to go, what you want to accomplish, your goal. From there you move backwards all the way to you, or your product, or your company.

Step 3: <u>Develop Your Personal Unique Value Proposition</u>

"To stand apart you have to be unique. To be unique you start with your Unique Value Proposition."

The title and premise of the book is "Stand Apart". By definition to stand apart you first need to stand together.

What is a UVP?

Your UVP is the VALUE you personally provide others. In business, the UVP will be the value the company can provide for you, your company and also your business. When you Stand Apart and create a UVP for your business, don't just think about branding your company. You have to separate a UVP for you, for your Products and Services and yet another for your Company. The number one mistake in branding is forgetting people identify with people; this is especially true with small businesses, as they don't have huge branding and advertising budgets.

What is the difference between UVP and USP? The USP or Unique Selling Proposition is the way you will market and sell yourself, your product or organization. The UVP is the value that you provide not how you market that value.

After you develop your UVP you need other people to know about it so you develop your USP (and you execute it). Simple, that's the formula for you to stand apart!

PERSONAL BRANDING AND UVP

The UVP in your personal branding is the value you provide to everyone. The value you provide not only in business but also in your family, to your kids, your spouse, parents, brothers, sisters, cousins, uncles, everyone. This value can include love, advice, humor, support, education, fitness, money, ethics, religion, time, and everything you provide that is of value to your family and friends.

These are a lot of values, but they are all unique. In your private and family life you can have many values and many ways of sharing them. You don't just need one unique value as you might need it in business for branding purposes. If you lack a few values that's fine, this is why you need to keep growing, learning, becoming smarter, in better shape, healthier, more educated. All of this is part of your own personal brand and when you grow your personal brand you grow your personal value to others. This starts with your family and extends to your friends and then to your colleagues, employees, partners, and customers.

I try to apply all the list of values and grow my own personal brand to add value to all my extended family. For all of this to work first you start with you, your personal brand, and then you add value to others. For example, I train friends and family in the gym up to five times per week. This means I better be in shape and educated on the subject. First I worked on myself, and then I helped others.

I also mentor friends and family on business and personal achievement. One of the topics I often use for mentoring is Public Speaking. The same rule applies here. If I mentor people on public speaking I need to be a good speaker first and learn how to mentor and teach the craft. From how to write speeches to how to deliver them in training, keynotes, or even to your friends and family. First I work on myself, and then I can help others. It's what we hear on the plane right? "In case of a lack of cabin pressure, oxygen masks will drop in front of you. Make sure you secure your own mask before helping others." Then you see a woman on the video securing her mask before helping her child. It's counter intuitive, but it's correct. You have to be able to help others, otherwise nobody gets helped.

YOUR BUSINESS UNIQUE VALUE PROPOSITION

One of my jobs is to help Executives stand apart, and to teach them how to make their companies and products stand apart from the competition. In working with dozens of senior level executives and entrepreneurs and listening to more than one hundred business value propositions per month, I see many mistakes and misconceptions about how to craft a value proposition. Many of my projects are in food, beverage and other consumer goods and many executives tell me, "My value proposition is that my product tastes great." This is not a UVP, this is a feature of your product. If every single company that calls me tells me the same thing, how can this be a Unique Value Proposition? Imagine that, if taste is your value proposition anyone can copy your flavor and take away that value from you.

Your business UVP has to be unique and create value for everyone involved in your company, not just customers. Your value has to extend to:

- Customers
- Investors
- Employees
- Management
- Stakeholders

Remember, *"To Stand Apart you first need to Stand Together."* This is my personal philosophy, and it has been a great personal branding and promotion mechanism by default. You can borrow it, steal it, live it, and use it.

About Jorge

Jorge S. Olson is President and CEO of Premier Brands Inc. He builds Beverage Companies!

Jorge is an international beverage industry expert and builds beverage and consumer goods companies.

He has successfully developed, marketed and sold more than 1,000 different beverages and consumer products in the United States and Mexico. He has more than a decade of C-level executive experience in consumer goods, beverages and wholesale distribution. He is the author of successful business resource books including *Build Your Beverage Empire* and *The Unselfish Guide to Self-Promotion.*

Jorge's expertise, which expands into sales, strategy and analysis for consumer goods, retail and wholesale distribution, is widely sought-after by consumer goods companies, entrepreneurs, and investors. He has consulted profitably with over 250 entrepreneurs, investors, and consumer goods companies.

As CEO, COO, and Vice President of Technology, Jorge has provided project coordination, direction and analysis for projects involving companies as diverse as Standard & Poors, SAB Miller, and a broad range of beverage and consumer product companies, including Coca Cola, Fiji Water, Hansen's, Red Bull, Rockstar Energy, Dr. Pepper, Snapple Group, Pepsi Bottling Group, and Vitamin Water. Consumer product companies he has worked with include Southern Wine & Spirits, Frito-Lay, Emergen-C, 5-Hour Energy, and Hershey's.

You can reach Jorge at: www.PremierBrandsInc.com

CHAPTER 24

ENHANCING SALES STRATEGY TO MAKE YOU STAND APART

BY KIP L. CARPENTER

Is your sales staff running a little flat? Has your sales team faded from their once brilliant showmanship, production and consistently high daily sales volume?

Since 2006, I have been reigniting once highly effective sales teams, turning GP margins from mid-30s to 50s, with sales volumes jumping immediately 20-40% and sustaining on average 10+% annually. It's not that the sales teams that I fixed were totally ineffective; after all, they were producing tens of millions of dollars in retail sales annually, but rather they needed a little something more that I will share with you shortly, to give them that extra edge.

Before diving in, I'll share a bit about myself to help you understand how I formulated these strategies:

I was born on Kodiak Island, Alaska – before it was part of the United States; an island known for having the most ferocious bears in the world, The Kodiak Brown Bears. My family left Kodiak just before the Great Alaskan Earthquake and settled in San Jose, California which really was the first influence on my sales strategy.

In elementary school, my parents were getting a divorce and my mother's anger boiled over onto me, creating a rough home life. In an attempt to gain approval from my Mom at home, I turned my punishments into accomplishments; practicing three instruments 45 minutes daily; reading 50 pages a night; practicing sports at school for years. I ran away from home entering High School, and moved into my Dad's house, while continuing to excel on my own; the pattern of over-excel (prove your worth) was set in my mind. Accomplishments included: Straight "A's"; playing three instruments; speaking five languages; Tournament fighter and Black Belt in Karate; lettering in sports in High School and College. Struggles are a part of life. How a person deals with them shapes how they grow. Each sales person will have different experiences but they are all relatable, make sure they share them to connect with your customers.

I left the San Jose area in my twenties because all my friends had opinions of my ability to excel that were different from mine. I knew I could one day run a big company, but up to that time I had only worked in smaller companies, so my friends put a limit on my upward potential and I knew that to be truly successful, I had to associate with, and mirror the actions of, truly successful people.

I moved to Newport Beach, CA. What a great place to get a new start. I didn't know anybody, and since no one knew me, I decided that when meeting new people, the adage would be 'what you see, is what you get.' I picked up the Wall Street Journal to look for a job and there was an ad that caught my attention. 'Chauffeur Body Guard Needed for President of Large Marketing Company, must be expert in martial arts.' Expert is a relative term, right?

I went and applied for the job and sat in a lobby with a couple other guys awaiting my interview time.

There was this guy there that was big, maybe 6'2", buffed, with short blond hair and wearing all black.

This guy looked like an expert and I couldn't help but think... "This guy will stuff my head in my tennis shoe if I'm not careful!" Someone later told me it was the actress Cheryl Ladd's body guard.

I was the last interview of the day, and as I took a seat in front of the executive desk, I was being asked questions by a woman that was filing papers with her back to me, I didn't even see her face. Question 5 was, 'How much do you want to make a year?' I paused and answered boldly, '$85,000!' She stopped filing and turned around to look at me. 'This job doesn't pay $85,000' she said. 'You asked how much I wanted to make,' I said. 'How much does it pay?' We both started laughing and talking; it broke the ice and I got the job because my personality closely matched that of the President of this company. Yeah! The President was a 6'5" Texan and maybe 220 pounds. I looked more like his son than I did his body guard.

So began a journey of driving a stretch limo and serving the wants and needs of a high profile person. I don't think I really imagined the long hours I would spend, most times 12 to 15 hours a day. I also didn't realize the great amount of knowledge I would acquire during those long hours together. I had two eyes to see, two ears to hear and one mouth to only ask questions occasionally. Learning to serve is a good personal trait to have and one that has stayed with me. When you're serving, you don't really have time to think about 'poor little me.'

I served as the Chauffeur for a year and a half; those very long days as a servant taught me how the President thought and what he found important, enough so that I was promoted to Vice President and assisted in building a sales force from 2,000 to 20,000 in 32 states, while sales volume rose to $1.5 Billion. Personal development seminars were a big part of my training, along with advancing the corporate image. Learning how and why he choose the high-producing sales people to join his company, educated me on the interview and selection process. This training has helped me focus in on how I can identify good sales people and reignite whole sales teams. Every business I joined, I became the leader, achieving #1 – whether there were 100 or 350 people there ahead of me. Why is that?

Highly effective sales people exhibit characteristic traits and mannerisms that I look for – eye movement, hand and head movement, pronunciation, accentuation on certain words in their speech. I look at the whole thing and ask myself: is this the complete package and would I buy something from this person? If these traits and mannerisms are present, I know I can fit this person in any place and they'll probably outperform a good number of the existing sales people.

Always be recruiting and running ads for sales people. The cost to run ads is nominal, and there's the likelihood that you may actually find someone with all the right attributes. Not long ago an existing salesperson referred a friend to interview with me. I agreed to meet this prospect in one of our retail stores. This person was a little rough looking; probably could have done something different with their attire, etc., but who am I to judge. I was there to focus on characteristic traits and look at the complete package, not just any one thing. Don't get judgmental before you have a chance to engage with the prospect. This person wowed me. They definitely had all the right attributes. We got into conversations about dogs and people and sales that had us both laughing. I hired this person on the spot, and they have done an amazing job for the company.

I've been asked what I look for in a sales person. Personality is very important of course, but also sales people that are socially comfortable in conversation. A person that is willing to talk and share information when asked, but knows when to shut it off, without having to be told. A little humble but still aggressive. I want someone with the right amount of social aptitude; smiley, great eye contact and willing to be open. The use of expressions in the sales process such as; 'I've experienced that before' – 'that hurt me too', shows an emotional connection and empathy for others. When sharing information, the sales person will pay close attention to the customer and as soon as the customer opens their mouth to speak, the sales person will close their mouth and let the customer talk and share the concerns or experiences they have had in the past. A good sales person will remember the weak points or concerns the customer was talking about and then bring them back into the close, describing how the product will help with the situations discussed.

In 2006, I was hired by a company that had been in business for approximately 50 years and was owned by the current proprietor for 7-8 years; ten's of millions in annual sales; with a large retail footprint in Southern California. I was unfamiliar with the inner workings of the industry, and the products, although valuable on a retail consumer base, had a real unknown value to me.

The company had a single owner; wealthy; young; well-connected with participation on the boards of well-known, top ranking companies and he has a commanding presence and knows what he wants to happen in his companies. Being a wealthy business owner and running one of many companies, he had high expectations and demands. I was there and more than willing to meet and exceed the high expectations of this business owner and this job assignment. Initial assignment: The Region of Orange County, California – bring it up in production.

I've been asked, 'How do I look at a company and their sales organization when I first go into a new situation?' The answer is that you can't really look at a whole company to try to solve its problems; you have to break it into pieces. Usually with sales teams of 50 to 350, break them into Regions or Districts. It's best to look at them in bite-sized pieces, so they can be analyzed one section at a time, and change can be effected one section at a time.

When I go into a Region, I'm really interested in the sales people, who they are, what their personality is like, and how they talk and sell. Since I'm regarded as a person that's here to bring about change, I will initially ask questions such as;

- What is this area about?
- What are the demographics like?
- Who is the customer in the area?
- Wasn't this area a higher performing area before?

It takes the focus off of the sales person and onto the region. Don't scare them, they are the reason you make money in the first place; instead, entice them to do better.

I ask questions like:

- Why was this area higher performing before?
- How has it changed?
- Have people moved out?
- Is there overbuilding in the neighborhood?
- Has competition moved into the neighborhood?

The responses are all relative because perhaps the sales person really is good; and the reason the Region or locations within the Region are not hitting the monthly or annual goals is because the area has changed; it's important to spend time listening to the sales persons responses.

I'll go through the Regions and talk to everybody and watch them sell. I do this analysis in a roundabout way and determine their competence, just by talking; just like I do in the interview process – I'm looking for the right attributes. Since I am dealing with highly effective sales people, I want to know where they are coming from, maybe there is a legitimate reason for low production or low gross profits, or maybe they just got tired. I lay praise on the sales people for the great job they've always done, there's no reason to tear them down.

Change is difficult for most individuals, but it's important to all companies. I think that all companies need someone that answers only to the Owner. In a sales organization, this person is outstanding in sales and has great management experience and can effect change the way the business owner wants and needs.

How do I determine which sales people belong where? Most assertive sales people want to sell in the number one location; but the number one location isn't for everybody because some people can't sell in that demographic. I listen and watch them with customers as they sell; by listening and watching you can tell someone's comfort zone in dealing with customers, young customers versus old customers, ethnicity, temperament, etc. Each region will have a distinct customer profile, make sure your sales people can click with it. I need to know and match not only the number one store, but all the stores with the sales people that match the demographics for whatever is being sold there. You as a business owner can do this, or you can designate someone on your behalf to complete this task; the results are worth it.

To complete the story on the initial assignment: The Region of Orange County, California – bring it up in production. For this company, the Orange County Region – with all its affluence and business savvy – had never been number one in this company, which was surprising. Six months later, Orange County was the Number One Region and remained that way for five plus years, with monthly GP's of 50+%, until I reignited another Region that took over for a short period of time.

'What is the next task as hand?' I asked the business owner.

'I want you to the fix the San Diego Region,' the owner said.

'Is there anything in particular you want fixed?' I asked out of respect for his ownership and direct financial involvement.

'From Top to Bottom!!' He barked at me.

[Note to Self: Never Ask that Question Again! Obviously he knows that I know what to do and don't need direction.]

The San Diego Region went from mid-30% to 52% sales margins, sales volume totaling a million dollars a month saw an increase of 5-15%. That's a good improvement with lots of money dropping to the bottom line!

I'm confident in what I do as a business professional reigniting once highly effective sales teams.

Is your sales staff running a little flat? I have a lot more I would love to share with you to help find you a solution.

To learn more about Kip L Carpenter and how he can effect positive change for your company,

Visit: www.KipLCarpenter.com. Call 949-226-8026
or email: Kip@KipLCarpenter.com.

www.KipLCarpenter.com

About Kip

Kip L. Carpenter was born on Kodiak Island, Alaska – before it was part of the United States; an island known for having the most ferocious bears in the world, The Kodiak Brown Bears. Kip's family left Kodiak just before the Great Alaskan Earthquake and settled in San Jose, CA. Much later he moved to Southern California.

In elementary school, his parents were getting a divorce and his mother's anger boiled over onto him, creating a rough home life. In an attempt to gain approval from his Mom at home he turned his punishments into accomplishments; practicing three instruments 45 minutes daily; reading 50 pages a night; practicing sports at school for years. Kip ran away from home entering High School and moved into his Dad's house, while continuing to excel on his own; the pattern of over-excel (prove your worth) was set in his mind. Accomplishments included: Straight "A's"; playing three instruments; speaking five languages; Tournament fighter and Black Belt in Karate; lettering in sports in High School and College.

Every business he joined, he became the leader, achieving #1 whether there were 100 or 350 people there ahead of him. Why is that?

A successful 30+ year career in business has produced: A Top Sales Producer and Sales Manager; conquering tangibles and intangibles. In a key executive position, he helped build a direct sales company to $1 billion in annual sales; he's served on the Presidents Clubs and Key Clubs of the Top Insurance Companies and Mutual Fund Companies in the world as an annual multi-million dollar producer; and he's achieved huge success in the retail marketplace.

What can he share with you? Since 2006, he has been reigniting once highly effective sales teams, turning GP margins from mid-30s to 50s, with sales volumes jumping immediately 20-40% and sustaining on average 10+% annually. It's not that the sales teams that he fixed were totally ineffective; after all, they were producing tens of millions of dollars in retail sales annually, but rather they needed a little something extra, that he provided to give them that extra edge.

'The Real Estate Housing Bubble', where money was abundant through financing and refinancing, was a economic period of great wealth. Sales during the housing bubble were great everywhere and sales people were added almost without thought, to meet the customer demand.

Kip states, "2007 forward saw a Recession and business slowed, producing a situation where our sales teams have become bloated with sales people that shouldn't be with us. We hired order takers to meet demand and when business slowed, we realized that we needed trained sales people... now."

If all Kip could do for you was methodically improve your sales, your GP's and your sales teams overall effectiveness, would you be interested?

During his spare time, Kip and his wife Chris, of 29 years, spend time with their 4 children. Daughter: Graduate, Vanderbilt University; Son: Graduate, USC Business School; Son: Junior, University of Notre Dame; Son: Freshman, Stanford University.

To learn more about Kip L. Carpenter and how he can effect positive change for your company, visit: www.KipLCarpenter.com. Call 949-226-8026 or email: Kip@KipLCarpenter.com.

www.KipLCarpenter.com

CHAPTER 25

YOUR ENTREPRENEURIAL FLIGHT™ – MAKE IT HAPPEN!

BY KIM LABRECHE

We are all a product of our own unique DNA. (I had to throw this in! ☺) Did you know that statistically, 40% of entrepreneurship is inherited and 60% of entrepreneurship is the result of learned or historical experiences?

I come from a strong entrepreneurial background. My father was and continues to be a visionary. Business came easy to him or so I thought as a young person. There was evidence of his successes in the new home, cottage and new cars that I grew up with. Furthermore, my grandmother who was a school teacher and taught my grandfather to read, loved flowers and had begun a floral business. She died while I was only four years old of lung cancer when second hand smoke was an unknown health risk. My grandfather took over this business so both prominent men in my life were successful entrepreneurs.

Entrepreneurs do not like to accept the *status quo*. My father decided that his English-speaking Protestant daughter, who happens to be me, should have every opportunity in her career choices so he decided to challenge the French School District to allow his daughter to attend a French Catholic School. In doing so, he understood that I would be able to maximize my opportunities for advancement in the bilingual city in which we resided. This of course was met with much resistance on the School Official's part, but in keeping with the mantra of "let's make it happen" vs. "let it happen", I was able to join my French friends at school. In fact, my French was at such an advanced level by the first Easter, that I joined my first language French-speaking friends in the regular French school curriculum. It was my first taste of success.

One of my greatest learning experiences came from having to survive the dreaded "D" word. My parents divorced when I was very young and in the years of separation, I was determined to succeed. I was in fact a survivor and would not succumb to any weaknesses. I started working at the young age of 15 to pay for my own personal expenses as my mother coped with the financial reality of being a single parent for many years. This experience enabled me to appreciate my independence and financial contribution to our real life situation.

As a female, I did not allow myself to be limited. In fact, I remember my father asking me what I wanted to be when I grew up and this made me feel like an adult, an equal. I always envisioned that I would be CEO of a large company in Toronto. At this time, I knew nothing of Vancouver and all of its natural beauty.

I was always fueled by drive and ambition, but I had a very soft piece to my DNA that allowed me to achieve success with heart, compassion and soul. I learned this from the females in my life. My mother sacrificed much for me to ensure that I was on the right path. My grandmother showed unconditional love for the man she taught to read (my grandfather) and married despite her family's objections. The women in my life were strong and a guiding light.

I brought these inherent DNA characteristics and my historical experiences together to form my own character. That is why at the age of 38 with a two year old son, I was not in the least afraid of purchasing an existing accounting practice. I knew that I could make it work and that I would do everything to make it happen. I had faith in myself and so did my husband. We borrowed 100% of the purchase price, entered into a five-year lease and assumed the existing staff members. I had no firsthand experience in running a company. I was only a child when my father had his company, but it looked easy and given that I shared the mindset of "make it happen," I knew that I would make sure that all was taken care of.

I had no problem growing the practice, ensuring that the work was done at the same high quality that I and my predecessor expected, meeting client expectations, collecting the money and paying the bills. I did this while being heavily involved as treasurer, a member of several Chambers, Rotary, being a wife and still the mother of a young son. When I reached a level that I could no longer sustain the business volume, I brought in a partner. I had known this person for many years. We hired additional staff with the qualifications and experience to allow me to pursue my passion to work directly with business owners. I took calculated risks when, in fact, more due diligence was in order. This partnership did not succeed, however, I am pleased to say that this learning brought me to the right decisions in my own Entrepreneurial Flight™ in that I brought in my husband as the right partner and I now have the right team members in the right spots! And what a pleasure it is to work alongside of them!

In my years of working with business owners as a Chartered Accountant, I have had the opportunity to understand their mindsets as I was also an entrepreneur myself, loving the shiny new objects, taking risks and being an "out of the box" thinker (I just recently purchased a massage chair for the reception area for the accounting practice as I always told clients that stress ends at the door!). I remain mindful of the fact that the success of my business starts with me. It is my responsibility as a business owner to ensure that I have a thriving and sustainable business that will ensure the ongoing operations of the company, and as such I will ensure the future prosperity of my family, employees, and professional colleagues. I am certainly no stranger to a challenge! With this foundation in place, I can now devote more time to working with business owners to do exactly what I have done.

THE ENTREPRENEURIAL FLIGHT™ MODEL

I have worked with the co-developers of The Entrepreneurial Flight™ for the past five years. It is the leading integrated model for accelerating the growth of entrepreneurs and their enterprises. It visually depicts the Entrepreneur's and the Enterprise's Flights. Take a few moments to look at the diagram on the next page.

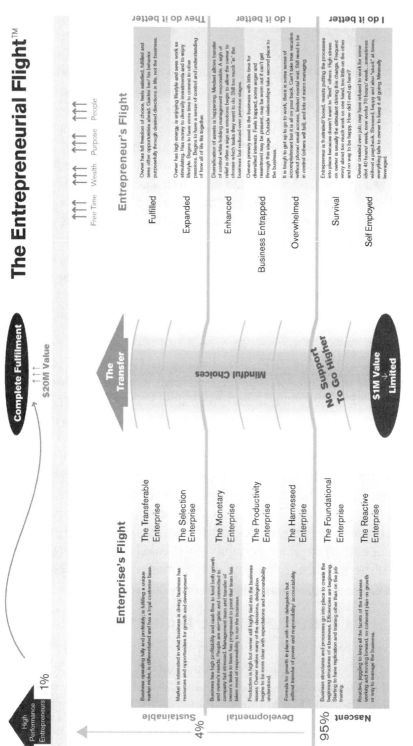

The Entrepreneurial Flight™

Complete Fulfillment

$20M Value

Free Time Wealth Purpose People

Entrepreneur's Flight

They do it better

Fulfilled — Owner has full freedom of choice, feels satisfied, fulfilled and sees other opportunities ahead. Guides her/ his behavior purposefully through desired directions in life, not the business.

Expanded — Owner has high energy, is enjoying lifestyle and sees work as stimulating. Has money to diversify investments and to enjoy lifestyle. Begins to leave more time to commit to other passions. Begins to have a sense of control and understanding of how all of life fits together.

I do it better

Enhanced — Diversification of assets is happening. Mindset allows transfer of control while holding management responsible. A sigh of relief is often a sign as emotions begin to allow the owner to choose which tasks they want to do. Still too much "in" the business but reduced over previous stages.

Business Entrapped — Owners primary asset is the business with little time for diversified interests. Feels trapped, some anger and resentment may be present, may be worn out if can't get through this stage. Outside relationships take second place to the business.

Overwhelmed — It is tough to get up to go to work, there is some sense of accomplishment but it is all on your back. Can't take that vacation without phone/ email access, limited mental rest. Still need to be in control (others will fail), and lots of micro managing.

I do it better

Survival — Entrepreneur is frustrated/ bored, resists putting the processes into place because doesn't want to "limit" others. High stress on owner is usually the stimulant driving this change. Frequent worry about too much work on one hand, too little on the other and no way to be happy. How did I end up here?

Self Employed — Owner created own job; may have refused to work for some idiot 40 hours/ week, now works 70 hours/ week...sometimes without a paycheck. Stressed, happy and also "stuck" at times, everything falls to owner to keep it all going. Minimally leveraged.

The Transfer

Mindful Choices

No Support To Go Higher

$1M Value → Limited

Enterprise's Flight

Sustainable

The Transferable Enterprise — Business operating fully and profitably, is fulfilling a unique market niche, is differentiated and has a loyal customer base.

The Selection Enterprise — Market is interested in what business is doing; business has resources and opportunities for growth and development.

Developmental

The Monetary Enterprise — Business has high profitability and cash flow to fund both growth and owner's needs. People are energetic and committed to company but stressed. Management team and transfer of owner's tasks has progressed to point that team has taken most of responsibility to run the business.

The Productivity Enterprise — Production in high but owner still highly tied into the business issues. Owner makes many of the decisions, delegation begins to be more clear with expectations and accountability understood.

The Harnessed Enterprise — Formula for growth in place with some delegation but without transfer of power and responsibility/ accountability.

Nascent

The Foundational Enterprise — Business structures and processes go into place to create the beginning structures of a business. Efficiencies are beginning. Starting to have replication and training other than on the job training.

The Reactive Enterprise — Reactive; juggling to keep all the facets of the business working and moving forward, no coherent plan on growth or way to manage the business.

High Performance Entrepreneurs 1%

4%

95%

Where do you fit as an entrepreneur? What level do you think your business is at?

If you could not work anymore, what would happen to your company?

- Who would make decisions? Would they be qualified to make the right decisions?
- Who would service your key clients and relationships?
- What would become of the company's culture without you?
- Who would keep the team members accountable?
- Who would assume your work assignments?

Wherever you see yourself on The Entrepreneurial Flight™, it is your choice…to stay where you are, to move down or to move up. In general, if you are in the Foundational, Harnessed or Productivity levels, it is difficult to stay there for long periods of time. The entrepreneur tends to get challenged and tired of living the Survival, Overwhelmed and Business-Entrapped life. Moving your business to and past the Monetary level or down to the Reactive level provides a more balanced life.

There are four key things that you must be able to do in order to move yourself, your business and your team up through The Entrepreneurial Flight™…..and I would like to share those with you.

4 KEY ENTREPRENEURIAL FLIGHT™ CHECKPOINTS:

1. Shift Yourself

We know that the entrepreneur must develop ahead of the business.

Most entrepreneurs start their businesses (and the first stage: the Nascent Stage of their Entrepreneurial Flight™) because they are good at delivering a product or service and want the freedom of "being their own boss." They are good at doing things themselves.

In order to move up the Entrepreneurial Flight™, the entrepreneur must be open and willing to shift their thinking and behavior. This, of course, implies that you must look inward to get to know "you." In most cases, we have a general sense of our strengths and weaknesses but we have not spent much time here as we don't like to see our flaws.

251

By diving in and gaining a clear understanding of "you", the entrepreneur acquires new knowledge. This knowledge enables new skills and behaviours to emerge, and as such, the entrepreneur now undertakes "mindfully guided actions" to move up the Entrepreneurial Flight™.

In the second stage, the Development Stage, the entrepreneur goes from being <u>good at their business</u> and doing it all themselves to <u>being good at business</u>, knowing how to work with and mentor others, learning business concepts to drive the business forward, and how to build a management team.

Once a strong management team is in place and the business is running smoothly, the entrepreneur moves into the last stage of the Entrepreneurial Flight™. This is the Sustainable Stage. Here, the entrepreneur has the choice of continuing to work in the business because it is still their life's passion or being completely out of the business and therefore just an investor in the business.

The movement between the levels involves a lot of change and is not accomplished quickly, but just think of the rewards....

Are you ready to shift yourself?

2. Create Opportunities for Others Intentionally

It is a great accomplishment in life to be able to create opportunities for others.

In creating a fully-sustainable company, you will move up the Entrepreneurial Flight™ and provide long term growth opportunities. You will be taking care of your family and the legacy that you began many years ago.

"What your mind focuses on, it sees." Entrepreneurs tend to have many ideas but they are not normally certain on where they are headed. By creating a clear plan, they are able to communicate clearly with others as to their vision, guide others, help them to be more effective, and in the end create more for all. Remember, you cannot move up The Entrepreneurial Flight™ by yourself!!

The development of the Strategic Flight Plan™ brings the team together. A facilitated retreat is a great way to get a great plan....it is efficient and always provides a better outcome for everyone involved. Teams with a written plan statistically outperform those without.

One important note: As you move up the Entrepreneurial Flight™ your business must strategically become more profitable and grow.

By being clear with a plan, setting it in motion and building a sustainable business that is making money and is providing growth for you and for all around you, you are creating opportunities for others.

3. Make your Business Perform

Establishing clear goals and targets is not always easy for most entrepreneurs. However, NOT to do so is like shooting arrows blindfolded. You will not be able to make the subtle adjustments in your aim to shoot accurately and hit your target performance without goals and targets.

Key Performance Indicators both financial and qualitative are those critical areas of your business that help you identify great performance or a problem early, so that you have time to self-correct your aim. For example, if you know that you need a certain level of sales to meet expenses, then it would be prudent to monitor sales to ensure that you are on track. Graphically, these are found on Dashboards. They are a quick and visual depiction of the areas that you need to watch for. They are made up of leading, current and trailing trends. Leading trends help you foresee incoming business, current trends give you information on the current state of your business, whereas trailing trends tend to be financial in nature. They are used to understand and clearly see how the business performs, how decisions are made and for teaching that next entrepreneurial team how you have run the business for so many years. As the entrepreneur reaches the Sustainable Stage, the dashboard will give insight into the business without having to be there physically.

To go up The Entrepreneurial Flight™, the business must perform. The business must be run well, run efficiently, and with sufficient cash flow to support growth in order to have the people and the business infrastructure (like a retreat, dashboard, trusted advisors, etc.) to be at the higher levels of The Entrepreneurial Flight™...that means you must *MAKE IT HAPPEN!*

As the entrepreneur, creating that thriving, profitable and sustainable business is one of the more important contributions that you will make in your life. In order to accomplish this, you must identify what is critical to your business, measure it, adjust to it and be accountable for it.

4. Live the Success

Entrepreneurism is to be celebrated. Entrepreneurs are the pioneers in our communities. They are building wealth for our families now and for generations to come. They are an integral part of our economy and the backbone of our countries.

There is a line of thinking that if you make too much money, you are being greedy, but where would we be as a nation without the entrepreneurial spirit that moves entrepreneurs to challenge the *status quo*?

So, to move up the Entrepreneurial Flight™, entrepreneurs must embrace success, for in sharing that success with others they are creating more opportunities for others and this is a "good thing." Go for it!

The benefits of reaching your Entrepreneurial Flight are:

- Harvesting the full potential of your company as it is no longer dependent on you.

- Freedom for the entrepreneur to stay in the business or transfer out…choices.

- Removal/reduction of business risk as a result of the early warning signals from the Dashboard.

- Empowering your Relationships as the owner ensures the continuity of employment to his staff and as a contributing member of the community in which the company operates.

What happens if you choose NOT to embrace these four keys in creating a sustainable company?

- Lack of control over the next transition. The chance of success without clear direction is greatly diminished.

- Erratic, poor business performance as a result of no monitoring or clear plan.

- Unforeseen challenges are likely as the team will burn out as they are not given a clear flight plan to conduct the day-to-day operations.

WHAT CHOICE WILL YOU MAKE WITH YOUR BUSINESS?

We all know that we each have much to offer in our own unique DNA way, and that our efforts and desires in large part are the only things in our path. When your child or grandchild asks you about your life's accomplishments, wouldn't you want to be able to say that you gave 110%?

Why not take your first Pre-Flight Check now, embrace the Entrepreneurial Flight™ journey and MAKE IT HAPPEN!!

About Kim

Kim LaBreche, CPA, CA has worked with thousands of individuals, entrepreneurs and executors to assist them with the complexities of tax planning and tax preparation, as well as business consulting at all levels from start-up to succession. She has been married for 22 years now to her loving husband Carl, and they have a 13-year old son, Justin. Kim loves to spend time golfing, camping, going to the beach and enjoying great wines.

Kim is passionate about making a difference in the lives of her clients and conducts "business with heart and soul." Her "Make It Happen" approach ensures that things will get done and her attention to detail in the delivery of her services is appreciated by those who work with her.

LaBreche Consulting is proud to be part of the vNacelle International Organization. The foundation of their collaborative consulting work is The Entrepreneurial Flight™, which is the leading business acceleration model integrating the entrepreneur and the enterprise.

DID YOU KNOW...

9 million of America's 15 million business owners were born in or before 1964, resulting in one business owner turning 65 every 57 seconds...... Businesses that are $10 million to $40 million are responsible for generating 65% of net jobs in the U.S. ... resulting in a great need for owners to be able to create sustainable businesses for future generations to come!

DO YOU HAVE A SUSTAINABLE BUSINESS?

To learn more about Kim LaBreche, LaBreche Consulting, how you as an entrepreneur can accelerate your Entrepreneurial Flight™ or to receive vNacelle's monthly vAccelerator reports on business, you can email Kim at: kim@labrecheconsulting.com or visit: www.labrecheconsulting.com

CHAPTER 26

PUT YOURSELF IN THE PALM OF YOUR CUSTOMER'S HAND:
HOW TO STAND APART WITH MOBILE MARKETING

BY LINDSAY DICKS

So you're out on the town with a friend – and, it turns out, neither of you really *know* the town.

That's because both of you just happen to be at a conference in a city you're unfamiliar with. Still, the sessions are over, it's a nice night and you want to find a great place with some amazing local cuisine so the two of you can catch up.

As you hit the street, you whip out your smartphone and Google the name of the place someone recommends, so you can check out the menu.

The problem is the restaurant's website isn't really made for smartphones. There are pop-up screens getting in the way of clicking where you need to click...and when you finally do click on the menu icon, you discover the menu is actually on a few PDF files that you have to download and try to read.

You do the download...your PDF app opens up the files...and, a few minutes later, you finally get to the menus. And that's when you find out the PDF type is tiny and almost impossible to read.

Luckily, while you're going through that ordeal, your friend spots a nice, upscale Sushi place on the corner, nudges you and points. And that restaurant you were going to go to? Well, they just lost that business. Why? Because they still don't understand the necessity for *mobile marketing.*

Do you?

You should – because otherwise, you might be like that first restaurant, and discover that potential customers aren't giving you the chance you deserve – or the revenue you need to earn!

THE ONLINE TIDE IS TURNING

As I write this, it's summer – and, according to a recent survey by Alliance Data Retail Services, *71 percent* of shoppers will use their smartphones to compare prices or download mobile coupons during their back-to-school shopping trips.

These are everyday moms and dads who, while driving from chain store to chain store, are looking for the best possible deals – and, of course, buying from those marketers who are most locked into leveraging their mobile presence!

From 2012 to 2013, according to an E-commerce Montetate report, the accessing of websites from smartphones and tablets *doubled.* More and more Internet users are using these much more convenient devices in bigger and bigger numbers – which is why sales of desktop computers keep falling and falling.

Obviously, people would rather access the internet where it's convenient for them (in bed, on the couch while watching TV, or, as noted, when actually shopping). Who wants to sit at a desk to search out something online – and feel like they're back at work?

That's why, as more and more people use smartphones and tablets to browse the Internet, marketers have to make some big adjustments to their approach – otherwise, like the restaurant with the unwieldy PDF menus, they're going to *drive* away their prospects rather than attract them.

Here are a few more startling mobile statistics from the Institute for Online Marketing:

- In 2013, close to a billion smartphones are expected to be sold.

- 53% of American consumers use online search engines on their smartphones – at least once a day!

- 4 out of 5 consumers use smartphones to shop.

- Tablets are expected to outsell PCs and laptops in 2013.

- 66% of Americans ages 24-35 own a smartphone.

- Going online through mobile devices is predicted to be bigger than fixed Internet devices (laptops and desktops) by 2018.

- Over 75% of mobile device users respond to *mobile-optimized sites* when making purchases.

- 64% of smartphone owners are now using their mobile devices to shop online.

And here's one more interesting statistic. It's my least favorite, but, hey, if the Institute of Online Marketing thinks it's significant...

- 75% of Americans bring their smartphones to the bathroom.

If that doesn't convince you that mobile devices have invaded every aspect of our lives – nothing will!

MAXIMIZING YOUR MOBILE IMPACT

Because mobile's explosive growth has been so recent – and because it has been on the heel of the explosive growth of the Internet as a whole – there's a temptation to treat it as an afterthought.

That's a big mistake. While marketers will certainly use many of the same online tools they used before – social media, email, websites, etc. – they have to think about using those tools in very different ways if they really want to connect with their mobile customers.

In this chapter, we're going to go through a few of the most prominent of these online marketing tools, and discuss how it's important to "change it up" for smartphones and tablets.

• Email

Almost half of all emails sent are now being opened on a mobile device. That means you have to seriously consider how to construct your emails so that they work the best on a mobile device.

First and foremost, you want to be as **concise and clear as possible with your messaging and your design.** Following this advice will improve the readability of your emails even on standard laptop/desktop screens (especially as our inboxes continue to fill up faster and faster and we have less time to consider every email that's comes our way), but, for mobile screens, this is an essential element that needs to be in place!

That means you want to **avoid multi-column formats** as much as possible. More than one column on a smartphone means you're either trying to scroll one way or the other to get all the information, or you're squinting as hard as you can to read all the tiny type in front of you.

And, speaking of tiny type, **avoid too-small fonts!** The minimum size for an email font should be 11 point for your body copy and 22 point for headlines.

In terms of content, try to feature just *one* strong Call-to-Action that's featured early on in your email copy - **tell people what you want them to do and make it easy for them to do it.** That means featuring a button or link that's easy for them to click on (remember, your readers are using fingertips instead of mouse buttons!).

Finally, **make sure there's a lot of strong contrast** in your email design (light colors against dark colors). Many people are using their mobile devices in bright sunlight and you want them to be able to see your message clearly. Also, **try not to rely too much on images**, as many mobile email systems turn them off by default – which means your recipients will be seeing a big box of white instead of that great photo you used!

• Facebook

Facebook currently ranks as one of the top three activities people engage in on their smartphones – with the average user checking on the social media site 14 times throughout the day.

Not only that, but, according to local marketing expert Balihoo, 91% of local business searches are done through Facebook. Yes, you read that right – 91%, or over 9 out of ten! And 63% of those searchers are more likely to buy from a business with information on a social media site.

So, guess what, marketers? Facebook is where you need to put your face!

Start by **checking out how your Facebook page appears on mobile platforms** – because it does end up looking differently. Make adjustments so that you look as professional as possible, even when you're down to handheld-size. Also, do what you can to make sure the information about your business is clear and as up-to-date as possible.

Next, **leverage the Facebook feature Nearby to your advantage**. If you're unfamiliar with Facebook Nearby, it will recommend businesses based on a user's "Likes," "check-ins" and "tags." That means you, in turn, should encourage as many people as possible to "Like" you on Facebook, to "check-in" when they patronize your business, and to "tag" you in photos.

The more of a presence you have on the site, the more you'll be recommended to other users who are friends of your current customers or clients. This is another reason to keep your business information as up-to-date as possible, even if you don't have a brick-and-mortar building that people come to.

Finally, **consider using Facebook paid ads** to really spread your business message. You can create a "virtual coupon" that can be redeemed online (and, yes, also on a mobile device), or **turn your posts into Facebook Promoted Posts** so they appear in other people's Facebook news feeds.

• Your Website

We're going to spend a little more time on this one, because it's so important.

Your website, of course, is a crucial sales tool. When you motivate online users to come there to check you out, it's a lot like a first date – in that, if something about you doesn't look quite right, the visitor to your site is not likely to "buy" into a customer relationship with you.

Odds are you've already done what you can to make your website as visitor-friendly and marketing-savvy as possible – at least if someone's checking you out on a desktop or a laptop. But...have you maximized your site for the mini-screens of mobile?

You've read all the incredible statistics so far that demonstrate just how many consumers out there are using their smartphones and tablets to make at-the-moment buying decisions, right? Well, I'm about to provide you with another one:

> *Despite* the mushrooming growth of mobile internet usage, only *26 percent* of small businesses have created a specifically-mobile website!

Scary, right? Especially, if you're among the 74% that haven't yet made the switch.

The first thing you need to know is that **a mobile site's web address is slightly different than the one for a full site**, in that the mobile version usually starts with an "m." In other words, if your name is Smith and you run a dental practice, your website address might be SmithDentistry.com – but your mobile site's address would be m.SmithDentistry.com.

Now, the user of the mobile device doesn't have to worry about that – he or she can just input the normal web address – and it should automatically redirect the user to the mobile site (of course, with all technology, it doesn't always work perfectly – so make sure you have a link to your mobile site at the top of your full site, just in case).

Now – how exactly should your mobile site differ from your full site? Here are a few important tips to keep in mind:

- Avoid using Flash and videos

Many mobile devices don't support Flash for videos or for website animation – so your site will just appear to be broken. Not only that, videos, of course, require a lot of time to load and eat up a great deal of data, so avoid them on your mobile home page. Your typical smartphone user will prize speed over a lot of time-consuming (and possibly non-functioning!) bells and whistles.

- Top off your mobile site with the most important info
Sometimes people are going to your site just to get a phone number or an address. So make sure that stuff is right at the top of your fast-loading mobile site! You'll want your name, address, contact info and a basic description of what your business is all about to appear before anything else!

- Make everything *EASY to READ!*
Have you ever gone to a website on your phone - and suddenly been stopped in your tracks by an endless procession of pop-up ads, videos, special offers and other frames that load on top of the website itself? And then – after you've done your best to clear all that away – you're left with a three column website that seems impossible to navigate on a screen that's two-plus inches by three-plus inches?

Again, a fast-loading simple straightforward design with easy-to-read type (in a large enough font) is the best way to go with your mobile site. And, as far as pop-ups go, try to avoid letting anything get in the way between you and your potential customer!

- Put everything "on tap"
Keeping in mind that your typical smartphone user wants information fast, so make it as easy as possible for them to get it. Have a button they can tap that will take them to a map of your location – and/or another button where they can tap to automatically dial your business number with their phone. Wherever possible, put that kind of crucial information at their fingertips – so they don't have to work too hard to get it.

- Put it to the test
Once you have your mobile site up and running, check to make sure it's working as it should – by taking a look at it on your smartphone, using your wireless carrier's data network. Type in your site's URL and see how long it takes to load – five seconds or less is awesome, ten seconds or more means you need to find ways to speed it up.

Ask your friends to also try it out on their mobile phones, especially if they have different phone models and different carriers, so you can get the full picture. Get their feedback on how easy your site is to navigate and whether it does the job for them.

Having a mobile-friendly site has become more and more critical to the success of a business. Google's own research has discovered that 74% of mobile users say they're more likely to return to a mobile-friendly site in the future – and 67% say that when they visit a mobile-friendly site, they're more likely to buy whatever product or service that site might be selling.

There are also a lot of *negatives* to not having a mobile-friendly site, according to Google, 61% of users said that if they didn't find what they were looking for right away on a mobile site, they'd quickly move on to another site. Not only that, but 48% of users say they feel frustrated and annoyed when they get to a site that's not mobile-friendly – and it made them feel as if the company didn't care about their business.

More and more, your potential new customers and clients are making their buying decisions on a mobile device – and they're anxious to engage with companies who understand just how big a small smartphone screen can be to their bottom line.

Whether you're a doctor, lawyer, entrepreneur, professional or business owner, mobile marketing is *the* platform to begin focusing on. The growth is undeniable and the opportunity is endless.

So put yourself in the palm of your potential customer's hand – and grab on to the future of marketing!

About Lindsay

Lindsay Dicks helps her clients tell their stories in the online world. Being brought up around a family of marketers, but a product of Generation Y, Lindsay naturally gravitated to the new world of on-line marketing. Lindsay began freelance writing in 2000 and soon after launched her own PR firm that thrived by offering an in-your-face "Guaranteed PR" that was one of the first of its type in the nation.

Lindsay's new media career is centered on her philosophy that "people buy people." Her goal is to help her clients build a relationship with their prospects and customers. Once that relationship is built and they learn to trust them as the expert in their field, then they will do business with them. Lindsay also built a proprietary process that utilizes social media marketing, content marketing and search engine optimization to create online "buzz" for her clients that helps them to convey their business and personal story. Lindsay's clientele span the entire business map and range from doctors and small business owners to Inc. 500 CEOs.

Lindsay is a graduate of the University of Florida. She is the CEO of CelebritySites™, an online marketing company specializing in social media and online personal branding. Lindsay is recognized as one of the top online marketing experts in the world and has co-authored more than 25 best-selling books alongside authors such as Brian Tracy, Jack Canfield (creator of the "Chicken Soup for the Soul" series), Dan Kennedy, Robert Allen, Dr. Ivan Misner (founder of BNI), Jay Conrad Levinson (author of the "Guerilla Marketing" series), Leigh Steinberg and many others, including the breakthrough hit *Celebrity Branding You!*

She was also selected as one of America's PremierExperts™ and has been quoted in *Newsweek*, the *Wall Street Journal, USA Today*, and *Inc.* magazine as well as featured on NBC, ABC, and CBS television affiliates speaking on social media, search engine optimization and making more money online. Lindsay was also recently brought on FOX 35 News as their Online Marketing Expert.

Lindsay, a national speaker, has shared the stage with some of the top speakers in the world, such as Brian Tracy, Lee Milteer, Ron LeGrand, Arielle Ford, David Bullock, Brian Horn, Peter Shankman and many others. Lindsay was also a Producer on the Emmy-winning film Jacob's Turn.

You can connect with Lindsay at:
Lindsay@CelebritySites.com
www.twitter.com/LindsayMDicks
www.facebook.com/LindsayDicks

CHAPTER 27

INNOVATIVE HOME SELLING STRATEGIES — GUARANTEED TO MAKE YOUR HOME STAND OUT, DRAW THE BEST BUYERS, AND GET YOU TOP DOLLAR

BY RIC GOODMAN

Back in the mid nineteen eighties, a close friend and I were sitting around my apartment drinking a few beers, when an infomercial came on the TV. It was about real estate investing with no money down.

A gentleman by the name of Robert G. Allen was hosting the program. He was the king of 'no money down' real estate and was conducting a 5-day teaching boot camp right here in San Diego. My friend and I quickly decided that we had to attend this workshop and learn from Robert Allen who was the best in the industry. Neither one of us had any money so we had to borrow the money to pay for the boot camp. We also didn't own any business attire, so we had no choice but to go to the nearest Thrift store to buy a suit and tie. The suits looked ridiculous on us. They were baggy and far from the right size.

The training, however, was amazing. We learned from some of the top real estate investors of the time – including Robert Allen himself. We became sponges for real estate knowledge and had to learn more from these people. Soon after the training, my friend and I became employed by Robert Allen and his company, Challenge Systems. Working with Robert Allen and his company allowed me to be exposed to other high level individuals that Robert Allen aligned himself with. Such great people as Anthony Robbins, Brian Tracy, Jay Abraham, Denis Waitley and others.

After several months with Challenge Systems, I achieved the level of Senior Property Analyst and was appointed a "Mentor" position. As a mentor I was sent out to different cities around the country to spend three days out in the field with a small group of investors –teaching them hardnosed real estate investing. This was awesome. I loved this work.

Unfortunately, it only lasted a few years. The company had some internal issues and scaled down drastically, forcing us all to find other work. I decided to get my real estate license and work in the mortgage/ real estate industry. However, I was still able to keep mentoring off and on for Robert Allen.

After working in the business for 14 years, the mortgage/real estate industry had become tainted by the unscrupulous lenders and real estate agents who had completely turned the industry on its head. …Not to mention the "Wall Street Kings" of unscrupulousness. I had witnessed so much of it first hand that I couldn't watch it any longer. I sold all my rental properties and I quit cold turkey…

I am an artist at heart, so I decided this was a wonderful time to explore the possibility of making a living in the art world. I went back to school and trained in new areas of computer arts. I loved every minute of the journey… except the part of not making money. Have you heard the term, "starving artist"? Well, there's a reason for it. The art world is a difficult place to make a living.

I then tried my hand in the restaurant business. I bought a restaurant in downtown San Diego, changed the name to Ricardo's Fresh Mex and proceeded to lose money at a record pace. It was only open for 11 months, so you've probably never heard of it.

During this three-year hiatus from the industry, while I was trying to market myself as an artist, I went back to the marketing strategies and teachings of Jay Abraham, who I was introduced to while working for Robert Allen. I studied his strategies and those of other marketing experts like Gary Halbert and Dan Kennedy. As I began to get really intrigued by leaning about marketing strategies, I also realized how much I missed the real estate industry. Both marketing and real estate turned me on and I thought combining the two would be a great idea.

The real estate industry had developed such a negative reputation that I had second thoughts about being associated with it. I had always worked hard and honestly with my clients. **There were real estate agents putting a client's property in the MLS and hoping it would sell, without putting in any other effort.** I thought **how WRONG it was that hardworking folks, in this day and age, couldn't get a fair shake, or an honest effort from their agent. If this economy isn't hard enough, you now have to worry about the agent who you've hired and trust, putting his or her own best interests in front of yours.**

If there is one thing I know well, it's real estate. And now with my strategic marketing knowledge, I can help people keep more of their money. I've developed some creative marketing strategies that help people do just that.

HERE ARE FOUR OF THESE STRATEGIES

I. Demand Indicator
First we need to know how much demand there is for our product. In this case, the product is your home.

Absorption Rate is something most sophisticated agents will use to try to gauge the direction of any given real estate market. Absorption Rate shows how many months it will take to exhaust the supply of homes on the market. This method tells us what has happened 2-3 months ago. This method uses a relationship between "Active" listings and "Sold" properties.

However, I use something far more sophisticated. I call it the **Demand Indicator.** This method utilizes the relationship between "Active" listings and "Pending" properties. (Pending properties are homes prospective buyers have already committed themselves to purchasing in your specific neighborhood and are waiting to close escrow). For example: If there are 6 "Active" listings within a one mile radius of your home, and 12 "Pending" listings within that same radius, we conclude that there are 2 prospective buyers for every 1 home in that specific market place. This would make for a fairly hot "Seller's" market and we would therefore price the home more aggressively knowing there is greater demand. On the other hand, if the numbers were reversed, if we had more homes on the market than buyers, we would have to price and market the home according to the low demand. What's most important about Demand Indicator is that it gives us a trajectory of any local market in "Real Time." We don't care as much about what happened 2-3 months ago as the Absorption Rate projects. We want to know what's happening in your specific neighborhood today, right now, in "Real Time".

I make sure that we have "Real Time" information that makes us the **smartest** principals in the negotiation with any buyer or their agent.

I perform a **Demand Indicator Analysis** every week your home is on the market. This will enable us to keep our finger on the pulse of what is happening in your neighborhood. We will always know the trajectory of the local market.

Now that we know what the Demand is for your home, we need to know who our best buyer is and who will be willing to give us "top dollar" for our home. Whether the demand is high or low, it still benefits us to have as many of the "right" buyers exposed to your home as possible.

That is where our next few strategies come into play. I call this next strategy:

II. Echelon Marketing
Echelon Marketing - is marketing to specific buyers, whether they are moving up in the echelon of price and amenities, or downsizing into the lower echelon of home prices and/or size., This demographic might include the Empty Nester who's children have all grown and moved out of the household, leaving the home too large for just the remaining couple.

What most of my competitors do, but I do differently, is "Randomly Market" your home to buyers. They simply try to expose your home to as many sources as possible and "pray" that they catch a buyer for your home. They really don't have any idea how to find the "right" or "most appropriate" buyer for your home.

Many of my competitors sometimes call Standard Services "Full Service" in an attempt to impress you. But honestly there are certain things you should expect to get when you list your home, no matter who your Real Estate Agent is or how much they charge for their services.

You should expect your Agent to:

- Hold Open Houses
- Get Colored Flyers
- Enter your home into the MLS
- Hold Broker Opens for your home
- Send out "Just Listed" postcards to neighbors
- Post your home on the web

This is where my **Echelon Marketing** strategy comes into play and will help me sell your home faster and for top dollar. With Echelon Marketing, I know to a 70% probability where your buyer lives, how far people move up in price when moving, how far away they move, and how long they stay in their homes before moving. I know how much money they make or need to make in order to purchase your home, and how much "Demand" there is for their home in case they need to sell in order to purchase your home.

We now know your "most appropriate" buyer better than anyone!

We take all of these statistics and information and turn it into knowledge. Using this knowledge we drive more potential buyers to our listings, which in turn creates multiple offers and higher sales prices for my clients. This is how we uncover the buyer who is willing to give us "top dollar".

III. Reaching our "Top Dollar" Buyer

Once we have established who our target buyers are, we need to reach out to them and let them know about your home. One way I have found that works great is through direct response mail marketing. It is imperative that our prospective "top dollar" buyers actually receive and read our offer or message. We can send letters or post cards to these prospects, but that doesn't mean they will actually read it.

Most people open their mail while standing over their trash can. If our message looks like junk mail, or mail they're not interested in, it gets thrown into the trash and never read. One way of better assuring that our message is received and read, is to get creative. I've tried many different avenues for this, and have found a great little niche. It's called object mail or 3D mail.

3D mailers are pieces that are not regular flat letters. They have some bulk to them. This creates curiosity. The person receiving this mail can't help themselves, they must open their mail and see what it is. One really effective way is to send our message in a large bright red "Express Mail" envelope with a little 'worry doll' stuffed inside. Our message would say that the homeowner can stop worrying about what to do with their lack of space and can solve their problem by buying a larger home. We show them how your home would be the perfect solution.

Another example is mailing our message in a vinyl "Bank Bag".. Think about it - if you were to receive a bank bag in the mail, wouldn't you want to know what was inside? We don't stop there, we make sure our message is tied to the bank bag. Our message might say something about how much money they will be able to bank away by downsizing from the large home they're living in now, to your smaller home. Another example is to send our message in a small "message in a bottle." This is an actual plastic bottle with our message rolled up inside. The bottom of the bottle unscrews for them to retrieve our message. Our message could be a little "treasure map" to the home we are marketing, with a few key details to pique their interest. These are just a few of the ways we can get our message into the hands of prospective buyers and actually read.

IV. Open House Done Differently

Once we've marketed to our target of buyers, we still need to expose the home to as many others as possible. A great way is by holding an open house. First we send out invitations to all the neighbors inviting them over for a "private showing" of our new listing. On the day of the Open House we strategically place signs around the neighborhood directing people to our event. But these aren't the regular signs you see other agents using. These signs are funny and entertaining. They use rhymes to describe a home's special features. We write them in a style similar to the "Burma Shave" signs of the fifties.

Here are a few examples:

- "You're going to smile when you see the style of this tile."
- "Grab your Spouse, you have to check out this House."
- "This home has a Kitchen that is absolutely bitchin."
- "You're going to be wiping off the drool when you see this pool."

We have over 50 different signs designed and ready that address a variety of amenities or attributes that could pertain to any home or situation. We use a handwritten style of font as we want the signs to look like they were created for each specific property, almost as if the homeowner themselves made the sign. We find that when people arrive at the home, they are more friendly and relaxed. It definitely sets a fun mood and also increases the volume of people that show up, hence increasing our chances of getting multiple offers and top dollar for the home.

So, there you have it, some cutting edge marketing strategies for getting "top dollar" for your home sale.

Remember that friend of mine? The one I was sitting around drinking beer with at the beginning of this chapter? His name is Chief Denney, and he is currently the star of the TV show "Flipping San Diego" on A&E. We are still great friends and still work together regularly. I help him find homes to flip and then strategically market the homes when they're finished to get him "top dollar."

"I've utilized Ric Goodman and his real estate expertise in locating and marketing real estate for many years. The strategies and marketing skills that Ric brings to the table make a world of difference in my bottom line. Due to Ric's hard work and knowledge, we were able to sell for more than I expected on several occasions. I frequently have large amounts of money on the line, and the immense trust I have in Ric makes it easy to sleep at night. I would highly recommend Ric Goodman and his services to anyone looking to buy, sell or invest in real estate.

- Chief Denney
Star of A&E's "Flipping San Diego"

About Ric

Ric Goodman is a San Diego native and has been involved in the real estate industry since 1989, where at the age of 25, he achieved the level of Senior Property Analyst for San Diego-based Challenge Systems, Inc. While working with Challenge Systems, Inc. he traveled the country teaching hard-nosed real estate investing with America's best-selling author, Robert G. Allen. Ric became a licensed Realtor in 1993 and has continued to teach and mentor buyers, sellers and investors in the wonderful world of real estate. During this time he's been a Mortgage broker and a Realtor, completing both parts of the transaction for his clients. Through over 20 years of experience, Ric has developed unparalleled negotiating skills, expert mortgage knowledge, created cutting-edge marketing strategies, and had gained extensive real estate wisdom. This makes him an indispensable team member to have on either side of your real estate transaction. Over the years he has honed his skills and is one of San Diego's premier Realtors.

Ric has studied under some of the top marketing experts in the country such as Dan Kennedy, Jay Abraham, and Gary Halbert. He has developed some of his own marketing strategies which he utilizes to obtain top dollar for his clients when selling their homes and investment properties. He still studies these experts and others to stay in tune with all of the cutting-edge strategies in the marketing world.

Ric is a member of the San Diego Association of Realtors, California Association of Realtors, and National Association of Realtors. This keeps his finger on the pulse of the real estate industry and informed about any changes that he and his clients may need to be aware of.

He works closely with some of this country's top-notch real estate investors including Chief Denney who is currently the star of the TV show "Flipping San Diego" on A&E.

If you'd like to contact Ric, you can go to his website at: www.GoodRicMan.com .

CHAPTER 28

SUCCESS IS WHERE THE SPIRIT LEADS YOU: THE SECRET OF SPIRITOLOGY

BY ROBERT FULTON

Some years ago, immediately after a church service, our congregation was having a cookout. A girl that I called Little Ruth was playing with a balloon – and, as often happens with kids and balloons, it got away from her and floated up into a very large tree. And there it stayed, caught in the branches – and too high for Little Ruth to reach and too high for anyone to climb.

Well, Little Ruth came over to me and begged me to get that balloon for her. With only a broomstick available, I kept reaching up in that tree to shake the balloon free but kept falling short. But she encouraged me to go on. She kept saying, "You can do it, Reverend Fulton, you can do!" Everybody at the cookout was watching! And somehow, I don't even remember how I did, but that balloon came down and everybody cheered with amazement.

Her words stay with me until this day – and it's the message I want to deliver in this chapter: You can do it!

This chapter is going to no doubt "stand apart" from the rest of the content of this book. I'm not offering nuts-and-bolts business advice. I'm not offering breakthrough marketing techniques. No – I want to talk about something more important than all that. It is, however, something that truly brings you success not only in the outside world, but also inside yourself.

You may not be a believer in spiritual matters, so you might not understand what I'm talking about. I have to laugh at myself when I wonder how I would react to this, if I hadn't had the experiences I'm about to tell you about. I might have the same mindset of doubt and disbelief that many of you may have.

But if you are indeed a "Doubting Thomas," someone who is not open to changing his mind about the message I'm delivering, this chapter may not be for you. On the other hand, if you're receptive to a change of your mind and your heart, if you are looking for someone or something to believe in, you just might find what you're searching for in my story.

RECEIVING THE WORD THROUGH SPIRITOLOGY

What I want to discuss is something I call Spiritology, a theological concept revealed to me by God through the Holy Spirit, as I was writing my dissertation for my doctoral degree. I asked the earthly question, "How can mankind – beings who are merely human and locked into a logical way of reasoning that only works in the physical world – connect, comprehend and truly experience a relationship with a spiritual God?"

That question was prompted by my study of a statement by the Apostle Paul, who said in 1 Timothy 2:5, "There is one God and one mediator between God and men, the man Christ Jesus," as well as by God's word as detailed in Isaiah 1:18, "Come now, and let us reason together, saith the Lord."

But how should we reason together? How can we truly achieve a meaningful relationship?

Surprisingly, the answer came to me directly from God, when I heard Him speak to me through the power of His Holy Spirit, softly saying, "We (referring to myself, God and Jesus Christ) are already in a Spiritological Relationship." God went on to reveal that 'a Spiritological Relationship' is only possible through His power of connecting the earthly with the spiritual, through believing in His Son, Jesus Christ, who came to us here on earth to forge an eternal link between the sacred and humanity.

Again, I'm sure there are some reading the above paragraph that might doubt this account. I was a doubter as a child and questioned everything and everybody. I grew up around the corner from an older cousin named Cricket, who was always trying to teach me things I didn't know about. I didn't always believe him, so I would always say, "Prove it, Cricket, prove it!"

It got to the point where he started calling me "The Prove It Kid" – and that's who I intend to be in this chapter, the person who will prove how the power of God transformed my life – and how He can transform yours.

HOW GOD PROVED HIMSELF TO "THE PROVE IT KID"

I'd like to tell you a little more about my journey before I discuss more of the specifics of Spiritology – because it's important for you to understand how He made me ready for our connection.

When I was a child, my whole household was full of music. My dad played the piano, my mother's twin sister played, her oldest sister played, and my older brother played. All I wanted to do was play too.

Luckily, I could always sing – most everybody else did too. Music was everywhere in my house and throughout the neighborhood. Since our home contained one of the few pianos in the area, many local people from the churches and other community groups would gather at our home. Me, I'd be sitting on the stair steps and watching, observing great musicians perform – and wanting desperately to be one of them.

I was about 11 or 12 and I would come home from school every day and run my fingers across the keys, pretending I could play. But I couldn't, I didn't have the gift and I would talk to God openly and ask, "Why, Lord? Why can't I play when so many others can?" The person who really inspired me was another boy my age who was a genuine prodigy – he ended up going to Julliard and actually playing piano for Jimi Hendrix.

So I wanted to play like him. I wanted to play like the greats, like Ray Charles and Errol Garner - I just wanted to play. I talked to God every day seemingly for several months, asking for this blessing.

Finally, one day, it clicked in – and I was playing a simple song, but I was playing it. I said, "Lord, you did it, I'm playing!" And I called Cricket and Gwen, my cousins who lived around the block – and they came running around the corner – to see the 'The Prove It Kid' prove himself. That was the first real miracle I experienced happening to me – and from then on, I knew to talk things over with God when I was pursuing an important goal or needed some higher spiritual guidance.

MORE MUSICAL MOMENTS AND DEVELOPMENT OF THE SPIRITOLOGICAL PERSPECTIVE

After more than 11 years as a founding member of the 60's soul group, The Emperors, and having not followed through on my dream and vision of our being recording artists that reached the world through music, I felt led to explore other avenues.

Fortunately, the Holy Spirit was there to lead me once again, after I left a rehearsal with a group I had begun playing piano for but had decided wasn't the right fit for me, God used a young saxophone player who I had only met two hours earlier to show me a new path. He said to me "You have a unique style of playing. I think that we should start a band and call it *The Bobby Fulton Trio*. Immediately, I recognized God's presence and agreed.

After recruiting a young drummer who the saxophonist knew, I again talked to God about a "hook" that we could use that would make our band "stand apart." He reminded me of the "Wednesday Night Prayer Meetings" that were a tradition in the church – and, right then, it came to me that our group would be billed as being "Soulville" and we would perform "Soulful Sounds from Soulville."

One more notable event happened. After showing up with our equipment at a nightclub that had given us a start and where we now played regularly, a club manager replaced the group's poster with a hand-made sign that read "Deacon Bobby Fulton and His Disciples from Soulville." When I asked what was the meaning behind replacing our sign, the bartender said "Your band plays Sanctified Music." That "Word" went by me - and it didn't return in a solid way until another "Musical Moment" that I will tell you about later, and when I was writing my dissertation and reviewing where God was trying to reach me earlier in life.

MOMENT IN THE POCONO MOUNTAINS – ONE DAY IN MY LIFE

When you are young, however, it's easy to draw away from God. For myself, it came to the point where I felt like a Jonah, caught up in the belly of a great fish. Instead of a whale, however, it was the world that had swallowed me up. My musical career had progressed to the point where I had experienced a great deal of success with The Emperors and with Soulville-Jaywalking Records; we had several successful singles in the 60's, including the Emperors' big Hit, "Karate," and the R&B hits by the Continental Four, "I Don't Have You" and "Day By Day."

After all that excitement, I finally made time to attend college, even though I was now thirty-three years old. One day, on a Saturday afternoon, I was in my one-room efficiency apartment, practicing on my Fender Rhoads piano for a program the next day at a local church nearby in the Poconos, and, after being unable to write a new song, I began to seek God's intervention as I played just a short chorus and sang these words over and over: "Show Me, Lord, Show Me, Lord."

In a startling moment, God caught me by surprise, as He spoke to me within through His Holy Spirit and His anointed voice of revelation.

For several hours, God spoke – and I listened – as He reminded me of my life, my youth, friends and loved ones, my music success, and my travels around the world, even how he brought me safely home from Vietnam. At that moment, images of Moses on the mountaintop and Martin Luther King famously proclaiming, "I've been to the mountaintop and I've seen the other side" flashed through my mind.

God said that if He happened to take my life that day, I should have no complaints. Now, He told me, there was something He wanted me to do for Him. "What's that?" I asked in my mind. He replied, "I want you to use your gifts and talents that you used with the Emperors and with Soulville, but, this time, do it for *Me*. I want you to testify and tell others what I've done for you and what I'll do for them, if they seek Me."

Astonished and befuddled, I asked another question, "What's the world going to say, those established preachers and teachers, and people that know that my entire life to this point has been devoted to R&B and Rock n' Roll music? I haven't studied any aspect of theology!"

God replied, "Just be my vessel, and I will tell you when to speak and what to say, and my Spirit will speak through you. " I believed the Lord and accepted His call.

My calling gave birth to Gospel Music Ministries International (GMMI) and its Christian Talent Search Crusade, to the Gospel Connection Outreach Church 'Coming to You' and 'Spiritology Institute.'

My work in Pastoral Ministry and Human Relations led to the Spiritological Deferral Method – whereby deferring to God's jurisdiction activates Spiritology's "Spiritological lens," that enables men to focus farther with more clarity and to discover hidden possibilities not readily available to the natural mind or eye. Similarly, but not Spiritologically, we see courts with cross-jurisdictional issues making deferrals from one jurisdiction to another.

MUSIC, HARMONY AND THEORY – OUR MODEL FOR SPIRITOLOGY

Being a musician, singer and songwriter led to my study of music, harmony and theory. During a masters class in Schools and Community, the Holy Spirit led me to study if there were any similarities or correlations between relationships in Music Harmony and Theory that could be useful in creating peace and harmony in schools and communities.

By lining up the four primary voices in music (soprano, alto, tenor, bass) with the four primary voices in schools (principals, teachers, students and parents), I found there to be correlations between Music Harmony and Theory dynamics and nuances impacting schools and communities.

SPIRITOLOGICAL KEYS

God revealed Music Harmony and Theory to be our model for Spiritology. As music has its concert key that allow instruments of different keys to play together, even voices of the universe, Spiritology has its 'Spiritological Keys' that allows men of every birth to enter into a Spiritological Relationship with God. Our GMMI Gospel Connection Outreach Ministries and 'Spiritology Institute' are testaments of my 'Calling to Ministry' and God's revelation to me of our 'Spiritological Relationship.' It's also a 'Thank You' to God of the Holy Spirit and to His only begotten Son, Jesus, who holds, and is, the Key to Spiritology. And that's the reason 'Spiritology' stands apart from everything that is only human and merely spiritual.

Obviously, Spiritology is a powerful concept that can and should be discussed over many pages. But space is limited here and I would like to conclude with a little tip that I learned about Spiritology's "Spiritological Keys" and how they can benefit you:

And that tip is this: Before I actually started playing the piano, I would run my fingers over the keys and *act* like I could already play! In other words, begin learning the keys and let God lead you to success. The lesson is the same one as I began this chapter with, and that is what the words of Little Ruth said to me: *"You Can Do It!"*

I came to know God through my music and through the gifts that God gave me. God wants to do the same for you when it comes to whatever your passion is. That is where you will be able to find God within yourself.

But you must seek Him. You have to *ask, seek, and knock*. Then, you'll find what you're looking for and that door that's been closed will be opened. As I've told you, God proved Himself to me, the original "Prove It Kid" – and he can make a believer out of you, if you're not one already. And if you aren't, I hope that you will make your connection and experience the benefits of a Spiritological Relationship.

It's really up to you. Which brings to mind the hit single, "It's Your Thing," performed by the legendary Isley Brothers, who I once had the privilege to play behind. As the lyrics to that song go, "It's Your Thing. Do What You Wanna Do!" When you don't seek God, that reminds me of another song, our first release for Soulville Records by the Soulville All-Stars – "Nobody to Blame But Myself!"

Thanks for taking the time to read my chapter. I hope that you will decide to step out and 'Stand Apart,' and let the Holy Spirit lead you to your success.

"You Can Do It!"

About Robert

Robert J. Bobby Fulton, Ph.D. is a Minister of the Gospel; Founder and Senior Pastor of Gospel Music Ministries International (GMMI) and the Gospel Connection Outreach Church Coming to You, home of GMMI Gospel Connection Outreach Missionaries, and Spiritology Institute; Producer of the GMMI Christian Talent Search Crusade and Arts Fellowship; Ordained a Bishop by the All-Faith Missionary World Outreach; an NCCA Licensed Clinical Pastoral Counselor and Diplomat of the National Board of Christian Clinical Therapists; an International Representative for the Sarasota Academy of Christian Counseling; former Western Regional Education and Community Services Supervisor for the Pennsylvania Human Relations Commission; later with the Pittsburgh Commission on Human Relations; Recognized as an Ambassador for Peace by the Interreligious and International Federation for World Peace; aka Bobby Fulton from Soulville: Musician-Singer-Songwriter-Bandleader; Original Member of the Emperors, Recording Artists of "Karate," (Mala Records); and the Soul-Exotics (Terri Records); Founder of Soulful Sounds from Soulville Productions and the Soulville-Jaywalking Records Group - Producers of the Soulville All-Stars, the Continental Four and various other artists; an Artist and Presenter of 'Soulful Sounds from Soulville: The Soulville-Jaywalking Records Story' compilation (GetHip Records); Songwriter for the Penna. Turnpike – 'People Are Falling In Love' (Perception Records); Founding Staff Advisor and Minister of Music for the East Stroudsburg University Gospel Choir; While Secretary of the Upward Bound Program at East Stroudsburg University of Pennsylvania, authored and composed the "Upward Bound" Song, adopted by the Pennsylvania and Mid-Atlantic Association of Educational Opportunity Programs; 2003 Distinguished Alumni Award Honoree by the Tri-State Consortium of Opportunity Programs in Higher Education (NY-PA-NJ); Entrepreneur - Bobby Fulton Enterprises and Supertown-Music of Pittsburgh; Business Management Diploma from La Salle Extension University; Degrees from the University of Pittsburgh, B.A, Self-Designed; East Stroudsburg University of Pennsylvania, M.Ed., Secondary Education; International Seminary, Ph.D. in Theology.

Contact information:
www.bobbyfulton.com
Tel: 412-488-7191

CHAPTER 29

STAND APART WITH YOUR OWN BRANDED FILM: USING STORYSELLING TO FUEL YOUR SUCCESS

BY NICK NANTON & JW DICKS

He always had a big mouth. And it was always getting him in trouble.

And he certainly wasn't good at dealing with authority – that was one of the big reasons he dropped out of college during his freshman year. Another reason was he wanted to start his own underground newspaper at the age of eighteen – it was the sixties and he had a lot to say.

Eventually, he built the paper up into a statewide success – and a national magazine came knocking on his door. He became a star writer there – and a few years later, he was promoted to editor.

But then he refused to run an article the publishers were adamant about putting in the next issue. He said it was inaccurate and overblown. They said…he was fired.

He had been editor for less than a year.

He sued for wrongful termination and settled the suit out of court for $58,000. But what was he going to do now? He was thirty-four years old and unemployed - with a reputation for being difficult. He knew he would quickly burn through the money if he didn't do something to get himself back into the spotlight quickly.

So…with the settlement money, he decided to make a movie about his hometown and the economic difficulties it was having in the late 1980's recession. But he made it what he called an "anti-documentary" – something that was entertaining and fun to watch. And he made himself the star.

In 1989, Michael Moore finished *Roger and Me* – and it instantly became a critically acclaimed financial success. And because Moore's face was all over the film, *he* instantly became a celebrity – and parlayed his newfound fame into more movies, a TV series, books, an Oscar win and a multi-millionaire dollar career.

And it all started with a Branded Film.

The Power of the Branded Film

Whether you're for Michael Moore or against him, we'd like you to look beyond his politics for the purposes of this book, and, instead, focus on just how a Branded Film jumpstarted his international success – and can also make you Stand Apart in the marketplace.

Now, if he hadn't been fired from the left-wing publication, *Mother Jones,* he might have done okay as a TV journalist – but no one would have offered him multi-million dollar movie and book deals on the basis of that.

Instead, he created a memorable logline – "A fat unkempt working class guy from Michigan takes on corporate America" – and brought it to life in a compelling narrative. And he did a magnificent job of StorySelling himself to liberal Hollywood and sympathetic moviegoers across the country.

There's no more effective way of branding yourself than telling the proper story about yourself – a process we call "StorySelling"™. And there's no better way to StorySell than with a film. You can actually bring your logline and whatever narrative you choose to life – and show your customers who you are and what you're all about in a persuasive and dramatic fashion.

And you don't have to make a documentary filmmaker to make this work for you. Anybody remember the inspirational sports movie, *Rudy,* about a 5' 6" kid with bad grades who worked his butt off to get into Notre Dame and into one of their games? Well, the guy who made his dream come true, Rudy Ruettiger, ended up working in a boring insurance company job after that moment of glory – but somehow convinced Hollywood to turn his college triumph into a feature film. Now, instead of quoting insurance rates, he began earning tens of thousands of dollars to tell his story to adoring crowds.

It took a Branded Film to make that happen.

WHY BRANDED FILMS WORK

There are many reasons Branded Films are essential to creating a powerful Celebrity Brand - here are a few of them:

- **Films Make Stars**

  …and isn't that just what you want out of your Celebrity Brand?

  In a Branded Film, you are the "star" - the central figure in your own story, who is presented as a likeable and magnetic individual. The audience responds to you on a gut level that just can't happen with the printed word. If Michael Moore hadn't put himself in his own movie, he never would have had the career clout he enjoyed after the fact.

- **Films Tell Stories**

  When the narrative behind your StorySelling is actually brought to life in a Branded Film, people take it in on a very deep level – and they *remember* it. Why? Because you're able to do your StorySelling in the most compelling and dramatic way.

  In any popular film, various time-tested film techniques - such as how you use editing, music, lighting and camera angles to create moods and effects - are put to work in order to make the story as exciting and suspenseful as possible. An effective Branded Film uses those same sophisticated techniques - and combines them with real people and real locations to give your narrative an authentic power that a Hollywood film can't match. Just ask Michael Moore – the only movie he made with actors and a concocted story (*Canadian Bacon*) bombed badly at the box office.

285

- **Films Control the Message**

  With a Branded Film, interviews and location shooting must be highly planned and scheduled, and the interview questions designed to shape the proper StorySelling narrative. It's one of the secrets of Michael Moore's success, by the way – he's been called out repeatedly for deceptive editing and shading reality to make the StorySelling in his films more pointed and dramatic.

- **Films Allow People to Know Who You Are**

  In a book, you can write that someone's attractive. In a film, you can *see* that a person is attractive. The difference is crucial - in the first instance, someone is telling you something that you have to accept as being true, in the second instance, *you see it for yourself.*

  Books are great at conveying ideas and demonstrating your expertise on a subject; they are essential to personal branding. Films do something else entirely - they allow your audience to experience *who you are* - how you walk, talk and look - and respond to you in a *personal* way.

- **There's Never Been a Better Time to Make One**

  A Branded Film is a relatively new arrow in the marketing quiver of entrepreneurs and business owners, for two key reasons, both having to do with technological advances.

  Reason number one: Creating and editing high quality films has become much more *affordable* in recent years. You no longer need millions of dollars to create a professional Hollywood-level production. Equipment is much cheaper, more people have access to train on that equipment, and post-production can be accomplished on computers not that much more powerful (or expensive) than your average home or office PC.

  Reason number two: Online video has exploded on the Internet, becoming much more prevalent and powerful. That means a branded film can be shared not only through YouTube.com, but also through popular social media sites such as Facebook and LinkedIn.

  Of course, for Celebrity Branding to really be effective, you need to stand out from the herd. Most Branded Films fall far short of the mark in this regard. Even though there are an incredible amount of videos and films being posted to the Internet, most of the ones that attempt branding do it in the most basic way possible; the person merely speaks to the camera and explains who they are or what they do. This is effective as a quick introduction to a website, or explaining a specific product or service, but, as far as StorySelling a brand goes, it only can do so much – especially if it ends up looking more like a hostage video than a real *movie*.

A successful Branded Film, in contrast, boasts high production values and an impactful emotional story. It raises the bar for the entrepreneur who really wants to present the most polished and professional brand possible, while, at the same time, make the strongest possible emotional connection to both customers and non-customers.

This is just the route the Justin Bieber management team took to boost their client's already red-hot profile when they released the Bieber documentary, *Never Say Never*, to theatres in 2011. This was the ultimate Branded Film event - and was a giant financial success as well, grossing over 70 million dollars in the U.S. alone. As *Forbes* put it, "*Never Say Never* was a brilliant way for the Bieber brand team to tell its story and, just as brilliantly, get it out there when the media wind was at its back. When you're on a roll, do what you can to keep the momentum going."[*]

PIXAR'S STORYSELLING SECRETS

As we've noted repeatedly, the most important facet to a Branded Film is the *story* you decide to tell. Storytelling is an art – so we thought we'd close this chapter with some winning advice from people who are today's leading practitioners of it. We're talking about Pixar, the most successful movie studio of all time, with thirteen feature films to its credit that have grossed over seven billion dollars worldwide as of this writing.

Pixar, originally funded by Steve Jobs, has enjoyed an unprecedented combination of artistic and commercial success. Probably the biggest reason for that success is that *they always put story first*. Recently, one of Pixar's storyboard artists, Emma Coats, revealed many of the guidelines the company uses for their storytelling process – and we're going to share a few of them with you, to inspire you to fully develop *your* Branded Film narrative.

---

[*] Allen Adamson, "The Secret Behind Justin Bieber's Brand Success," February 25th, 2011, *Forbes Magazine*

Pixar Story Point #1: Once upon a time, there was _____. Everyday, _____. One day, _____. Because of that, _____. Because of that, _____. Until finally, _____.

No, this isn't Pixar's version of Mad-Libs; filling in these blanks allows you to flesh out the backbone of any story. When you're constructing your narrative for your Branded Film, you want to make sure the story keeps moving forward – and has a beginning, middle and end. If you watch Michael Moore's first movie, Roger *and Me,* you'll see his attempts to personally confront the head of GM becomes the running narrative – you are hooked because you want to see if he's ever able to pull it off.

Pixar Story Point #2: Keep in mind what's interesting to your audience, not to you.

In a Branded Film, you want to avoid spending too much time on stuff *you* care about, but the people you want to reach probably *don't*. That can actually turn a potentially disastrous corner; we've all seen celebrities go on and on about subject matter that not only doesn't appeal to their fans, but might just actually offend them (anybody remember Tom Cruise lecturing Matt Lauer about psychiatry a few years ago?).

Pixar Story Point #3: You admire a character more for trying than succeeding

We all fail in our personal and professional lives at one point or another. We don't like for it to happen, but it's a part of life – it can't be helped and, many would say, it's actually *good* for us; it helps us to learn and grow. But because we all do fail, it's incredibly relatable. So don't shy away from past mistakes within your Branded Film, as long as you come out a winner at the end.

Pixar Story Point #4: Give your characters opinions.

Pixar adds to the above guideline, *"Passive and malleable might seem likeable to you, but it's poison to an audience."* In other words, if you don't stand for anything, you don't mean anything. It's more than okay to have a point of view in a Branded Film – as a matter of fact, it's a must; otherwise nothing about you will be all that memorable.

Pixar Story Point #5: What are the stakes? Give us reason to root.

As all of the plotlines we've discussed make clear, audiences get more invested in a story when there are big challenges that must be overcome. What are the challenges you can portray in your Branded Film? They could be in your personal story or they could be an integral part of your business (for example, an investment counselor trying to protect his clients' savings in a difficult economic time). StorySelling requires some tension – that tension comes from facing obstacles that can seem insurmountable.

Pixar Story Point #6: Get the obvious out of the way: Surprise yourself.

Nobody wants to watch a movie where they can already guess the ending – unless there are enough surprises along the way to make it fun and interesting. It's all too easy to do what's expected in a Branded Film – that's why we always try to come at our subject matter from unexpected directions and you should too. Obviously, most of these kinds of movies end up as success stories, because you want to StorySell yourself as someone who's good at what he or she is doing. What you do along the way to get to the positive feel-good conclusion, however, should be as unexpected as possible – and reveal things that the audience never saw coming.

Pixar Story Point #7: Honesty lends credibility

Branded Films succeed not because they're full of the overhype of an infomercial selling some new crazy weight loss system, but because they're fairly low-key and feature *real* people in *real* locations speaking honestly about you, your life and your business. This approach works for any type of business.

But it actually goes beyond that. When you watch a good movie, you become involved in the characters' lives and what's going to happen to them. You root for them to do well and succeed. And you want to see more of them – that's why Hollywood is so big on sequels.

There are a lot of reasons for this, but it comes down to this: by telling your story, especially in a Branded Film where viewers can actually see what you're all about, you and your company become a *shared experience* with the public. They are magnetically drawn into your professional and personal life, they feel like they're a part of your success story – and they want to see you continue to do well.

And that, in turn, makes them *want to do business with you.*

This all happens on a deep psychological level, because a properly produced Branded Film triggers an amazing amount of empathy that draws viewers closer to you and your business. And, again, it doesn't matter what kind of business it is!

So consider creating a Branded Film to StorySell your business – and "Stand Apart" by putting your story onscreen for everybody to see. You may not be the next Brad Pitt or Sandra Bullock - but you just might take your business to the next level of success.

About Nick

An Emmy Award Winning Director and Producer, Nick Nanton, Esq., is known as the Top Agent to Celebrity Experts around the world for his role in developing and marketing business and professional experts, through personal branding, media, marketing and PR. Nick is recognized as the nation's leading expert on personal branding as Fast Company Magazine's Expert Blogger on the subject and lectures regularly on the topic at major universities around the world. His book *Celebrity Branding You®*, while an easy and informative read, has also been used as a text book at the University level.

The CEO and Chief StoryTeller at The Dicks + Nanton Celebrity Branding Agency, an international agency with more than 1800 clients in 33 countries, Nick is an award winning director, producer and songwriter who has worked on everything from large scale events to television shows with the likes of Steve Forbes, Brian Tracy, Jack Canfield (*The Secret*, Creator of the *Chicken Soup for the Soul* Series), Michael E. Gerber, Tom Hopkins, Dan Kennedy and many more.

Nick is recognized as one of the top thought-leaders in the business world and has co-authored 30 best-selling books alongside Brian Tracy, Jack Canfield, Dan Kennedy, Dr. Ivan Misner (Founder of BNI), Jay Conrad Levinson (Author of the Guerilla Marketing Series), Super Agent Leigh Steinberg and many others, including the breakthrough hit *Celebrity Branding You!®*.

Nick has led the marketing and PR campaigns that have driven more than 1000 authors to Best-Seller status. Nick has been seen in *USA Today, The Wall Street Journal, Newsweek, BusinessWeek, Inc. Magazine, The New York Times, Entrepreneur® Magazine, Forbes,* FastCompany.com and has appeared on ABC, NBC, CBS, and FOX television affiliates around the country, as well as CNN, FOX News, CNBC, and MSNBC from coast to coast.

Nick is a member of the Florida Bar, holds a JD from the University Of Florida Levin College Of Law, as well as a BSBA in Finance from the University of Florida's Warrington College of Business. Nick is a voting member of The National Academy of Recording Arts & Sciences (NARAS, Home to The GRAMMYs), a member of The National Academy of Television Arts & Sciences (Home to the Emmy Awards), co-founder of the National Academy of Best-Selling Authors, a 16-time Telly Award winner, and spends his spare time working with Young Life, Downtown Credo Orlando, Entrepreneurs International and rooting for the Florida Gators with his wife Kristina and their three children, Brock, Bowen and Addison.

Learn more at www.NickNanton.com and:
www.CelebrityBrandingAgency.com

About JW

JW Dicks, Esq., is America's foremost authority on using personal branding for business development. He has created some of the most successful brand and marketing campaigns for business and professional clients to make them the credible celebrity experts in their field and build multi-million dollar businesses using their recognized status.

JW Dicks has started, bought, built, and sold a large number of businesses over his 39-year career and developed a loyal international following as a business attorney, author, speaker, consultant, and business experts' coach. He not only practices what he preaches by using his strategies to build his own businesses, he also applies those same concepts to help clients grow their business or professional practice the way he does.

JW has been extensively quoted in such national media as *USA Today,* the *Wall Street Journal, Newsweek, Inc.,* Forbes.com, CNBC.com, and *Fortune Small Business.* His television appearances include ABC, NBC, CBS and FOX affiliate stations around the country. He is the resident branding expert for *Fast Company's* internationally syndicated blog and is the publisher of *Celebrity Expert Insider,* a monthly newsletter targeting business and brand building strategies.

JW has written over 22 books, including numerous best-sellers, and has been inducted into the National Academy of Best-Selling Authors. JW is married to Linda, his wife of 39 years, and they have two daughters, two granddaughters and two Yorkies. JW is a 6th generation Floridian and splits his time between his home in Orlando and beach house on the Florida west coast.

CHAPTER 30

AMPLIFY:
15 STEPS TO LAUNCH FAST, GET TO CONTRACT AND CASH CHECKS

BY THOMAS K.R. STOVALL

CLEAR…TO…CLOSE. October 13th, 2006 was the first time I ever heard those words. What I didn't know was that in the near future they would soon become music to my ears…and in the not so distant future, the pursuit of those three words would be my undoing. Naiveté, what a beautiful, dangerous drug. It was upon me.

At 26 years old, I considered myself a relatively seasoned and well-studied entrepreneur. Though I graduated from Tennessee State University with a degree in Electrical Engineering, I had never actually worked a day of engineering in my life. I started my first business at the age of 19 out of my college dorm room, selling luxury custom wheels and performance tires online from New York to California. As a college student, it was great owning a business making a few dollars and doing something that I enjoyed. I advertised my business by driving a tricked out car that I would put a new set of chrome wheels on every few months, but it was all a mirage…I was broke as ever.

In the years that followed, I started another business creating, promoting and producing large special events. Within a year, I had raised over $30,000, secured over 60 sponsors, and produced two major events for the public that were my own brainchild. These events were highlighted in every major news publication in the city, and one received actual news coverage. Special events were a way for me to provide an interruption, if only for a moment or an evening, in the monotonous rhythm that our lives can easily fall into. Being a catalyst for inspiration is my passion, but once I moved past all the intrigue and excitement and got down to brass tacks, my big "special events" were all either losing money or barely breaking even. Another year gone, and I was STILL broke as ever.

The year before that fateful day in October of 2006 that forever changed my life, consider the reality I now found myself immersed in. I'm 25 years old, and for the last six years I've literally been working on my businesses day and night, 6 to 7 days per week. In all those years in business, while I had spearheaded some major accomplishments that I was proud of, I'd barely made enough to support myself. I attended countless business conferences and courses and read every personal development and business book I could get my hands on. *Rich Dad Poor Dad, Think & Grow Rich, The E-Myth, The Power of Positive Thinking, The 48 Laws of Power* and *The Art of War* were just the tip of the iceberg.

I was a sponge, I devoured anything business related. I was willing to outwork and outstudy ANYONE and EVERYONE, and for all intents and purposes I did, yet I still had no money. I understood the difference between being self-employed and being a business owner thanks to Robert Kiyosaki, and Michael Gerber had taught me to understand and build my business with a franchise model in mind. I studied, I practiced, I produced tangible and significant results, but I didn't produce any significant amounts of money. There was something Trump and the others weren't telling me in their books and courses...what was it?

In 2005, I moved to LA to contract with a real estate private equity investment firm. Can you imagine seeing real estate investing at the monopoly board level? Learning at the tender age of 25 that all you'd been taught about money was false? In this private equity world, money was simply 1's and 0's on a computer screen, more an IDEA than a tangible thing to touch and hold. Money moved in conversations and handshakes, and it was all grounded in trusted, vetted relationships. The deals were done before people sat down at the table, and you didn't get an invitation to transact at the table unless someone already in the room put their reputation on the line and vetted you. It didn't matter how hard you worked or how much you knew, these people valued trust above everything else, and with trust in the background of every transaction, things moved FAST. Conversations weren't about hundreds or thousands; they were about millions and hundreds of millions.

On the foreclosure auction floor I held cashier's checks for 7 figures. In the office, I helped prepare presentations for multi-billion dollar institutional investors we approached for capital. In the boardroom, I saw people get paid $250,000 just for making an INTRODUCTION. It was clear to me that relationships were the currency, and trust was what gave that currency its value. From that point on, I had a different mindset about access to money, and I also understood the true value of relationships and maintaining the integrity and trust inside of them at all costs. What I didn't know was that I still had no clue how to leverage relationships to MAKE money and KEEP money.

In early 2006 I returned to Chicago, intent on starting my own real estate investment and consulting firm. I had spent the last year consulting with the private equity firm in LA, and while I learned a great deal, I had made no money to speak of. On October 13th, 2006 I heard those words, CLEAR TO CLOSE. The same day, I parted ways with my employer. 18 days later, on October 31st, 2006, I closed on my first building. Over the next 12 months, over half a million dollars passed through my company's bank account.

By the time year 2 in business was complete, I had raised close to $250,000 in private investment capital and $1,169,886 of revenue had passed through my bank account. Sounds great right? Well unfortunately, this story does not have a happy ending. I was precise in my project management, process management and people management, and I never lost money on a deal, but the actual management of the business as it grew incredibly fast was where I failed. I had no mentorship, I had no team, and my house of cards crumbled. By the age of 30, I had amassed over $2.5MM of real estate holdings in my portfolio, but in the end I lost everything, including my $350,000 dream condo which I had proudly purchased a few years earlier. Again, BROKE AS EVER.

When I closed the real estate investment business in mid-2010, I had NOTHING. Credit ruined, no money in the bank, my name was now mud with my investors, and my confidence had taken a major hit. I knew that my journey was far from over, but I had no idea what I would or could do next. Through trial and error over 10+ years as a business owner, I had already identified how to build a new business from scratch and produce significant results incredibly quickly with no money to begin with; I had done it three times. Through the mindset shift of working in private equity and the practical experience of building my real estate investment and consulting firm, I had finally made the transition and actually learned how to generate significant amounts of money, FAST. What was missing was my ability to make the explosive growth and revenue generation sustainable over time, and I knew it.

On July 21st, 2010 I began participating in a scarcely known and highly specialized business philosophy and curriculum, and I soon realized that I had finally found the secret formula I had been searching for all those years – that filled in the gaps of how to build a scalable business. As I had suspected all these years, it WAS scientific and predictable. I could now see and articulate clearly why I had been unable to produce SUSTAINABLE results up to that point that were consistent with what I was committed to producing. There WERE specific steps to take in a specific order that produced reliable, predictable results. After 2 years of intense study, practice and application of what I learned from this curriculum, I finally found a way to couple all that I had learned there with my unique pre-existing skillset and personal process for building businesses.

Over close to 15 years of detailed study, personal development, business apprenticeship, successes, AND plenty of failures, I've learned that the highly elusive and "unpredictable" path we must take to achieve success is, counter to common belief, quite systematic and HIGHLY predictable. The answer to the puzzle had finally presented itself in an incredibly agile business methodology for entrepreneurs that I call "Amplified Growth."

Without a dollar to my name, in November 2012 I launched my most recent business venture, a real-time market research mobile app for enterprise executives called "CANDID Cup." Using my Amplified

Growth process, within 6 months of incorporation I secured signed letters of commitment from multi-billion dollar global companies and nationally-recognized speakers to use the app upon launch, created a $500,000 technology partnership with an enterprise application development company, raised over $100,000 in private money at a $3,000,000 valuation, got Version 1 of the app completed and approved in the Apple App store, and brought on three seasoned business development experts. Within 2 weeks of being approved in the Apple store, it was named the official feedback app of a VIP online marketing and social media conference in downtown Chicago – featuring some of the top-paid and most well known online marketing experts and technology company founders in the world. This process works.

In my Amplified Growth methodology, there are 6 Stages and 35 specific sub-categories of business growth and development that a company must move through in order to build a scalable structure, focus its time and resources, and create exponential growth. Below, I'm going to offer you a practical 15-step guide that gives a CliffsNotes style overview of my process. If you follow these steps in order, you WILL amplify the growth of your business and produce explosive results.

Step 1: <u>Be Afraid, Do It Anyway</u>
The fear NEVER goes away, just hit the go button. Total failure is a concept that doesn't really exist, there's only FAILURE TO MEET A GOAL that you set. That said, fail fast, dust yourself off, re-assess and do it again.

Step 2: <u>Set Your Coordinates</u>
Clearly articulate your vision and mission, because if you can't see it, you can't say it; if you can't say it, you can't do it. You can't get to a specific spot on the grid if you don't know the coordinates.

Step 3: <u>Be A Narrowist</u>
Don't be a generalist. Define your specific, ideal customer. It's counter intuitive, but the more niche and specific you get, the easier it is to find them, and the easier it is for them to find you.

Step 4: <u>Accurate Thinking</u>

Vet the idea with experts and REAL PEOPLE immediately, and have them poke as many holes in your balloon as possible as quickly as possible, then make the adjustment.

Step 5: <u>Remove Your Ego</u>

Do you currently have the specialized knowledge, track record and skillset to stand up in front of ANY investor, customer or strategic partner and get their buy-in? If not, get over yourself and transact for the help of a specialist who does and get them on your team ASAP.

Step 6: <u>Trusted, Vetted Relationships</u>

Everything and everyone you need is already in your network or one degree away, you're just not asking. Money, specialized knowledge, talent, access; it's all there. Go deep inside your network and make powerful requests, you'll get results much faster because you're moving inside of trust.

Step 7: <u>Identify Your Weaknesses - Bring On Specialists</u>

Self-employed mindsets try to be expert at everything and trust no one in their business. Business owner mindsets master identifying what's needed, then recruiting and effectively managing specialists in every area of the business who are smarter and more seasoned than themselves.

Step 8: <u>Look The Part</u>

Move with the knowledge that EVERYTHING you say, everything you do, everything you wear, everything you present, everyone who is associated with your business is ALL a reflection on the perceived quality and viability of your business and your level of competence or ability in fulfilling on the mission as the owner.

Step 9: <u>Gnat's Ass Detail</u>

Be painfully and annoyingly specific in your internal and external documents as you define your vision, mission, target, as well as your brand identity and narratives. Every

word matters, every detail matters, every pixel matters.
That doesn't mean perfection, it means precision.

Step 10: <u>Show Me The Money</u>

Clearly Define How You'll Make Money. Build it and
they will come is a fantasy, and at best, it slows down the
pace of exponential growth potential. Define the actual
strategy and objective numbers associated with growing
the business and closing deals with your specific customer,
by day, by week, by month, by year.

Step 11: <u>Build Your Team On A Budget</u>

If you don't have cash to pay people, barter, create strategic
partnerships, call in favors, and leverage relationships to
form your team initially. Start with creating a solid Advisory
Board of highly seasoned business people who believe in
you and trust you, and they will help you define and attract
the other team members you need.

Step 12: <u>Documentation</u>

NOTHING exists outside of contract. Do NOT move
in the world of "good intentions." Have people sign
confidentiality agreements and contracts for everything.
No gray space, clear expectations.

Step 13: <u>Time...Friend or Foe?</u>

Time is of the essence, and every single second that goes
by once you launch the business is either building your
track record, or diminishing it. Stay in stealth until you
go live, but once you officially launch, you had better be
ready to pull the trigger.

Step 14: <u>Master The Invitation</u>

Whether you know it or not, the single most effective
tool in building a business extraordinarily fast is creating
tremendous first impressions. When done properly, a
masterful and compelling invitation closes business and
secures the buy-in of strategic partners before you ever
begin the presentation. Ponder how to be extraordinary in
your approach.

Step 15: <u>**Make 'Em Smell You, Leave Your Scent Behind**</u>

Your collateral materials are everything. At a minimum, you need a Power Point with rich, visually-engaging graphics and concrete facts, figures and case studies. Invest in a video and a website. If you can't afford a professional, go to the local college and find a top-notch student to do it. Present yourself and your business in ways that are so compelling and creative that you are forever imprinted on the memory of your prospects.

About Thomas

Thomas K.R. Stovall, widely regarded as The Business Amplification Expert®, is an entrepreneur with over 14 years of real world business experience, specialized study and training in the areas of business amplification, project management, leadership development, sales, viral marketing, transformational learning and ontology.

While attaining his Bachelor's degree in Electrical Engineering at Tennessee State University, he started his first business – selling luxury custom wheels and performance tires to online customers from California to New York out of his dorm room – and has been an entrepreneur ever since.

At a glance, Thomas' business experience includes private equity, real estate investment, large-scale event production, business amplification consulting, and business amplification software. Thomas owns the nation's first Business Amplification Firm, specializing in helping C-Level executives and seasoned entrepreneurs identify blind spots in their businesses to rapidly increase their bottom line. Thomas is also the Founder of CANDID Cup, the first real-time market research mobile app for enterprise executives, top level decision makers and business owners. In 2013, Thomas was featured in two books by best selling authors as a Business Amplification expert. His first personal title, *AMPLIFY: The Entrepreneur's Bible - Launch Fast, Get to Contract, Cash Checks,* is forthcoming in 2014.

For more information about Business Amplification:
www.BusinessAmplification.com
or Email:Info@CandidCup.com

Thomas K.R. Stovall - The Business Amplification Expert®

CHAPTER 31

ESSENSENSE:
HOW TO STAND APART

BY LAURA J. VAN DEN BERG SEKAC

INTRODUCTION

When I was 16 years old, I got suddenly ill. Many months in the hospital, and 2 years later, I was told I had rheumatism, and I had to prepare myself to end up in a wheelchair. At the time in my life when I had just started to become autonomous, my plans for a great life were interrupted. A decision thundered through my mind: NO. Not in this life. In this life I say no to such a path. I won't allow my vision of glorious life to be destroyed.

A couple of weeks later I had a dream about a dilapidated, filthy house. I took it seriously because I had dreams with foresight before. I understood it was a message from some wiser part of myself about what was really going on. I suspected I had to learn more about myself, something I was eager about anyway. It put me on the path of self-knowledge that I would never leave.

During the same period of time, I read an article about a young French woman. At a certain point she stated: "In this life, I decided to be happy."

Her sentence touched me deeply. I had free choice to decide how I would feel! I could sense the truth of her words - it was the same kind of decision I made earlier myself. Now it was apparently time to commit again. So I stated firmly with all my heart, like the young woman did,

"Yes, in this life I DECIDE to be happy. I won't allow anything to spoil my life." Because, you know, although I experienced plenty of challenging times in my younger years, I always felt happy and full of joy inside, for no reason, and I just loved that feeling.

In this way her words became an important mantra in my life, a trusted compass I could always rely on. I often was thinking about her, how everyone had something important to share, and I decided I wanted to enrich other people's lives, too.

Little by little I regained my health. Thanks to my dream that brought me to healthier habits and a better attitude, the illness was gone. As far as my health, there was nothing to really worry about.

Until years later. Out of the blue, my little finger itched. From itching it went to pain, and from pain it changed into a finger that looked like arthritis. I immediately recognized what was going on. Yet I didn't want to know, let alone to act on it. I considered my health habits to be satisfactory, my attitudes sufficient, and in general, I still was happy and joyful inside.

To keep the story short, I was wrong. If I didn't want to end up in the same situation as earlier at the age of 16, major action was required.

I always was talking about how important it was to be truthful to yourself. And in a certain way I did walk my talk, but I had to admit I never expressed myself fully. Although it was my nature to do things in my own way, I never dared to fully stand apart, and clearly and loudly show the real me. I thought I was doing well but I was fooling myself. Without knowing it, I kept myself much too small.

I felt the urge to achieve great things, but in order to perform something outstanding, one can't be small. Playing small doesn't lead to great deeds. So this time it seemed I had only one option: dare to really stand apart and live my fullest life, or return to being miserable.

I knew I had to take bold action. I needed to reconnect with my core values and the essence of who I was in a deeper way. My biggest challenge was how to handle disparity. How to stay connected to others while setting healthy boundaries, how to remain grounded in my origins while being open to the truth of others, how to express my deepest wisdom and desires that a part of me felt ashamed or guilty of?

This is the reason why you find my story on these pages. I know that I'm not the only one with these challenges, and I'm curious about your experience.

But there's more to why I wanted to write this chapter. While working with clients for over two decades, I discovered that they often had a deep and common longing for being free to express themselves in their own original ways.

They felt that being free to do what they loved to do, in a way that was their own, would give their lives more meaning because they'd have something to give their hearts and souls to.

They felt there was more, and at the same time, their biggest frustration was that they didn't know HOW to make a change, or that they recognized that what they assumed to be an authentic expression of themselves was actually not authentic at all: the values they were holding on to were, in fact, in conflict with their own true values – which was why they couldn't really move forward in their lives.

The interesting thing was that as soon they learned what their true longing was, they mostly found the courage to take the necessary steps. Some changed the course of their life and moved to be closer to nature, some decided to break into their creativity choosing the path of the arts, some left draining relationships and unsatisfying jobs, others created new businesses, shifted their tactics, or simply focused more on what was important to them.

Soon magical things began to happen. They started to do things in a distinct way – which gave them something special, something intangible, something … unique. Their eyes started to shine with excitement, their health and relationships thrived and so did their work and businesses.

They began to Stand Apart.

TO STAND APART IS IMPORTANT

What caused my clients to Stand Apart? What is Standing Apart *exactly*? And why would you want to sing a different tune?

To answer the last question, it's because being unique is your natural state. It's important to fully express it. When you neglect your uniqueness, you lose contact with who you truly are – your inner fire and passion extinguish, and your dreams fade away. At the end you may give up your happiness. But when you give up your dreams and happiness, your soul bleeds to death leaving you empty behind, feeling dead among the living.

Another reason is because, even if it sounds like a cliché, the world needs people who dare to step out and take actions that inspire.

Yet another reason may be that the things you do with love radiate that love out. They are better, more beautiful and are of higher quality. They improve and embellish the world and your own life as well. We all long for a better world, and in order to create a healthy, wealthy and peaceful world, we have to live it first.

So what is *Standing Apart*? According to dictionary, it refers to things like: *be distinct, appear clearly different from other things or people, be off the beaten path, be unequalled, be of high standard or quality, show contrast, and (I like this one) stand apart from the drama.*

In summary, it refers to standing free, out of the ordinary, apart from what is common place, standard or prescribed, doing something original to you, without borrowing from other people's ideas.

In my own definition *Standing Apart* means *to Step Into Your Genius, and Live it Fully.*

It's to do something unique in your own particular way that nobody else does or can do. However, you cannot act in such a manner unless you bring it into line with your personal core values. These represent your true standards and belong to you from the very moment you were born. They are not inherited or borrowed from others. They just are yours.

This was why my clients stood apart. Because they connected to their core values, to what was really important to them, and then started to implement such in their relationships, work and health matters, and the way they treated themselves, their authenticity became visible.

TRUSTFUL GUIDANCE

In changing times or when you want to expand, you need trustful guidance. Your personal core values provide this. If your choices are in accordance with those values, then your choices are in sync with who you are.

How to recognize if a value is your core value? By my definition, its central characteristic is that it always results in more beauty. This may translate as effectiveness, Zen simplicity, esthetics, an eye for detail, humor, and so on. A core value always enriches your life and those of others.

Sometimes however you may have lost your sense of YOU. Your values may be so deeply buried inside that you have no clue what's crucial to you. To reconnect, you must find out what matters to your heart.

HOW TO RECONNECT?

You must look inside yourself. When do you feel happy and why? When is your heart soothed and your soul excited? What does it emanate that you love – beauty, flow, adventure?

And what breaks your mood and vitality? How do you allow other people to upset you, how do you put yourself down? What do you do over and over all your life? Some limiting beliefs and negative emotions may arise. These stand in the way of getting in touch with your core values.

So instead, change your perspective. Ask yourself: "What is the strongest encouraging belief and feeling I'm able to feel? Which one do I love the most? Is it trust? Is it wonderment, honesty, gratitude? Or is it optimism, freedom or maybe exploration?"

When you're really happy, what heartfelt feeling prevails? What mood gives you the most energy and makes you feel the most joyful, grateful, at ease and excited? Look also at the activities you love the most. What feelings are involved? And then, put all those feelings together, and ask yourself again: "Which feelings are the dearest and the most important to me? Without what feeling or value do I feel dead?"

Those are your (essential) core values. To be in sync with your true self, everything you do must contain them.

YOUR ESSENSENSE

But we're not done yet. Ask yourself once more: "When I'm feeling and expressing those values, what is beneath all this? And beneath that? And beneath that?"

Finally, you may come up with a raw sensation of movement, perhaps flow, focus, peace or majesty. Sometimes it's difficult to describe.

This underlying raw sensation is your *EssenSense*. In this state you can *feel the essence of YOU* – a unique, basal feeling of power that goes together with feelings constituting your core values such as serenity, joy, independence, and with an inflow of insight and motivation. *You can say then that the way you access your power happens THROUGH serenity, joy and independence.*

When in a state of EssenSense, you may get brilliant innovative ideas for your business, find ways to improve your relationships, grow your wealth, or get insights to solve situations that were stuck for years. It's also a very healing condition for your body and mind.

When you touch your EssenSense, you immediately touch your authentic self as well. Your heart opens, and your body may start to tingle, sensing that immense power, joy or freedom in each part of it. It's a kind of magnetic, falling-in-love feeling that forms the foundation of your core values. It adds something special to you; something that Beyoncé, for example, has; that Apple had with Steve Jobs; or that girl in the bakery, when you always leave feeling uplifted because of the way she smiles. However, EssenSense is not charisma. It's what *causes* it. It's what you're here on earth to express and to bring forth.

People may share the same kind of EssenSence, but its expression differs from person to person because the manifestation of their EssenSense depends on their personal core values.

ESSENSENSE IS YOUR TRUE FUNDAMENT

Since EssenSense and your core values represent what you're here to accomplish, they need to be at the base of everything you do.

When your EssenSense is, for example, expansion, then your life has to be about expansion in all its aspects such as growth, innovation or prosperity. If you force yourself into a job with lots of routine, it will make you ill because expansion and new experiences are as vital to you as routine can be to someone else. You then need to reinvent yourself and upgrade your life from time to time. That also may be why you feel the urge to travel, leave jobs, move to other places, learn new skills, or engage in new activities all the time.

If your core values are joy and optimism, you must take actions that cause you to feel delighted. If it's integrity, you must not lie to yourself and force yourself to do things only for the sake of not disappointing others. When it's beauty, then you must surround yourself with what you find beautiful, have a job that enables you to express beauty, and have a significant other who also loves it. If not, you'll feel disconnected, unheard, and unimportant.

ORIGINALITY BROADENS YOUR PERSPECTIVE

When you manifest what truly matters in your life, it makes you unequalled without requiring any effort. The more you do what's important to you, the more authentic and original your thoughts, words and deeds become. You feel lucid and energized, and you reach your goals more easily because clarity keeps you motivated and vitality gives you the stamina.

In such a state, challenges turn into opportunities. You become inventive, magnetic and inspired. You learn to cope with paradoxes and recognize how your actions lead to consequences – but not in the way you might think:

- Your fear to take action brings about your anger that you hold yourself back. Therefore, you understand your anger, and stop blaming others.

- The more you follow an existing path, the more you get stuck in it – so you leave it.

- The more time and energy you spend on useless activities, the more time and money they will cost. For that reason you don't waste it anymore.

- If you doubt what you have to give, others will be hesitant to receive your gifts. Now you understand bad sell results.

- The more you adapt to others, the less they adapt to you. So you respect yourself more.

- The more you respect and love yourself, the less egoistic you become. So you choose self-love.
- Bad is not the opposite of the good – it's ignorance. The good has no opposites, only complements. So it's not about 'not being good enough.' It's about being unaware of who you truly are.

In short, your vision broadens, and so does your perspective.

So how about you and your core values? Do you dare to stand apart and embellish the world?

About Laura

Laura J. van den Berg Sekac, M.A. is an author, creator, entrepreneur, and international expert in the field of self-knowledge and personal transformation. In 1993, she founded the former well-known personal development School of Earth Teaching in the Netherlands.

She also is the founder and SEO of **Essenticals**™ that is created to offer a way of living based on what is fundamental in your life, relationships, health or career so you can create a lifestyle that really fulfills your heart and soul.

EssenSense™ carries the name of a method developed by Laura to define your unique fundamental energy, the 'inner fire' that drives you, and that is at the base of your life's purpose. Each person has his or her own EssenSense™ yet very few are actually in touch with it.

With more than 20 years of coaching and consulting experience, using her knack for seeing the patterns and connection between underlying behaviors and events, Laura has helped thousands of men and women to gain clarity, larger perspective and deep understanding of themselves and their life, in order to unpack their inner power, joy and creativity, and achieve greater personal and professional happiness.

Her passion is to develop new, often unconventional methods to empower and get the best out of the people she works with as she explores how events that occur outside them connect to what they do inside. A great example was her feature appearance on Dutch TV where she worked with horses and her clients in order to unveil the hidden inner attitude of the person who works with them.

Laura is a strong believer in each person's ability to reach their innate strength and higher potential in every part of their life, and she loves to teach her clients how to step into their full power, stand apart and become change-makers.

Laura J. van den Berg Sekac now lives in the French borders of Geneva, and works from there internationally.

To learn more about Laura and **EssenSense**™, please visit: www.Essenticals.com or contact her at: infoEssenticals@gmail.com

CHAPTER 32

THE ABC'S OF A USP —
MARKETING FOR
EXPONENTIAL GROWTH

BY RICHARD JOHNSON

February, 1990. I had just finished a week of marketing training from one of the country's foremost marketing experts - Jay Abraham. I was ready to start my own marketing/sales consulting and training practice. And, a new son, Taylor, was born that month as well. The pressure to produce and provide was on.

I returned home to start calling on business owners. I called on all types of business owners – owners of retail, wholesale, manufacturing, professional practices and service businesses. I mailed letters, made phone calls, made presentations to Chamber of Commerce groups all around the state. I offered complimentary consultations to those business owners interested. I advertised in a local business publication. I asked for referrals.

I listened. These owners expressed several marketing and sales frustrations. They were wondering how to make sense of all the marketing voices and strategies bombarding them? Where do they start? What's the next step? Is there any system to marketing? How do I measure my marketing and sales performance? How do I know if my advertising is working? How do I do marketing when I'm not a marketing guy? How can I sell more without having to keep lowering my prices? How can I get more out of my salespeople? How can I get more sales without having to spend more money? These frustrations continue today with on-line, Internet marketing.

From Jay's training, I knew a good USP – Unique Selling Proposition – would go a long way to eliminating their frustrations. But, I was amazed at how many businesses did not have a USP. I asked one business owner, "What is it that makes you come to work everyday?" He replied: "I don't know." I said: "Then I recommend you get out of business." He said, " O.K." Two days later I called on him and the doors were locked and shut. Another owner said that because he had a PHD in engineering that should be enough. I replied: "No one cares about your PHD."

 What is it that makes you, a business owner, passionate and persistent enough to go to work every day? Do you have a USP? In asking about a USP, most respond: "We have the best quality, lowest price or superior customer service." These are not USPs. All of these are minimum levels of expectation to even stay in business. *What makes your business "stand apart?"*

Since 1990, *The Exponential Sales Marketing System* has been helping business owners eliminate these frustrations by first creating a USP. And then, growing their sales and profits exponentially. There are licensed marketing coaches in the US, the UK, Nigeria, Luxembourg, Australia, Greece, Ireland, Canada and Holland using the system to help small businesses grow exponentially in their area.

HOW THE SYSTEM WORKS - IT ALL STARTS WITH A USP - UNIQUE SELLING PROPOSITION

Within every business are marketing opportunities or marketing assets. These include:

owner expertise, staff and employee expertise, time in business, credibility, performance, policies and procedures, customer service, current marketing and sales processes, current customers, average customer sale, conversion rate, prospective customers, past customers, location, customer retention rate, and more.

The four steps of the exponential sales marketing system leverages and optimizes all of these assets for maximum revenue and profit opportunity.

These four steps are:

1. Develop and create a USP - Unique Selling Proposition.
2. Integrate and communicate the USP in all company departments - especially sales and marketing.
3. Database marketing with your new USP.
4. Alliances, affiliates and marketing partnerships - built around your USP.

Implementing these four steps effectively grows your business three ways simultaneously:

- Increases the number of qualified prospects contacted.
- Increases the conversion rate of prospects to paying customers.
- Increases the value or worth of each customer to the business.

And, this growth can happen quickly - sometimes in as little as 60 to 90 days!

Traditional marketing and advertising strategies focus only on number one - increasing the number of leads or prospects contacted.

The Exponential Sales Marketing System is the only marketing system or plan that grows all three - systematically. That is why it can create exponential sales. And, it is guaranteed to perform. That's *The Exponential Sales Marketing System's* USP! The USP is not in the names or steps of the system but in the order and tactics of execution! The graph below illustrates the impact the marketing system has in growing all three revenue lines simultaneously.

Three Ways to Exponential Growth

Growth Objective 20%

	Number of Prospects		Closing Ratio		Number of Customers		Average Customer		Gross Sales
Now	200	x	20.00%	=	40	x	$1,000	=	$40,000
1)	240	x	20.00%	=	48	x	$1,000	=	$48,000
2)	200	x	24.00%	=	48	x	$1,000	=	$48,000
3)	200	x	20.00%	=	40	x	$1,200	=	$48,000
4)	240	x	24.00%	=	57.6	x	$1,200	=	$69,120
							Actual Growth Achieved		72.80%

Small Improvements in Each Area Will
Give You Dramatic Growth Overall – AND THIS CAN HAPPEN BOTH
DOMESTICALLY AND INTERNATIONALLY

Do you track and monitor the growth in these three areas for your business? Do you know what your numbers are? Run the numbers - you'll get very excited!

That's it. Pretty simple. It works. If it fails, it wasn't executed properly and did not have a strong USP.

THE FOUR STEPS

STEP ONE: USP - Unique Selling Proposition

In the book *Differentiate or Die*, author Jack Trout credits Rosser Reeves with coming up with the USP idea and says there are three parts to the definition:

1. Each advertisement must make a proposition to the consumer and say to each reader: "Buy this product, and you will get this specific benefit."

2. The proposition must be one that the competition either cannot, or does not, offer.

3. The proposition must be so strong that it can move the mass - pull over new customers to your product.

Does your business have a USP? I would suggest 9.5 out of 10.0 businesses do not. They might have a slogan, logo, tag line or mission statement hanging on the lobby wall. These are not USPs. A USP should fill a void. It should matter to the customer. A slogan might introduce a USP. LensCrafters - in about an hour. Great USP. Walmart owns the low price USP. Target can build a store right next to Walmart and do great. Why? Different USP. Target goes after a different customer than Walmart. Kmart has been trying to compete with Walmart and is losing. One night I saw a commercial that said: "Kmart - the stuff of life." Wow, now that's unique! A USP is not claiming you have good quality. That's expected. It's not good customer service. That's expected.

You might have to innovate the demand of your customer. Papa Murphy's pizza - bake your own. That's a USP. Instead of competing on Pizza, they shift our demand away from buying pizza to baking our own. Talk to your employees. Ask them what they think makes your company unique. Talk to your top salesman. Are they selling a USP? Research the competition. What are they doing that's unique?

A USP is the most important strategy in marketing. If you don't have one, you're losing thousands if not millions of dollars in sales. A USP optimizes the marketing assets of owner and staff expertise, policy and procedures, customer service, product quality, etc. It impacts ALL three ways to grow. It attracts more of the right prospects, helps convert more prospects to paying customers and helps increase the value or worth of each customer. All working to grow sales and profits exponentially.

Without a strong USP, it will be hard to grow your business sales and profits in a significant way. A good USP helps you create your own demand. Create your own economy. You take more control of your business because you know what it is you really sell! That's the power of the right USP.

STEP TWO: Integration of the USP and communicating it over and over again

To be successful, a USP must be integrated into all parts of your business. Especially the sales and marketing processes. Salespeople must be sold on it or it's dead in the water. Involve them in creating one. Help them integrate it into their phone calls, contacts with prospects, presentations and closing. Successfully integration and communication will increase the conversion rate of prospects to paying customers.

Get the USP integrated into all pages of your website. Include it on business cards, emails and all promotional materials. Make sure production, shipping and customer service departments understand and support it. Measure the success of a USP by measuring the three ways to grow: How many prospects are being contacted? What is the conversion rate? What is a customer worth? Are these numbers increasing weekly? Monthly? These are three numbers to run and manage your business.

STEP THREE: Database marketing - with your new USP

There are three groups of customers in your business. Past customers. Present customers. Prospective customers. How often do you communicate with them? How well do you follow-up with prospective customers? Do you have an "autoresponder" follow-up system? Do you capture contact information of prospects from your website? Do you try to reactivate past customers and bring them back to your business? Especially with a new USP? Customers need to understand clearly why

317

they should do business with your company. If you don't have a USP, they will shop with their wallets and shop for the lowest price.

Do you regularly try to get current customers buying from you again and again? Most customers leave a business because they get a feeling of "apathy" from the business. Do you understand the lifetime value of your customer? Can you beat the competition at keeping your customers loyal to you? Are your sales dependent upon the salesperson or do they buy your company USP? Good database marketing with a strong USP will increase the value or worth of your customers to your business and contribute to exponential sales.

Communicating your USP with a specific offer and call-to-action will optimize your marketing efforts. Feedback from customers will also tell you when your USP might need to change. They often tell you what the competition is doing and that feedback is most important in keeping your USP current. Dominos Pizza had a great USP twenty or so years ago when they offered to deliver your pizza in 30 minutes or it's free. Soon, all other pizza companies were delivering pizza in under 30 minutes. It is no longer a USP. Dominos needs to change their USP. Will they? What's their new one?

STEP FOUR: Marketing alliances/partnerships built around your USP for more leads

Again, the order of these steps and the execution of each tactic within the steps is what makes *The Exponential Sales Marketing System* so powerful and unique. Traditional marketing's first focus is more leads. Here, it is last. There's a reason. Why would you go get more leads and prospects if you're not managing and leading the current prospects well by implementing steps one, two and three? Why waste more money? If you're marketing/sales system is broken don't waste more money on more leads!

Put the first three steps in place first. Then, go find more leads. Only this time do it with alliances and marketing partnerships. Get affiliate partners on the web marketing for you. If you have dealers and distributors, do more partner marketing with them. Teach them the three ways to grow. Help them make more money and they will perform better for you.

Search out from your customer base those that might have customers you want. Ask them for an endorsement to their customers. Endorsements are a powerful way to attract new prospects. Identify complementary businesses that have customers you want. Form a marketing alliance with them to promote your products/services to their customers. In return they can promote their products/services to yours. You're optimizing the marketing assets of relationships and trust to generate more prospects.

Don't do partner or alliance marketing with businesses that don't accept or believe in your USP.

The graph below illustrates all four steps working together to create exponential sales.

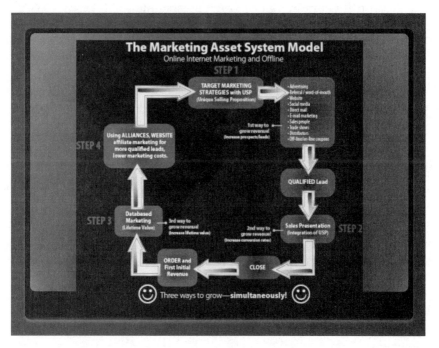

These four steps should be your marketing plan. Every marketing strategy can fit under one of these four steps. Before you do any other marketing, make sure these steps are in place. Otherwise, you're wasting marketing dollars. You're missing out on a lot of cash that could be yours. The opportunity cost of not successfully executing these four marketing steps is huge. You don't want to afford that.

MARKETING PROBLEMS SOLVED AND FRUSTRATIONS ELIMINATED! GETTING MORE OUT OF WHAT YOU ALREADY HAVE!

Successfully executing the four steps of *The Exponential Sales Marketing System* optimizes for maximum revenue and profit the marketing assets sitting in your business right now. Why spend more money to add more marketing assets if the current ones could deliver you more cash now? And, do so quickly! Perhaps in as little as 60-90 days! You'll get more out of your policies and procedures, your customer service, your current sales and marketing processes. You'll get more out of your marketing message. You'll get more out of your salespeople.

You'll get more out of the talent and expertise of owners and employees. You'll be able to spend less and get more in the new economy.

As a business owner, you'll be more excited to lead your company. The prosperity of you and your employees will increase. You'll be happier.

EXECUTION AND TRAINING - A SYSTEM

Finally, a marketing/sales system that is just that - a system. It all starts with a good USP. Then you successfully integrate that USP. Increase your customer value with effective database marketing. Finally, go get more leads with marketing alliances and partnerships. That's it. Four steps. Your marketing and sales now has order. You can now track the growth of numbers using the three ways to grow. And, it works on-line as well as off-line. It's a blended marketing system.

Don't do any other marketing until these steps are in place. Then do all you can. Do all you want. Watch your revenue and profit go up! Exponentially!

You now have a marketing system for your marketing and sales team. Have them report weekly on the three ways to grow and the progress they are making.

You don't need to be a marketing expert. You have a system to follow. You have systems for other parts of your business. Now you have one for marketing and sales.

MAKE MORE MONEY - INCREASE CASH FLOW

Regardless of the situation your business is in, *The Exponential Sales Marketing System* can help you make more money and increase cash flow quickly. You control the system. Implement it as slowly or as quickly as you'd like. The system delivers cash more quickly because you're getting the cash out of marketing assets you already have! You're not risking marketing dollars to create more assets with strategies that may not work!

For over twenty years, *The Exponential Sales Marketing System* has delivered exponential sales for businesses and their owners. It is guaranteed to perform. Get it into your business – now!

www.exponentialsalesmarketing.com

About Richard

Since 1990, Richard Johnson has been helping small businesses in all industries grow sales and profits exponentially using his Exponential Sales Marketing System. These include retail, wholesale, professional, service and manufacturing businesses.

Richard is founder and CEO of 21st Century Marketing Systems, Inc. and is the creator and developer of the company's four-step Exponential Sales Marketing System. His system is an approved growth system for manufacturers through the U.S. Commerce department's business development division. The system is licensed with nine Manufacturing Extension Partnership centers around the country. In 2007, Dell Computer Marketing Centers began to include steps of The Exponential Sales Marketing System as part of their learning system.

Since 1994, Richard has trained and certified hundreds of marketing consultants and coaches worldwide including the US, the UK, Nigeria, Luxembourg, Australia, Greece, Ireland, Canada and Holland. These consultants help business owners in their local areas implement The Exponential Sales Marketing System.

His book, *Twenty-five Ways To Improve Sales Without Spending An Extra Dime On Advertising,* was published in 1999 by CRISP business publications. Richard is now in the process of launching his new eBook : *The Exponential Sales Marketing System.*

With his marketing and sales expertise along with a Masters in Business Degree, Richard is continuing to make *The Exponential Sales Marketing System* available to small business owners worldwide.

Richard is married to his wife Melanie, and they have four children. He enjoys music, reading, sports, history and grilling.

He can be reached at:
richard@exponentialsalesmarketing.com
www.exponentialsalesmarketing.com

CHAPTER 33

ON BECOMING WHAT YOU THINK

BY TRAVIS McLAREN

I have won the lottery twice in this life and I'm confident my good luck is going to continue until I leave this earthly plane. My first win was the day I was born, April 3, 1985. Two amazing individuals, Neil and Darlene McLaren, brought me into this world. I was born in Saskatoon, Saskatchewan and moved to Brandon, Manitoba when I was in Grade 4. My parents were very hard working individuals who spent most of their corporate careers in the banking industry. Their careers in finance have aided in making me a well-rounded entrepreneur. They raised me to have a banking mindset and nurtured my visionary mindset and allowed me to dream.

After high school, my parents and I moved to Calgary where I attended the University of Calgary. Within the first semester, I realized that university was not for me at the time. This became a very dark time in my life, which I never talked about to anyone. I had everything one could want materially, but found myself in a large university with no friends and a limited ability to make new connections. I was in a lonely place in life, with suicide thoughts that crept into my mind. I was just not in a good place. Reflecting back, I was stuck in my own head with the inability to slow down and understand that I was not alone. In that moment, everything seemed so difficult; I understand now that it's in those moments of great difficulty that amazing things in life seem to start unfolding. That's exactly what happened to me and one day I made a drastic change. The opportunity arose for me to join a high school friend and backpack in Australia for an indefinite period of time.

That radical change was one of the best decisions of my life. I experienced a different culture, adventure, life without a schedule, but the most dramatic realization, was just how grateful I was for everything I had in Canada. This trip dramatically helped me grow and mature into a much different person. The result of this adventure shifted my confidence level and engrained certain values like generosity, responsibility and growth that continue to resonate with me to this day.

When I returned to Canada, my parents were living in Kelowna, BC, so that is where I lived for the next 12 months. I was floating through life working an average job earning just over minimum wage. It wasn't until my life flashed before my eyes in a near-death experience that I got the message of what was my next move in life.

I was driving a white Jeep Liberty with two passengers. I remember the snow storming down, so I ensured the truck was in 4x4. Before I knew it, we passed a sign on the side of the road that said, "Leaving City Limits"; the road started to bend and wrapped around a mountain. Moments later, I crossed the point on the road where the snowplow had stopped its clearing. In hindsight this is the point where I should have turned around.

Listening to Eminem in the background, I persevered. It was little more than a minute when the back end of the Jeep started to drift. Within seconds the back tires slipped off the road and the Jeep immediately flipped on to its roof. We ended up slamming from tree to tree as we ricocheted down the mountain face. Every window shattered, but I remember only silence. No screaming from anyone, no Eminem playing in the background, no glass shattering, just stillness. Thankfully, the truck had a roof rack installed, which ended up getting snagged on a tree, stopping the Jeep feet from going over a 100 foot embankment. I remember hanging there upside down in complete darkness. Each of us checked to ensure the others were uninjured and started, one by one, to climb out the drivers window being as careful as possible, because the truck was swaying back and forth with just the tree branch holding us. When the truck was recovered the next day, I remember being in awe because all of the three seats that were occupied were fine, but the one spot where no one was sitting was completely crushed. My life was saved that night for a reason. I have never forgotten that fact.

After this experience, another light bulb (aha) moment flashed through my mind.

I decided that I wanted to become a police officer and help others. I moved to Abbotsford, BC and started studying Criminology at the University of the Fraser Valley.

In the second year of my university studies, I was accepted in the Abbotsford Police Department as an Auxiliary Constable; essentially a volunteer uniformed member without a gun. This served as a perfect sneak peek into the life in the police force. This was complemented by two summers as a Park Patrol officer at Cultus Lake, BC. After two-and-a-half years with the police department, I realized law enforcement was not for me, as I did not want to spend my career immersed in negative energy. I remember a few cases where it was my responsibility to bag the body of a deceased person before transferring them to the morgue. It was dark moments like these that made it easier for me to understand what I don't want. I was at a major crossroad in my life and knew a decision needed to be made.

During the school year, I also worked as a server at a restaurant. One evening something amazing happened to me. A friend introduced me to the idea of 'floating' or sensory isolation tanks by giving me a book he was reading, "The Book of Floating" by Michael Hutchison. Within a week, I had read the book in its entirety and soon ventured south to Seattle to experience my first float.

If you have been in Europe or are a fan of Joe Rogan (Comedian and UFC Commentator), you may have heard of floating or sensory isolation tanks, but for those to whom it's brand new, here is a brief description of what it is.

Floatation Therapy is a very unique experience. Imagine a space where you effortlessly float, there is no gravity, no distractions, you are safe, warm and relaxed. Floating has been compared to going back to the womb. There are many reasons why people hop into the tank and keep on coming back to experience 'nothingness.' The three main reasons people float are for relaxation (both physical and mental), pain relief and spiritual growth.

The float units are approximately 8 feet long, 4 feet wide with approximately 11 inches of water at skin temperature allowing the mind to forget the difference between the body and the water. There is also approximately 900lbs. of Epsom salt in the water, which allows a person to float effortlessly at top the water. This eliminates the effect of gravity on the body, allowing you to float like an astronaut. After about 20-30 minutes, the brain goes to a very slow brain wave frequency (theta brain waves). This deep meditative state allows a person to reduce stress, enhance creativity, <u>reduce</u> chronic physical pain, and improve normal sleep.

After a few floats I was hooked and began dreaming of starting my own float spa even though the resources required were out of reach. My thought processes were changing. I became increasingly aware of the energy each person carries, the law of attraction and spirituality. I began reading more books on these subjects ranging from *The Secret*, *Think and Grow Rich*, *The Power of Now* and *As a Man Thinketh,* to name a few. These books opened my mind and my level of belief to the possibilities of the mind and the infinite power we all possess.

Instead of returning to Park Patrol for another summer, I did various landscaping jobs with a good friend. It was that summer when my entrepreneurial journey began. I remember it clearly. As we were landscaping a realtor's office we started envisioning the business 'Naked Boxer Briefs'. I knew I wanted to open a Float Spa but this entrepreneurial journey with Naked Underwear felt like the perfect avenue for me to explore. We spent the rest of the summer brainstorming and creating as we worked. What came from all the hard work was a high-end seamless men's underwear made from Italian fabric and packaged in a high-end box. I remember telling my business partner that we should try to get on *Oprah* or the *Dragons' Den* TV show. The *Dragons' Den* TV show is a board of angel investors where hopeful entrepreneurs pitch their business ideas with the goal of landing an investment. It was not much more than a couple months after putting this intention out there in the universe, that we were flying to Toronto to pitch our unique business to the *Dragons' Den*. We were in the infant stages of sales at that time, which resulted in us leaving the den with no deal. However, there is not much that compares to appearing on National TV in solely your underwear!

The following year, I parted ways with my business partner to complete my University studies with my dream of opening a Float Spa still in my mind. After graduating in 2010, I felt that I needed to find a corporate job to help generate the savings needed to start the float spa. I started at Cintas, a uniform provider company, as a carpet cleaning assistant. Within 30 days I got promoted to having my own sales and service route, resulting in the income goal of $50,000 to $60,000 a year.

After a year and a half of running my own route, I was in line for another promotion at Cintas, a Plant Supervisor position. However, something didn't feel right; it was more money, but something was off. I went through three separate internal interviews to get this promotion; I had completed two with the last one scheduled for the week after Easter in 2011. I travelled to New York that Easter long weekend to visit a float spa to learn and absorb as much information as possible about running a float spa as one could do in four short days. While I was there, I got to enjoy three floating sessions, which I utilized to do some deep reflection on my life as the big interview awaited my return to Canada. It was not until my third float that something clicked and I realized exactly what my next move was. Upon my return to work, I met with the General Manager to advise him that I was giving a month's resignation notice. This caught the management staff off guard, as I was running a successful sales route for the company and was in the running for a promotion. The GM of Cintas was supportive of my dream and we parted ways on a positive note.

From there, Cloud 9 Float Spa began to take shape. I had saved enough cash to open a two-tank spa, which was my initial vision. This is the time that I won my second lottery; Cloud 9 opened its doors August 1, 2012 and was the first Float Spa in British Columbia. We started on a grass roots level, in a rural city outside of Vancouver in the basement of my house. The initial business learning curve was daunting. With no other float centers in the area to rally alongside, I learned by trial-and-error for the first few months. Very quickly, I had people traveling vast distances and over four hours with the sole intention to float. I knew that a larger commercial location was needed. Within 13 months we were able to open a new location over double the size in Metro Vancouver, allowing even more people to experience the blissful state of "nothingness" that floating offers.

Floating has personally touched and changed the lives of many clients at Cloud 9. One client, who was driving a gas-guzzling truck, was bothered by the cost and its harm on the environment, however was still hesitant to make a change once finished his float. During his first sensory deprivation experience he reflected on this situation, and on his way home he drove to a Toyota dealership and traded his truck in for an environmentally friendly car.

Another client had been struggling with fibromyalgia (chronic widespread pain) for the last 34 years and had been in constant pain for decades because of that ailment. She shared with me that after five minutes of being in the tank she burst into tears because it was the first time in decades that she was pain-free. It was an emotional and physical release like she had never experienced before. She now utilizes flotation therapy as part of her pain management protocol. Other fibromyalgia sufferers have followed suit.

One of my personal experiences in the tank that was enlightening for me and expanded my belief in the unlimited possibilities of the tank happened during an evening float. I put out the 'intention' before my float that I would like to come in contact with one or some of my life guides. 'Life guides' can be viewed as an entity that remains a disincarnate spirit in order to act as a guide or protector to a living incarnated human being. Quickly, I started to relax and slow down to a nice theta state and time drifted away. While floating, my Reiki Master who is an individual who can attune other people to Reiki (a form of hands-on healing) was meditating in New Westminister. During my float, I proceeded to astral travel, appearing before Tina and proceeding to give her a huge hug. She was surprised and decided to text me to ask what I was doing. After I emerged from the tank, I was not fully unaware of the astral experience and having left my body. I saw that I had a text message waiting on my phone. I proceeded to call her and confirmed I was floating at the time I appeared to her. It's experiences like this and those of our clients that continue to expand my 'belief' that we, as humans, have untapped power and potential.

Being able to offer the service of floating to people feels amazing. Creating a space and offering a tool that allows people to grow, heal, expand their consciousness and beliefs, is a dream come true. My next vision is to see Cloud 9 Float Spa franchises all over North America!

Through operating a float centre, I meet amazing, unique individuals every day. About two months into business, one customer, who is now a great friend, really changed my life. My Reiki master Tina, introduced me to Reiki. Reiki practitioners transfer universal energy (ki energy) through the palms, for healing and bringing the chakras back into a state of equilibrium. Tina has enhanced my ability to connect with others and myself on a level that I have never experienced before.

I was also introduced through a client to an amazing private success club that has opened countless doors in my life. When I was in University, I became aware of the 'law of attraction,' primarily via *The Secret*, but was never taught and instructed how to actually utilize the Law.

I have learned four tips that I would recommend you consider:

First, recognize that 'You become what you think about most of the time.' The average person has dreams, goals and ambitions in life, but they spend most of their waking hours focusing on their apparent 'problems' in life. When they give attention to their 'problems' they only attract more of those situations into their life. It's one of my full time jobs to be "mindful of my mind." Successful people have problems, but they learn how to become conscious of these problems and use it to their advantage all the time.

Secondly, make an attempt to shake up your routines. This sparks new connections in your mind and promotes continuous growth. Go for a walk, take a different route to work, go to a new restaurant, learn something new, and never stop progressing.

Third, write down a list of your dreams and goals for your life (all dreams, no matter the size). Pretend that money doesn't matter, that it's flows naturally to you. Remember you are your own personal genie that can produce anything on your dream list. Now re-arrange your list, with the dreams listed at the top that you believe you can attract first. These dreams must 'feel good' when you think of them and not be in a state of stress, because it's too grand an idea or that you can't get it for whatever reason. Focus daily on those initial dreams that make you "feel good." Create a movie in your mind and imagine yourself with those dreams at the top of your list. When you have attracted those dreams, move down your list. By starting small as you attract your dreams, your level of belief will increase and things will manifest easier for you. Make sure you have fun with this; you are a movie director for your own life!

Fourth, this is a point from Herb Cohen who wrote the book '*You Can Negotiate Anything.*' He said, "In life and in negotiations you have to care, but not that much." We are here to grow and prosper, not to suffer and feel sorry for ourselves. It's important for us to remember to take life a little lighter, smile more, hug people more and enjoy the process. Inducing positive energy on to others will create a circular process and you will revel in the same rewards.

Knowing that floating and the positive energy I bring forward helps individuals heal and aids in their growth in this life, feels amazing. This amazing feeling that resonates in me is a true indicator that operating and growing Cloud 9 Float Spa is my current calling in life.

I'm so thankful that this is my life and that I didn`t coast through it, settling for average experiences. The future holds infinite possibilities for me. The future holds infinite possibilities for you. The infinite is in your mind and the journey you take and the way you experience it is entirely up to you.

About Travis

Travis McLaren is the founder and owner of Cloud 9 Float Spa. He initially pursued a career as a police officer, earning his Bachelor's Degree in Criminology at the University of the Fraser Valley and obtaining over three years of experience as an auxiliary police officer. Travis is now living out his dream, embracing the five year journey that has seen him transition from a police officer to a Float Spa owner.

In 2008, Travis co-founded Naked Boxer Brief Inc., a company that produces high-end men's underwear. He and his previous business partner were featured on the *Dragons' Den* in 2009, and in 2013 the company went public.

While attending university, he competed in rowing at the national level. Travis believes rowing is a perfect combination of mental fortitude and physical power, balanced in perfect harmony. While competing, he recalls visiting a hypnotherapist to strengthen his mental preparation for competitions.

One of Travis' goals is to introduce the float tank to high performance athletes who wish to take their game to another level, through enhanced mental training and rapid physical recovery that floating provides. Another primary goal is to introduce sensory isolation to those who suffer from chronic pain, providing opportunities for people to feel relief, not only while in the tank, but for extended periods which can last several days beyond. Floating reminds such clients what it feels like to live pain-free again.

Travis is a Reiki practitioner and is enthusiastic about what can be achieved through "energy work." He wishes to introduce floating to those who are open to enhancing the "mind-body connection."

> *"We are all energy – We must love life, take time to laugh and feel good."*
> ~ Travis McLaren

CHAPTER 34

ARE YOU LOOKING FOR A FITNESS AND NUTRITION PROGRAM FOR YOUR CHILD?—
DID YOU KNOW THERE ARE PROGRAMS THAT WILL GUARANTEE YOUR CHILD'S WEIGHT LOSS, INCREASE THEIR CONFIDENCE & SELF-ESTEEM AND SET THEM UP FOR A LIFE OF SUCCESS?

BY TONI MARTUCCI

How are you teaching your child how to live healthy, have a positive attitude, to be self-motivated and to set and attain goals for themselves?

My name is Toni and I have made it my life mission to help children fight back against not only being overweight, but fight against the negative impacts it can have on their life. You may now be wondering what other impacts, besides health issues, that being overweight can have on a child's life. This is a great question and I am going to show you now.

Throughout my entire adolescent years, I was unhappy and insecure about my body. Feeling this way on the inside was shown on the outside, which made me the victim; I was always the one bullied at school, picked on for my weight or for something else.

When I went away to college, I told myself I could be anybody I wanted to be! I was going to run for president of my class, join a sports team, and just be involved. That was until the first day of class when the minute I walked into that room and I felt like everyone was talking about me. I sat in the very back row and I would bet money on it that everyone was just thinking something horrible about me, and every time they whispered to each other, it was about me.

It took me into my third year of college before I realized, there must be something wrong with me not everyone else in the world. It always boiled down to my weight; I had such a lack of self-worth it was keeping me from even setting goals, let alone actually achieving them. It was making it impossible for me to accept myself.

It was at this time that I met my now husband. He owned a fitness center and he inspired me and motivated me and taught me how to take charge of my life and my body. He helped me establish a goal and he gave me the tools and the direction I needed to get there. When I finally reached my goal of having the body I had always wanted, I felt so empowered and confident, it was such an amazing feeling to be able to see something I wanted, work towards it and then actually achieve it.

He had inspired me and became my mentor, that's when I realized that is exactly what every child out there in my position needed, a mentor. Someone to teach them how to exercise, eat properly, motivate them and help them achieve their goals. Which ultimately is how I have ended up here writing this chapter.

I have now been training and educating overweight children in the New York area for years and I have encountered a seemingly endless number of children lacking self-confidence, self-esteem, self-respect, and self-discipline. The deficiency in these developments manifested itself in children in multiple forms: some children could not focus for more then a few seconds, others were slower learners than their peers, and many of these children were not doing well in school or social situations because of their low self-esteem and lack of self-confidence.

I have an attachment to children in this type of situation because I was one of these kids through my adolescent years. I know from experience that with the right guidance, education, and motivation, their lives can be changed significantly for the better! I promised myself years ago that I would not stop until I could help every child battling this war to become more confident in themselves, and that starts with weight loss.

I know my husband and I want to ensure that our daughter has the very best opportunities available and I know every other parent feels the same way. However, what I have found in this situation is that many parents are simply not aware of all the options that are available for their children to lose weight and live a healthy lifestyle.

As a result, many parents end up making choices that could be ultimately holding their child back, physically and physiologically, in ways that they don't even realize. I have had the privilege of working with a large number of children and parents, and this experience has given me the knowledge and understanding of how impactful a fitness and nutrition program can be for a child. It has also shown me the opportunities that can open up for the child as a result and how much children are missing out on chances that could help enhance their lives in so many ways.

I hate seeing so many parents not making the very best choices for their child's health because of a lack of information, or falling for the lies some programs make up in order to make a quick sale when in reality, the program will never deliver what the child really needs. I have built a list of five questions for you to ask any fitness and nutrition program that you are considering in order to find out if that program would be a perfect fit for your family and child.

And I have included the #1 Biggest Secret that Children's Fitness and Nutrition Programs Don't Want You To Know. *This could be the difference between a lifetime of "dieting" and a lifetime of "happiness and health for your child."*

I want to make sure that you, the parent, have the right information in order to make the very best choices for your child, so your child can gain all of the benefits that come along with weight loss, and that you are confident about your decision after you choose a program.

FIVE QUESTIONS + THE #1 SECRET CHILDREN'S FITNESS AND NUTRITION PROGRAMS DON'T WANT YOU TO KNOW!

#1 - How will this program help my child lose weight?

– *Losing weight is a simple concept, to ensure your child's weight loss they need to focus on two elements:*
1. Fitness
2. Nutrition.

– Incorporating fitness- For a child's body to change, he or she has to incorporate cardio and strength training for optimum results. Your child needs a solid exercise plan; he or she needs a curriculum to make sure all ten physical skills are being met:

• Cardiovascular/respiratory endurance

• Stamina

• Strength

• Power

• Speed

• Flexibility

• Agility

• Accuracy

• Balance

• Coordination

The key is to trick your body. When you do the same workout every day, your body will get used to it; when your body gets used to a workout, it no longer has to work to complete the exercise and you will stop seeing results from that workout. You need each workout to be different, so your body is always working with 100% effort to ensure you are getting the most benefits from that workout.

– Incorporating nutrition- *80% of losing weight is what you eat.* This means if you are looking into a program that is solely based on exercise and does not teach your child about proper nutrition, chances are pretty good your child will NOT achieve the results they desire.

#2 - How will this program fit in with my child's daily routine?

Scheduling is the number one reason so many people fail in a fitness and nutrition program. They claim they don't have the time for it. *If you want something bad enough, you will make the time for it.*

The issue is, however, that if a program starts off at working out five times per week, for an hour per day, it equals five hours a week. Does your child currently spend five hours per week just sitting there doing nothing? Probably not.

You want a fitness and nutrition program for your child that can get him or her into the habit of exercise in a progressive way, instead of breaking down the foundations of his or her life and forcing the program in. What do people do when someone is intruding into their homes? They kick them out. But if someone knocks on the door, and you open it and then show them around, the feelings about that person being in your home are much more positive.

Finally, you want a program that starts off only taking up a little bit of time, maybe an hour or two per week. Then, as your child feels more and more welcoming to that one or two hours, you can add on more exercise time.

#3 - How will this program help my child achieve goals in every day life?

It may sound simple, but goal setting and goal achieving can be complex, especially for a child; even more so for a child that may already feel beaten down or defeated, maybe from being bullied or their own emotional insecurities because of his or her weight.

Being able to set a goal, work for it, and then achieve it takes a great amount of confidence. If a person, child or adult, is lacking in confidence, he or she will not be able to set goals for himself or herself to achieve, and yet achieving a goal is the best confidence booster. So how do we get around this double-edged sword?

Most of the time, children are lacking confidence and self-esteem because of the way others treat them. Many children keep this inside, but I have seen it an innumerable amount of times myself: children being teased, bullied, stared at, and talked about because of their weight. This type of negative attention has the power to pull a child's confidence so

337

deep down that it can have a serious lasting impact on the rest of your child's life, into adulthood.

The best type of program is one that is not only going to get your child to lose weight, but through the process of losing weight they will learn to set goals for themselves. As they achieve these goals they will gain confidence, and when enough goals are achieved, your child will really believe in him- or herself. This is how a fitness and nutrition program will help your child set and achieve goals in daily life.

#4 - How will the program help prepare my child for the future?

When you consider any type of program for your child, one of the biggest questions is how this program will prepare your child for the rest of their life.

There are many programs out there that will have your child dancing around your living room for 30 minutes a day, so if you are simply looking for a program to say that you are doing "something" for your children's health in between their favorite shows then this question is irrelevant for you. However, some parents recognize the fact that everything is an opportunity for children to learn and develop skills that will enhance their lives in ways that aren't shown on the surface.

If your child sticks with a fitness and nutrition program for even just two years, exercising in front of the television for even just three hours a week, that's a total of 312 hours, or 13 days! That's 13 days of either dancing around your living room, or learning life skills, proper nutrition, and exercise techniques that they can use for a lifetime.

Before choosing your child's fitness and nutrition program, I advise that you ask for stories of children who have been in the program for a couple of years, and look at the progress they have made in other areas of life as a result of what they have learned in the program.

#5 - How will the program help my child realize their full potential?

Do you want to see your child achieve the best results possible in all aspects of his or her life? Of course you do, every parent does. However, sometimes the challenges of real life make parents feel like they have to accept something less than the very best for their child. This never has to happen, and I am going to tell you how.

I have witnessed children achieve greatness through my program and push themselves to levels of success they never thought possible. The key aspects to their success normally include:

- **Confidence**- learning to believe in themselves
- **Motivation**- getting energized enough about something to take action on it
- **Support**- getting help from those around them
- **Purpose**- knowing exactly what they want to achieve
- **Recognition**- praise and encouragement from others for what they have accomplished
- **Perseverance**- committing themselves to success

This list incorporates all of the qualities your child can learn and develop from a great fitness and nutrition program. Being competent in these skills and qualities will change a person's life dramatically and it will help him or her achieve any dream they desire.

Your child's dreams and goals will start coming true when they have the right tools and support to achieve them.

THE #1 SECRET MOST CHILDREN'S FITNESS AND NUTRITION PROGRAMS DON'T WANT YOU TO KNOW

This is the biggest secret that children's fitness and nutrition programs don't want you to know: The hidden "cost" of the program you're choosing, and I do not mean the monetary cost of the program.

The *biggest* question you should be asking is how your child will benefit from the time they spend in the program. This can be broken down into two questions: What is the benefit your child will gain while actively participating in the program, in this case while they are physically doing the workouts? And: What benefit will the program give the child during the hours he or she is not physically participating in the program? Most programs for children will not be able to give you a good, straight answer to that question.

This is the truth: Most children have many hours free outside of the time they spend in school. Many programs are designed with the sole purpose of giving a child a day's worth of adequate physical activity in one hour or less. From my studies, these have mostly been programs containing solely "aerobics" workouts, not strength training, metabolic conditioning, or any other form of cross training. Not only do you want a well-rounded fitness program to get your child into great, healthy shape, but you also want your child to be advancing in other areas of personal development. Just as you develop your body, you also need to develop your mind.

Fitness and nutrition programs that are not teaching life skills are therefore limiting children's potential, harming their future, and wasting their opportunity to improve.

Choosing a great fitness and nutrition program can ensure that your child does something in that time that helps him or her become more disciplined, self-confident, motivated and academically successful, and therefore, you give them a massive advantage in life.

About Toni

Toni Martucci is a Best-Selling Author and creator of KidFit, the nations leading at-home Child Fitness and Nutrition Program. She has been seen on ABC, NBC, CBS, and FOX as one of the World's Leading Experts in Child Fitness and was recently on the television show "America's Premier Experts" speaking on the effects and cures for Childhood Obesity.

Toni is on an unstoppable mission to cure childhood obesity. Being brought up in the average American household, in a world of fast-food, T.V. and video games, she battled weight issues throughout her adolescent years and has now made it her life mission to stop this issue amongst our youth and prevent the negative life-long side effects that come with this disease. Toni began a child's fitness and nutrition program inside of her husband's fitness center after graduating from Adelphi University. Toni's program thrived with such success and had such a great impact on the children in the program that she wanted to be able to help children all around the world.

Toni developed her program to help overweight children lose weight, but that wasn't her only goal; her curriculum revolves around developing life skills and goal setting.

The concrete pavements of her program include these qualities along with the development of self-discipline, improved concentration and a positive mental attitude. Her goal is to have children build their confidence by losing weight, teaching them how to use their newfound confidence to set and achieve their goals, and helping them see their full potential. Most importantly, she wants children loving and believing in themselves. Through Toni's experience with childhood weight loss and extensive knowledge in nutrition, she has developed a program using her proven formula to guarantee weight loss results.

In addition to expanding her award-winning KidFit program worldwide, Toni is a renowned motivational speaker. She speaks at venues and schools across the country – teaching parents and children about proper nutrition and exercise and how they can be a foundation for increased self-esteem, confidence, and success in life.

You can stay connected with Toni at:
Toni@TonisKidFit.com
ToniMartucci.com
https://www.facebook.com/tonimartuccis.kidfit

CHAPTER 35

COURAGE IS KEY

BY VANESSA WIEBEL

"I believe everyone's instrument counts, standing apart with unique resonance, and at a crucial moment, making the music played together compelling, so we all can leap forward in our evolution." ~ V.Wiebel

Let me tell you a bit of my story, how standing apart matters and is related to mental and physical fitness and matters beyond oneself.

At age 11, I saw a little boy being beaten. I was not popular. I was an outcast. I was bilingual, spoke different and held two sets of cultural values in my heart, one German and one British. It was at a time when cold war politics ruled the social behavior in Northern Europe. As the boy was being beaten, at that moment something rose inside me. I stood up for the first time matching my values of both countries that I embodied, and I thought, "How cruel and unfair, I have to do something!"

I walked up to the bully, a girl taller than I was. Looking back I do not know where the strength came from – it was a visceral feeling of an internal rising "super hero" in me.

"Why don't you start fighting with someone your own size," I yelled.

Until that day I had enjoyed being more or less invisible in a school of 2000. By speaking up and shaming an 'in' kid publicly, I had disrupted the game.

The boy was safe, and I was the new target! I got pushed to my new place with social repercussions! From that day on, I had to fight for myself. I had no allies and I lost my loyalties. I had left the crowd paradigm. I became very reactive, fearful, and socially very clumsy. I was not prepared to stand tall continuously. "My hero journey began as I learned to stand for my values."

Like many, I dared to stand up for my integrity for a while, and then dove back into the soup of the invisible crowd. Every human has this survival response to stay alive. We naturally have an instinct and are neurologically wired to hide and self-protect, as standing out could be dangerous.

Only as we mature healthily, we develop more skills to self-manage; we evolve and stay in a place of conscious mindfulness – daring us not to duck.

My quest to be non-reactive developed throughout my professions, as a Physiotherapist, Acupressure Therapist (Shiatsu Master) and Co-active Life Coach; and in the evolution of my life, I learned:

To make a choice instead of to react is beneficial, by learning to access "who we want to be" and therefore rendering beneficial outcomes. By staying in choice we take advantage of the ability to learn and apply new lessons, going beyond selfishness operating for a constructive Meta-view.

Being a thoughtful human, making conscious choices, is key to fulfilling your collaborative destiny. Only then can you stand apart and have the potential to be a true leader. Following your inspiration, and leading by your vision, you stand apart.

Standing apart I see as an authentic expression of the unique treasure each one of us brings to this time to be needed and to be utilized today.

WHAT ENABLES YOU TO STAND APART?

The key ingredients I see needed for you to stand apart are *confidence, courage, and vision.* Dare yourself to be exposed to unknown pressures and forces, believing you will make it through the journey. You risk your being in order to succeed!

Our sense of self-value and self-worth is determined early by the response we get for being noticed by caretakers. If standing out rewards us in a way we enjoy, we will naturally learn how to pursue standing apart and want more. Commonly, if startled or shocked, we develop a more suppressed pursuit to rise, and we tend to become reactive for self-preservation (hesitant, defensive: Brene Brown).

WHAT WOULD'VE HAPPENED IN YOUR LIFE IF YOU HADN'T STOOD APART?

WHO WOULD YOU PERSONALLY BE IF YOU WEREN'T STANDING APART FROM YOUR PEERS?

Let me continue my story and may it inspire you to realize standing apart is an important social contribution each one of us makes in a unique way. Besides the already mentioned key ingredients – Courage and Confidence – others are needed as well.

Mental and physical fitness have to be in sync; your personal choices and actions have to align with your personal goals and values.

So simple; tougher to practice in the socially turbulent waters of today's life and its modern demands.

I did not have confidence or courage spoon-fed by praising parents. The setting of Europe in the '80s was an intense environment of political activism, feminism, anti-war companies and the first sparks of environmental awareness. I went to events alone; I became a fiercely independent woman. Though I was in groups, I was scared deeply from being bullied, feeling lonely, and shamed. A moment came when faced with Skinheads wanting to rape and beat me up in Hamburg in 1987, and I managed to handle them, so I was unharmed.

It was the first moment I recall I leaned into the pressure and remained successful protecting myself by trusting my skills. This was a breakthrough in my learning, and my confidence and courage rose, and I learned to trust myself and become internally calm.

A huge cornerstone: "I know I can!"

My courage and confidence grew together. I began to step up seeking a more peaceful place within me and in the world. And the world responded to me with whirlwinds of test runs. I immigrated to Canada facing divorce, stripped of my credentials, having to re-train and establish myself professionally and socially. I was constantly learning how to maintain, obtain, sustain success and stay sane and healthy.

Reaching a peak in 2013, I had to put all my learning into a personal 'Mount Everest' climb. I was faced with my mother saying that she was ready to die. I flew to Europe from Canada. Everyone in the family, including doctors, believed she was going to die within a week or two.

Before I left Canada, I vowed to myself not to be triggered by my past or my family dynamics. - Naturally everyone is triggered by their parents, as they are the deepest neurological hard-drive setting we have. I planned to counteract being emotionally hijacked by applying all the self-managing skills I obtained in my professional and personal training as I interacted in an extreme setting of life and death. I vowed to my mature self not to have any expectations towards my parents and parent my own inner soul compassionately. Indeed, would I manage my emotions and physical needs so that I could be fully present at all times – no matter what happened or what my family needed. This time I was prepared for the pressure I had to face. I handled the pressure, I had emergency allies. I planned to utilize Internet access to reach trusted friends for assistance, affirmed personalized mantras and follow a planned self-care routine – all of which I could transfer to Europe. Despite the fact that I was recovering from a car accident, which compromised my physical being, I went. Different since age 11, today I obtain skills that are sustainable and allow me to be mindful and acting in choice.

In Europe, I observed mom, unconditionally loving. I shared information from Canada about Parkinson's from Michael J. Fox Center and Anthony Faulkner. I got her to be less reactive while my family members remained reactive, resisting change due to their own fear.

After 8 days of what felt like being in a horrible emotional 'gong show' pointing towards my mom's passing, the moment came when I began to see paradoxes in my mom's behavior. There were insynchronicities that made no sense, the alignment was not there. My practice of presence, and gift to read body signals like a book, allowed me to remain curious and open-hearted. I felt all my feelings and applied my professional know how as I engaged from a place of choice. I was surprised at my own calm. My inner voice grew stronger. I dared to speak what mom really never wanted to hear. It required all my courage and all my confidence as I knew I was standing against the grain of my family's values to 'be silent, do not stir and bear suffering.' I risked as I did as an 11 year old, to be bold, only now I had more training in standing apart and being ok after.

I faced my mom:

"Mom, I have felt bodies who died in my presence and right now as I hold your hand and connect with you, I don't feel that you are at death's door yet!" Could my observation be true? "Mom, I wonder what is making you feel so suffocated?"

In that moment my mom's eyes flared at me, as if she fired a gun. I found out her truth and her body answered when her mouth was silent! The acknowledgement of the white elephant made my mom melt and share what she hadn't dared to speak of – the fear she felt about 'being a burden and of no more use.'

What followed was a very private midnight conversation in which I was required to continuously stay present, courageous and responsive, confident in my answers. I could stand the pressure and be mature, loving, compassionate and kindhearted. I was grateful for all my shortcomings as they trained me for this big job. I applied all the tools I could think of, all that I had learned in my personal and professional journey. Trust broken before I was even born was fundamentally transformed, and healed years of family pain keeping us all apart.

The next morning, to the surprise of my father and me, mother got up for the first time in months. She prepared breakfast and asked us to join her. In the classic British statement, she said: "Vanessa, you were so right."

I was confused about what that meant. I needed to understand. "Mom, what exactly was I right about?" She announced, "I want you both to know you are right, I still have lots to live for, even if I am dealing with Parkinson's, let's have breakfast."

Dad and I were flabbergasted; we couldn't quite believe what was happening in front of our eyes. The transformation was so fast, visible and aligned in my mom's actions. From bed-ridden and depressed to upright, slow-moving and rosy.

I will never forget that moment, and I realize I had stood as a beacon in the family storm. My client practice had trained me to bring healing to my core family. It transformed all to the better, staying in a state of open-hearted choice is the key. By standing apart, I took leadership for the well-being of my family beyond myself and that really matters. I knew how to navigate fierce individualists struggling alone, how to reach collaboration and join them in jubilation and success. Standing apart in my family at a crucial time required courage, confidence and for me to really manage my emotions and physical being, so I could be present in the moment to really be able to navigate through pressure and forces. Following my heart, I needed to take the lead in my family.

As if the universe would say 'thank you' for choosing to live, my brother announced three months later, "Mom, you're becoming a grandmother."

Therefore I know in my work and in everything I do, everyone matters. It is important that we care for each other and that we encourage each other to be uniquely individual. It is important that we know who we are so we can stand apart and recognize each other, understand each other, connect with each other, be with each other, interact and have relationships with each other, and create aliveness with each other and love.

All of us do not need to be "historic figures" like Gandhi. In our own areas of life, we need to be great beyond ourselves, to be of service to others so that we can all live together in a peaceful, joyful, enjoyable life now. Experience today and be present in a place of inner calm. I believe we, as a species, CAN leave reactivity behind and be respectfully responsive to each other.

For this reason it is important that we stand apart no matter if you are the violin, the trumpet or the little piccolo, it is important that at the event at any given moment when it is your turn to stand apart, that you play and give it your all, that's what makes the world go around.

For your inspiration I have put together seven tips to develop your ability to stand apart to build your confidence and courage:

1. **Stand in front of the mirror** in a superhero posture two minutes a day, and you will notice your confidence will increase – it increases confidence hormone levels. (Thanks Amy Cuddey for this one.)

2. **Differentiate your body sensations**: being reactive vs. making healthy choices. Listen to your body signals. Notice the difference. (Great to practice to share with someone as their feedback helps you learn faster.)

3. **Now choose** – reading your body signals only follow and feed the sensations you enjoy long-term and create more of them. (Tip: Follow what is sincerely heartfelt, enjoyable and invigorating.)

4. **Feel your successes to steer better:** give yourself credit, treat yourself, and then share it with others who are your cheerleaders. If a friend chooses to not cheer you – Then it is great practice opportunity to continue cheering yourself and reinforcing your values anyways. See your vision ahead so you know what you're steering for and cheer for yourself in the storm!

5. **Embark on the hero's journey. Follow your courage while you practice the most important:** self-care, self-compassion and self-kindness – these include regular sleep, laughter, regular moderate food and regular exercise, and good company. I am not kidding...in that order!!

6. **Practice something new everyday.** If you get reactive, do it slower or change the setting so you can stay present and in a choice mode. You will notice it's fun and as you learn things your life enjoyment makes a difference, you matter beyond yourself.

7. **Space for your individual personal Courage buster.**

I welcome your thoughts and comments, you can reach me at: www.vanessawiebel.com and if you're stuck, my website may inspire you to see www.vanessawiebel.com for inspiration for you and your loved ones.

About Vanessa

Vanessa Wiebel's motto is: "Yes you can LEAP ...it's In You."

As an established exceptional Confidence Coach, being a Certified Professional Co-active Coach and Multi-disciplinary Bodyworker, she assists professionals in leading positions aligning their confidence with their courage to get the job done with integrity. She has been an insider secret for high-end executives in the Vancouver area and professional migrants, facilitating them to get back up and run again where others had given up or been told not to bother.

Vanessa is the Expert on aligning body, heart and mind with your inner confidence courage to achieve sustainable success. She matches your lifestyle and setting so you enjoy life far more.

Being a Success-building Expert, she knows transitions can be horrifying and a trigger for most people, preventing dreams or success. Vanessa turns the uncomfortable into comfortable by empowering. She educates with practical applicable simple lifestyle shifts of "know how" expertise proven in her 20-year practice. "Yes, you can LEAP ... it's in You," defeats the fear experience in the process.

Since 1996, Vanessa earned her BSc. in Germany, Certified Professional Co-active Coach through ICF, Physiotherapist and Zen-Shiatsu Master. She is a highly skilled knowledge merger. Working with her, you experience the advantage of all perspectives of conventional medicine and effective eastern modalities of health management now packaged in her Expert coaching methodology.

In her life, Vanessa is quite the trendsetter always rising to the challenge. She emigrated from Germany to Canada in 1994. Due to her migration, she was stripped of all her credentials, upgraded and managed a divorce simultaneously. Undefeated, she got re-accredited and in 2000 opened one of the first multidisciplinary holistic health clinics (Holistic Therapy Center) in Vancouver, learning how to collaborate and successfully run a joyful and profitable Center.

As president of STA of BC, she facilitated national recognition of alternative healing modalities, now recognized by several mainstream insurance companies. She has created and facilitated numerous workshops, aligning participants with their wellbeing passion and ability to dare to take a big leap and be successful contributing to local and international communities.

Today, Vanessa is undoubtedly the expert on "how to rise after a fall." Her simple "Yes you can LEAP… it's In You" approach has facilitated businesses and families in Europe and North America to remain intact regardless of the storms life throws at you. She teaches the ability to align multi-faceted complex dynamics of social dynamics with simple practical methods, so your "fear does not take you out of your game." Her methods get you to simply leave survival and strive forward. Besides offering workshops and lectures and one-on-one sessions, she is now publishing her work to make her applied coaching methodology accessible to the masses.

Vanessa is a spirit that rises together with her team. To learn more about Vanessa Wiebel, the Expert on aligning yourself to sustainable success, visit:

www.vanessa.wiebel.com
Or call toll free: 778-991-5822